T0320030

More praise for
Good Counsel: Meeting the Legal Needs of Nonprofits

"Essentially a one-volume guide to the entire practice of law relating to nonprofits—a remarkable achievement!"

—Kelly Kleiman, *The Nonprofiteer*;
Principal, NFP Consulting (Chicago)

"A remarkable, comprehensive, thoughtful, wise, and useful book. *Good Counsel* will be of immense value to new and experienced board members, regulators and commentators, and counsel. I have not seen anything like this in a publication. An exceptional tour de force, drawing upon Rosenthal's incredible range of experience as a General Counsel."

—Scott Harshbarger, former Attorney General
of Massachusetts

"*Good Counsel* serves as a layman's legal primer for nonprofit organizations. It is everything about nonprofits that you need to know, and a must read for its leaders, boards, and donors."

—Philip L. Milstein, Trustee, Columbia University

"Lesley Rosenthal's *Good Counsel* fills a much-needed void of information for the nonprofit world. It is an invaluable resource in furthering the public good."

—Damian Woetzel, Director, Aspen Institute

"*Good Counsel* was desperately needed, and Lesley Rosenthal was the perfect person to write it."

—Jeannie Suk, Professor of Law, Harvard Law School

"*Good Counsel* is an invaluable first-stop reference for anyone who now does—or has ever wanted to—work or volunteer as a nonprofit lawyer or executive."

—Victoria B. Bjorklund, Head, Exempt-Organizations Group, Simpson Thacher & Bartlett LLP, and co-author, *New York Nonprofit Law and Practice*

" . . . an absolutely invaluable book for any lawyer who does pro bono work for nonprofits . . . "

—Jeffrey S. Tenenbaum, Chair, Nonprofit Organizations Group, Venable LLP, Washington DC

"*Good Counsel*, Lesley Rosenthal's extraordinary work about the legal issues, problems, and obligations facing nonprofits, is a magnificent resource, full of practical advice for officers, directors, trustees, employees, and corporate partners. Anyone so engaged should purchase *Good Counsel* for frequent reference."

—John P. McEnroe, director of a family foundation and The Irish Repertory Theatre

"I've read many books and guides for these various audiences, but never something this comprehensive and accessible. Lesley Rosenthal has done a terrific job in striking all the right notes. Easy and fun to read!"

—Marnie Berk, Director, Pro Bono Programs, New York Lawyers for the Public Interest

"*Good Counsel* is a valuable contribution to members of the nonprofit bar and all those who seek insight into the world of inhouse lawyers: their day-to-day responsibilities, what motivates them, and the issues they confront."

—Michael S. Solender, Americas Vice Chair and General Counsel, Ernst & Young; Lecturer, Yale Law School

"*Good Counsel* is an indispensable training manual on corporate governance. It is a must-read for anyone serving the legal needs of nonprofits."

—Tracee E. Davis, Trustee, Literacy, Inc.

Good Counsel

Good Counsel

MEETING THE LEGAL NEEDS OF NONPROFITS

Lesley Rosenthal

WILEY

John Wiley & Sons, Inc.

Published by John Wiley & Sons, Inc., Hoboken, New Jersey.
Published simultaneously in Canada.

For general information on our other products and services or for technical
support, please contact our Customer Care Department within the United States at
(800) 762-2974, outside the United States at (317) 572-3993 or fax (317) 572-4002.

Wiley also publishes its books in a variety of electronic formats. Some content that
appears in print may not be available in electronic books. For more information about
Wiley products, visit our web site at www.wiley.com.

Library of Congress Cataloging-in-Publication Data:
Rosenthal, Lesley, 1965–
    Good counsel : meeting the legal needs of nonprofits / Lesley Rosenthal. — 1
    p. cm.
    Includes index.
    ISBN 978-1-118-08404-5 (cloth); ISBN 978-1-118-22279-9 (ebk);
    ISBN 978-1-118-23667-3 (ebk); ISBN 978-1-118-23683-3 (ebk)
    1. Nonprofit organizations—Law and legislation—United States. I. Title.
KF1388.R67 2012
346.73'064—dc23

                                                          2011039741

Printed in the United States of America
V10002580_072518

Contents

Part III   For Good Counsel Only

Preface

Every nonprofit organization I have served has had a tiny or non-existent legal team. From the modern dance company with a shoe-string budget I helped out as a fledgling attorney, to the child care advocacy organization I served when its outside pro bono general counsel suddenly passed away; from my childhood summer camp that tracked me down as an adult and invited me to join the board, to the foundation of one of the greatest violinists in history and to the largest voluntary state bar association in the nation with 75,000 members—the total number of in-house counsel in each organization has been binary: zero or one.

Even when I arrived at Lincoln Center for the Performing Arts, Inc., the world's largest and most comprehensive performing arts center, from Paul Weiss Rifkind Wharton & Garrison, a 500-lawyer major law firm in Manhattan where I had practiced for the previous 13 years, Lincoln Center's Legal Department consisted of just an executive assistant and me. When friends who knew the size of my previous practice setting asked me how big Lincoln Center's staff of lawyers was, I would look myself up and down and joke, "Oh, around five-foot-five!"

These experiences are not at all unusual: Of the nation's one million charitable organizations, only a minuscule fraction has regular access to counsel, whether in-house or outside, paid or voluntary. The organization's first hire is its executive director, usually its founder; next come program managers: drug counselors for drug treatment programs, teachers for educational organizations, curators for museums, and so on. Successive hires may include fundraisers, financial and accounting staff, and an administrative manager to take care of personnel and office matters. Public relations may soon follow, and if the organization has physical facilities to operate and secure, someone will eventually be hired to oversee and coordinate that work. Early on the organization may have an outside accountant, an outside public relations firm, management, and/or fundraising consultants. But unless the organization has an unusually high-risk profile or is particularly savvy about legal matters, it is generally not until the organization has reached a much larger size—perhaps the hundredth employee—that consideration will be given to putting an attorney in charge of the organization's legal affairs.

Until now. Tectonic shifts in the nonprofit landscape are persuading directors and senior executives that it is necessary and desirable to bring on counsel to oversee the organization's legal function at a much earlier stage in the organization's life. Fortunately, there is a great deal of goodwill for nonprofit organizations among public-spirited lawyers, and there is more time and willingness to serve among the legal profession than has been fully tapped to date. Lawyers can serve nonprofits as in-house counsel or from the outside, at law firms. Outside or in-house, paid or volunteer, there should be one person—a general counsel—in charge of overseeing the legal affairs of most tax-exempt nonprofit corporations.

With this book, I hope to show nonprofits how to better recognize their legal needs and, at the same time, to inspire and empower a new generation of lawyers and law students, whose primary exposure may be far afield of the issues facing nonprofits, to help meet those needs.

My arrival at Lincoln Center in 2005 coincided with a budgetary mandate to significantly cut the Center's expenditures for outside legal fees in order to ensure that scarce mission-critical funds would go to core program areas such as arts and education.

Meanwhile, the organization's legal, governance, and regulatory complexities were about to grow exponentially. Already a highly visible organization at the center of New York's vibrant cultural scene, Lincoln Center was planning a $1.2 billion expansion and rejuvenation of its 16.3-acre complex. After nearly five decades of artistic excellence and service to the public, Lincoln Center was undertaking 37 projects to fully modernize its concert halls and public spaces, renew its urban campus, and reinforce its vitality for decades to come. In addition to renovating and expanding infrastructure and many of its storied performance and educational facilities, Lincoln Center also embarked on a plan to make the public areas of the campus more welcoming, user-friendly, and expressive of its arts and educational mission. The new design incorporated elements of glass where there was once opaque travertine marble; sunlight where there was darkness; innovative visitor information systems where there was once a vexing lack of signage; grass, trees, and free wireless Internet access where there were underutilized public areas; and safer spaces for pedestrian circulation. In addition, for the first time the complex would have a visitors' center, which would feature a community gathering place with ample seating, another free Wi-Fi node, free weekly performances, food service, a relaunched tour program, a staffed information desk, clean public restrooms (a rare commodity in New York City), a centralized ticket location, and a same-day discounted ticket booth.

The organization's board itself, ably led in turn by chairs Bruce Crawford, Frank A. Bennack Jr., and Katherine G. Farley, was about

Mark Bussell/Lincoln Center. Reprinted with permission.

The Revson Fountain at Lincoln Center

The Josie Robertson Plaza at Lincoln Center, renovated in 2009 as part of a series of 37 redevelopment projects at the complex, provides a welcoming entrance to the world's largest performing arts center.

to undergo a substantial enlargement, both in terms of number of members as well as engagement through expanded committee work and a major capital and endowment campaign.

If you are in the habit of spotting legal issues, you will have identified a range of legal needs in the areas of corporate law and governance, real estate, construction, fundraising, financing, community and government relations, environmental law, consumer regulation, technology, and many more.

But that was not all. Lincoln Center's innovative president, under the leadership of an extraordinary board and executive team, also envisioned a simultaneous redevelopment of our economic model. This economic redevelopment was building out our sources of revenue far beyond the traditional two streams—ticket revenues and contributed income. Our balance sheet would soon include income and expenses from all sorts of start-up ventures: media deals, an international consultancy practice, leases, licenses, and brand expansions into fashion, book publishing and beyond. Each of these strategic initiatives, too, would present novel legal challenges and complexities.

At the same time of the redevelopment of the complex, the growth of the board and the diversification of our lines of business, the nonprofit sector as a whole was coming into a new phase of increased regulatory scrutiny. Arising from several highly publicized nonprofit scandals in the early 2000s, and following in the footsteps of spectacular corporate governance failures of Enron and Arthur Andersen in the private sector, there was a palpable move by charities regulators at the federal, state, and local levels as well as by organizations themselves to import new Sarbanes-Oxley-style accountability measures into the nonprofit world. These moves counseled adding or enhancing audit committee charters, conflict of interest policies, whistleblower policies, executive compensation committees, and other oversight structures to a degree previously unknown in what once was a sleepy backwater called nonprofit governance.

There was no way our leanly staffed legal department could take all of that on ourselves. Fortunately, coinciding with my arrival, Lincoln Center's President Reynold Levy and board members Bart Friedman and Richard K. DeScherer envisioned that the organization could build a council of in-kind supporters to take on this vast expanse of legal work on a voluntary basis.

Working together, we quickly began to assemble the council, which I dubbed the Counsels' Council. Initial members included those law firms already represented on our Board of Directors, such as Willkie Farr & Gallagher and Cahill Gordon & Reindel. The law firm that had been my professional home for the prior 13 years, Paul Weiss Rifkind Wharton & Garrison, unhesitatingly accepted my request to join. To their great credit, so did Weil Gotshal & Manges, and in particular R. Bruce Rich, who was adverse counsel in one of my longest-running representations.

Today, the Council boasts over 25 members, including large law firms, the General Counsel of major companies, and even a professor or two. We lined up the legal needs—reviews of pledge agreements, government relations matters, real estate transactions, labor and employment issues, corporate governance developments and more—with willing and able providers. Together, members of the Lincoln Center Counsels' Council have helped the organization meet the strategic and legal challenges and take on projects on a pro bono basis. The total value of this work in a little over six years is close to $8 million. The net result is a significant increase in our legal productivity and acumen—substantially greater than if we were either to do the work ourselves or to try to find the funds to pay for outside help of this magnitude.

This book came into being because the efforts of the Lincoln Center Counsels' Council came to the attention of the president of the New York State Bar Association, Stephen P. Younger, and the Chief of the Charities Bureau of the New York State Attorney General's Office, Jason Lilien. Messrs. Younger and Lilien had the idea to gather a statewide group of attorneys willing to serve as pro bono counsel to help meet the legal needs of tens of thousands of under-resourced and deserving nonprofits. I promptly accepted their request to help organize this effort, then started looking around for training materials.

I felt strongly that there should be a common set of materials to train the people on both sides of the attorney/client relationship: the volunteer lawyers, who may be seasoned in their own areas of the law but not necessarily knowledgeable about the legal needs of nonprofits; and the clients, leaders of worthy but unrepresented nonprofits, who may be quite sophisticated about running and overseeing their organizations but not in recognizing the range of legal needs, framing the issues, and taking the advice of counsel. In initiating a new and productive relationship between lawyers new to nonprofit counseling and nonprofit leaders unaccustomed to working with lawyers, it was important that both the lawyers and the clients play from the same playbook.

Many fine books have been written about nonprofit law, addressing such topics as what is a nonprofit, how to form and govern a nonprofit corporation, how to obtain and comply with the tax exemption, and so on. But nonprofits have business law needs besides those directly arising from their nonprofit status. Nonprofits also have employees; contracts; physical locations or facilities to operate; intellectual property; communications strategies; insurance, and more. Some excellent, although somewhat scattered, resources explain the basics of each of these complex areas in the nonprofit context: articles, associations of nonprofits, and bar groups. Yet I could not locate the book I was looking for: a single volume for attorneys counseling public charities as well as nonprofit professionals, board members, volunteers, and students of the sector who need a concise, accessible overview of the legal needs of nonprofits.

The purpose of this book is to fill that gap.

I stand in awe of the work those nonprofit executives, staff, trustees, volunteers, and other friends of the sector do with such passion, energy, and commitment. I am also inspired by the public spiritedness of the great (and sometimes maligned) legal profession, which has a tradition of volunteering free legal services—*pro bono publico*, for the good of the public—that I believe is unsurpassed by any other profession.

The aim of this book is to build on these efforts, to empower and facilitate even more productive relationships between and among nonprofit executives, their governing boards, and public-spirited attorneys.

This book is dedicated to them.

Lesley Rosenthal

Acknowledgments

This book would not exist without the extremely generous contributions of time and know-how by many people.

Supporters: Ted Rosenthal, Aron and David Szanto, Reynold Levy, Dan Rubin, Karen Levinson, Alicia Glekas Everett, Roy and Jenny Niederhoffer, and Cecelia Gilchriest.

Wiley editors: Susan McDermott, Jennifer MacDonald, and Donna Martone.

Overall research and drafting assistance: Adam Ness, Cardozo Law School LLM 2011; Elizabeth Dann, Georgetown Law School 2012. Case studies: Josh Sekoski, Harvard Law School 2012. Focus questions: Amy Perry, Spelman College 2012. Chapters 2 and 3: Michael Cooney, Nixon Peabody LLP; Deborah Hartnett, Music Theatre International; Mark Hoenig, Weil Gotshal & Manges. Chapter 4: Elizabeth W. Scott, Major League Baseball; Emma Dunch, Dunch Arts; Megan C. Bright, Fordham Law School 2012; Simon J. Frankel, Covington & Burling. Chapter 5: Emma Dunch, Dunch Arts; Jeffrey S. Tenenbaum, Venable LLP; John Sare, Patterson Belknap Webb & Tyler; Jane McIntosh, Lincoln Center and Columbia University Teacher's College. Chapter 6: David Sayles, BlackRock Solutions; Kara Medoff Barnett, Shilla Kim-Parker and Clive Chang, Lincoln Center for the Performing Arts; Susan Leeds, New York City Energy Efficiency Corporation; Erin S. Gore, UC–Berkeley; Kenneth B. Roberts, Hawkins Delafield & Wood LLP; Lisa B. Herrnson, Proskauer Rose (pension law section). Chapter 7: Allan S. Bloom, Paul Hastings Janofsky & Walker LLP; Jeffrey S. Klein, Weil Gotshal & Manges; David R. Warner, Venable LLP; Debra Osofsky, Harvard Law School 1989; Philip M. Berkowitz, Littler Mendelson; Stephanie Marks, Wormser Kiely Galef & Jacobs (immigration law section). Chapter 8: Elizabeth W. Scott, Major League Baseball; Emma Dunch, Dunch Arts; Keith E. Danish, Hiscock & Barclay (trademark law section); R. Bruce Rich and Caroline Geiger,

Weil Gotshal & Manges; Barry Agdern, Hearst Corporation and Donald Saelinger, Covington & Burling (sweepstakes issue-spotter). Chapter 9: Suzanne St. Pierre and Peter S. Britell, Dewey & LeBoeuf LLP; Debra Sapp, Katsky Korins LLP; Elizabeth B. Stein, Environmental Defense Fund; Andrew A. Lance, Gibson Dunn & Crutcher; John Tiebout and Sara Chang, Lincoln Center for the Performing Arts. Chapter 10: Brittany Uthoff, Harvard Law School 2011; Alexandra Megaris, Venable LLP. Chapter 11: Thomas J. Ostertag, Major League Baseball; Lewis M. Smoley, Davidoff Malito & Hutcher LLP; Cory Greenberg, Alvin Ailey American Dance Theater; Andrew J. Lauer, Yeshiva University. Chapter 12: Liza Parker, Lincoln Center for the Performing Arts; Debra Sapp, Katsky Korins LLP; Sharman Propp; Amanda B. Horowitz, Paul Weiss Rifkind Wharton & Garrison; Lisa Williams, Office of Public Interest Advising, Harvard Law School. Chapter 13: Brandon N. Egren, Dewey & LeBoeuf, David A. Rosinus, Covington & Burling.

And those patient souls who reviewed the manuscript in draft: Hon. Judith S. Kaye, Skadden Arps, and Chief Judge Emerita, New York Court of Appeals; Jay Topkis, Paul Weiss Rifkind Wharton & Garrison; Prof. Mark Kleiman, UCLA School of Public Affairs; Gary E. Friedman, Schacker Realty; Rebecca Sayles, Copland House; Phyllis Isaacson; Nancy Fadem, Americana Student Center; David Munkittrick, Proskauer Rose; Thomson Kneeland; David B. Ramsey, Harvard Law School 2005; Alan H. Fallick, Newsday; Joy A. Fallick; Julie Lineberger, Vermont Businesses for Social Responsibility; Prof. Tobie Stein, Director, MFA Performing Arts Management, Brooklyn College, The City University of New York; Kelly Kleiman, NFP Consulting and The Nonprofiteer; Scott Harshbarger, Proskauer Rose and former Attorney General of the Commonwealth of Massachusetts; Marnie Berk, New York Lawyers for the Public Interest; Caroline Geiger, Weil Gotshal & Manges; Prof. Brian Glick, Director, Community Economic Development Clinic, Fordham University School of Law; Richard Speizman, KPMG; Prof. Robert Holmes, Director of the Community Law Clinic, Rutgers School of Law; Betsy Vorce, Lincoln Center for the Performing Arts; and Sean Delany, Lawyers Alliance for New York.

My deepest thanks to all for their good counsel.

L.R.

Introduction

America's one million charities represent a gorgeous array of goodness.

These nonprofits lead our efforts to prevent or cure disease, alleviate poverty and hunger, advance education, address environmental and social concerns, and ennoble through culture.

Our nation's robust charitable sector includes such powerhouses as the American Red Cross, the Mayo Clinic, the National Council of YMCAs, and major universities, as well as community-based organizations including neighborhood drug-prevention programs, local wildlife refuges, small community theaters and religious and secular charities.

These organizations not only work hard to fulfill their missions; they work hard for our economy as well. As a sector, nonprofits employ over 10 million people, or 7 percent of the U.S. workforce. More people work in nonprofit jobs than in finance, insurance and real estate—combined.[1] Charitable nonprofits in America account for some $1.4 trillion in revenues and expenditures annually— more than all the holiday shopping for three strong Christmas seasons a year—making the sector a powerful economic engine as well as a force for the good.[2]

In addition to jobs created and dollars expended on worthy causes, charities harness the volunteer labor of millions more good-hearted people, carrying out the organizations' missions through generous contributions of time spent serving, teaching, assisting, visiting, consoling, enlightening, and more. The estimated value of the over eight billion hours a year spent volunteering in the United States is close to $175 billion.

The sector is large and growing—in scope, scale, and complexity, including legal complexity. Every one of these organizations faces legal issues, and yet most do not have regular access to counsel. The purpose of this book is to offer practical and compact guidance about the panoply of issues likely to arise.

Business law issues pertaining to contracts, fundraising, personnel, real estate, operations, intellectual property, financial and other matters are omnipresent across the sector, in organizations small and large; but the issues can be daunting and difficult to navigate. Many nonprofits either lack the acumen to spot legal matters, or they hesitate to address them head-on for fear of untold expense or of opening Pandora's box. Still others subscribe to commonly held negative views about lawyers and the law and try to avoid dealing with them at all. The unaddressed legal issues may disappear for a while, but they have a way of recurring and mushrooming, and occasionally they result in a spectacular blowup that sends good institutions reeling and causes shockwaves throughout the entire sector.

The widespread legal underrepresentation of America's nonprofits is needless. More attorneys are willing and able to represent the sector, either on a pro-bono or paid basis, in-house or as outside counsel, than currently serve. Willing counsel may feel they lack the training, and there may be some sector-wide inefficiencies in matching up willing attorneys and law school clinical legal programs with needy nonprofits. If this book sensitizes nonprofit executives and trustees to the latent legal needs of their organizations, and at the same time educates willing counsel and up-and-coming law students, inspiring confidence in them and laying groundwork for them to step up and serve, the book will have advanced its purpose. If the book creates a forum for nonprofit leaders to meet willing counsel for co-learning, networking, and matchmaking, even better.

Who Should Use This Book

Good Counsel is for:

- Executives in the nonprofit sector looking to gain important legal perspectives on their organization's affairs.
- Board members who are entrusted with governing and overseeing the organization.
- Volunteers assisting the organization with business and other needs.

- Legal counsel in the nonprofit sector, both seasoned and novice.
- Law firm lawyers expanding their practices to include serving as outside general counsel in this thriving sector.
- Law students, business students, and others interested in learning more about this vibrant and growing area.

Features of the Book

Take a walk through the halls of a nonprofit organization with this book in hand, and it will show how legal needs arise in each department or function. The book identifies a wide variety of legal matters that affect an organization's corporate, governance, program, fundraising, finance, human resources, marketing, public relations, operating, and government-relations areas.

Working with the checklists and illustrative cases in this book, an organization's leadership, together with counsel, can:

- Envision and execute new business initiatives that tie into the mission and support the goals of the organization.
- Improve risk management, financial and operational efficiencies.
- Facilitate communications about legal matters between lawyers and non-legal staff, many of whom have never worked with a lawyer before.

Good Counsel also reveals:

- How an incoming attorney can organize, structure, and manage a nonprofit's legal function like a pro.
- How willing attorneys and nonprofits in need can find one another.
- How they can work together to leverage other legal resources, on both a paid and voluntary basis.

Practice pointers throughout the text call out points of particular interest to attorneys and law students.

Focus questions at the end of Chapters 1 to 10 provide students—and other readers in a spirit of self-reflection—with an opportunity to consider what they have read and test their working knowledge of important concepts.

Work plans for Chapters 1 to 10 also provide users with the tools they need to perform an organization-wide assessment of legal needs. The process of working through these assessment tools at the end of each chapter provides an invaluable perspective to the organization's leadership, while at the same time equipping lawyers and law students to serve their clients.

These work plans are also included as part of this book's companion web site at www.wiley.com/go/goodcounsel. In addition to accessing the work plans, please visit the web site to download an array of materials, including:

- Chapter-by-chapter glossaries of the specialized terms of interest to nonprofit executives that appear within the chapters in *italics*.
- Detailed write-ups of the case studies from the book.
- Links to additional materials and information.

How This Book Is Set Up

This book is intended to serve a unique role: a singular playbook that enables an organization—its executives, directors, staff members, volunteers, and counsel—to take stock, together, of the organization's legal needs.

Part I summarizes what is unique about the legal profile of nonprofit organizations:

- Chapter 1 provides an overview of the legal context of nonprofits.
- Chapter 2 encapsulates nonprofit corporate law and the requirements of the tax exemption.
- Chapter 3 explores nonprofit corporate governance and maps out counsel's role in supporting good governance.

These chapters will be of interest to trustees, the CEO, and counsel looking to establish the basic terms of their working relationship on behalf of the nonprofit.

Part II is a backstage tour with the general counsel; a department-by-department survey of the business law topics that most often arise in running a nonprofit. Each chapter is targeted toward the executives who are responsible for each function, to help familiarize them with the legal needs that often arise. These chapters are also useful for lawyers who are not conversant with these areas of law or could use a refresher.

- Chapter 4 introduces the common legal needs of the Program department (contract law, introduction to intellectual property law, safeguarding the organization's copyrighted works).
- Chapter 5 provides an overview of legal needs that arise in the Fundraising department (laws governing charitable solicitations, restricted gifts, planned giving, in-kind gifts, grants, pledges, gaming and raffles, corporate contributions, joint fundraising and more).
- Chapter 6 takes us to the Finance department, where legal issues may commonly arise pertaining to audit and control functions, profits and reserves, statutes governing endowments and investments, considerations of insurance and risk management, pensions, taxes and more.
- Chapter 7 summarizes laws pertaining to Human Resources, such as employment contracts, employee handbooks, minimum wage and hours laws, executive compensation, labor and immigration law, while highlighting particular areas where laws may differ, or special considerations may arise, in the nonprofit setting.
- Chapter 8 introduces the legal needs that commonly arise in the functions of Communications, Marketing, and Public Relations: trademark law, rights clearance, truth in advertising laws, and consumer regulatory laws applying to membership/list-building activities such as text clubs, e-mail lists, giveaways, social media, and more.
- Chapter 9 tackles the legal needs of the Operations department, addressing such diverse matters as real estate arrangements, procurement, compliance with building codes and other applicable laws, leasing, and construction issues.
- Chapter 10 reviews the key legal constraints pertaining to the Government Relations (lobbying) function and the prohibition against public charities intervening or participating in political campaigns.

This department-by-department approach provides non-lawyers and non-specialists with an overview of the complex and diverse legal needs of an operating nonprofit and explains the fundamental legal concepts.

Part III takes the reader to counsel's inner sanctum: the Legal department. Returning to more of a personal point of view, these chapters are primarily addressed to lawyers who want to use their training to help meet the legal needs of nonprofits.

- Chapter 11 shares tips for how the new counsel of a nonprofit can take charge of the legal function, while overcoming the natural suspicion against lawyers. Executives and trustees, too, can read this chapter to learn how to help foster a healthy, trusting, and productive relationship between counsel and the rest of the organization.
- Chapter 12 shows job-searching lawyers how they can find a coveted position in the nonprofit sector.
- Chapter 13 explores how nonprofits and the lawyers who serve them can cultivate and keep valuable relationships with the legal sector at-large. These pages also discuss how good-hearted counsel can match up with good-hearted organizations, on either a paid or voluntary basis, all to the betterment of the organization and the public at large.

By the end of the book, it may be hoped that hundreds of thousands of idealistic, underutilized lawyers, law firms and law students will have found their dream role serving the legal needs of nonprofits, and that hundreds of thousands of unrepresented yet worthy organizations will have induced top legal talent to join their cause.

An ambitious agenda? Yes, but no more so than our sector deserves.

Preliminary Observations

Observation 1: The "General" in General Counsel Is Literally True

Surprisingly little of the in-house lawyer's work pertains directly to the mission of the organization, although of course all of it supports the mission ultimately. The Lincoln Center General Counsel job attracted me because in addition to being a lawyer who is absolutely passionate about the law, I am also a violinist. My husband is a noted jazz pianist, composer, and educator, and both of our children play instruments. We live a life in the arts, and I thought that putting my legal skills to work in the service of the arts would be a dream combination. In fact it is, but not exactly in the way I expected.

If you looked at the matters currently on my desk you would see that about 85 percent of them have little to do with the arts, and everything to do with general business-related legal matters. A small part of my professional time is spent directly on program, such as preparing or reviewing contracts for Lincoln Center's performing arts programs and educational activities. Even fewer hours are spent specifically on nonprofit governance matters, such as board agendas and resolutions, bylaws, committee charters, and meetings minutes. The rest of my portfolio looks much like the work of the general counsel of any business with a large physical complex to operate, a $100 million operating budget and 500 employees.

The legal department I lead includes only two full-time lawyers and a superb executive assistant. We may spend much of the day handling matters that relate only indirectly to the organization's mission of sustaining, encouraging, and promoting musical and performing arts. One moment may be spent on the contract with the elevator service contractor, and the next moment I could be helping figure out whether our outside fundraisers are complying with 45 different state laws. After that it may be off to a meeting with Human Resources with a question about hiring or terminating an employee or resolving a pending matter with a labor union. At lunch I may notice a new business has popped up in the neighborhood or online, styling itself as Lincoln Center Groceries, Mostly Mozart Café, or Facebook Friends of the Lincoln Center Institute. Upon returning to my desk I'll send out a polite but firm letter clarifying who has the right to use our name and under what circumstances. I may spend part of the afternoon sorting out which nation's tax treaty applies to conducting fees of a Spanish performer with a British agent. Before the end of the day I may be putting finishing touches on board meeting minutes and draft resolutions for an upcoming meeting.

Fiscal year end may find me helping Finance review our insurance arrangements, meeting with auditors for year-end activities, or consulting on certain governance elements of our tax returns. At calendar year end we review our public disclosure documents

to ascertain that we are in compliance with the continuing requirements of our public financing. Because so many of these legal issues
can arise in almost any business setting, there are some days I feel
that I could be general counsel of a widget factory! My colleagues
and counterparts at other kinds of nonprofit organizations tell me
their experiences are similar. But whether our workday challenges
pertain to governance, nonprofit law, or other general business law
issues, the work is satisfying. It takes on additional meaning because
it is part of something bigger, something that matters. It is all interesting, and even more important, it is all to the good.

Observation 2: Maintaining Independence While Being a Team Player Is a Balancing Act

One important role of a general counsel is common to both the
for-profit and nonprofit sectors: ensuring the good governance
of the organization. Notable corporate failures of the past dec-
ade have been caused by failures of governance. While they generally involve a toxic combination of greed, inattentiveness, and
wrongdoing at the CEO and board levels, many could have been
avoided, cut short or at least mitigated by the presence of a strong,
independent, fully empowered general counsel. Governance shortcomings sometimes arise not because the organization lacks sound
policies and procedures, but rather because it lacks an enforcer
to make sure they are communicated, understood and followed—
even at the cost of some personal embarrassment, discomfort, or
disfavor with those in charge. An independent counsel is one who
understands deeply that the client is not the managers, the CEO,
nor the trustees, but the organization itself. The close working relationship between counsel and trustees or managers of an organization should not be misconstrued as an attorney/client relationship
between the lawyer and any one individual.

On the other hand, some think that ours is an age of hypervig-
ilance; that following a few high-profile governance failures in the
for-profit and nonprofit sectors, regulators have devised one-size-fits-
all solutions to yesterday's problems. Do tiny nonprofits struggling
just to survive and meet urgent community needs really require a
whistleblower policy for accounting matters and a document management policy? In interpreting these requirements, counsel should
keep an eye on context, foster trust among team members, educate
colleagues about the law and attorney/client privilege, and be a

source of strength in the exceedingly unlikely event that wrongdoing is alleged against the organization or its leadership.

Observation 3: Good Practices Are Good Enough for Good Counsel

The breadth of the legal and governance matters that arises makes for stimulating and challenging work. It is great fun for a generalist, yet infinitely frustrating for anyone who yearns to delve deeply into a subject area and come up with the pluperfect analysis of a legal conundrum. There is simply neither the time nor enough organizational resources to achieve perfection as an in-house counsel, particularly not in a high-performance organization where management seeks to effectuate change and bring about greater goodness in the world at a breathtaking pace. One of my boss's favorite phrases is, "Let not the perfect be the enemy of the good." For that reason among others, this book is called *Good Counsel*, not *Best Counsel*. You will not see the phrase *best practices* in this book. The phrase is too confining, suggesting there is one and only one best way to do something. I prefer, and will use, the term *good practices* instead.

Illustrative Cases

Specific cases help illustrate the critical role that general counsel can play in maintaining good practices and good governance at a nonprofit. The cases are set forth in full on the companion web site at www.wiley.com/go/goodcounsel. They are summarized here. The chapters ahead will refer to these instructive examples.

Case 1: Audubon String Quartet

The Audubon String Quartet is a case of a band fight gone bad. The quartet enjoyed a significant reputation for excellence, winning awards and high praise from critics, providing a livelihood for its musicians through concerts and its coveted position as Quartet in Residence at Virginia Tech. In forming a nonprofit corporate entity through which to carry out its musical enterprise, however, the quartet's members took on a raft of legal obligations that they didn't seem to realize would coexist with their artistic pursuits. Unfortunately their adherence to corporate form was considerably less virtuosic than their musicianship. In 2000, years after the quartet was formed and incorporated, three members decided it was time to replace the fourth. The three members, some of whom appeared confused between acts undertaken in their personal capacity and acts of the corporation, did not undertake proper business procedures to effectuate their decision. The first violinist sued the other three members, and in 2005 a judge ordered the quartet's corporation *and* the individual members to reimburse the discharged first violinist some $611,000 to cash out his economic interest in the ongoing quartet enterprise. The remaining members faced the sale of their homes, instruments, and music libraries, and ultimately all three filed for personal bankruptcy. The fundamental error was not that the quartet mixed corporate law with a creative mission—indeed, this decision provided certain tax advantages and fulfilled important business objectives—but rather that the quartet observed the corporation's legal existence, nonprofit status, and fiduciary duties only in the breach.

Case 2: Stevens Institute of Technology

Stevens Institute of Technology is a highly respected technical university in Hoboken, New Jersey. Although the school is close to 150 years old and engages in a significant range of educational and research activities, until recently it had no general counsel or professional corporate secretary. In 2009 the president and board chair were alleged by the state attorney general to have acted together to overcompensate the president with a high salary and forgiven loans; to plunder the endowment in violation of certain donor gift restrictions; and to keep much of the rest of the board in the dark about the organization's weakening financial condition and poor internal controls. Because the attorney general concluded that the lack of legal and governance advice deprived the organization of a valuable source of checks and balances, the settlement of the civil charges, which did not involve admission of wrongdoing, included a requirement to institute certain corporate governance changes *and hire a general counsel and corporate secretary* to help implement and oversee them.

Case 3: Smithsonian Institution

The Smithsonian Institution, the world's largest museum and research complex, experienced a profound governance crisis in 2007. An independent review committee established by the board found problems with excessive compensation of the secretary (i.e., the chief executive); incomplete disclosure of compensation matters to the board; senior staff expenses that were not fully reviewed for reasonableness; substantial absences by the secretary and the deputy secretary due to vacation and compensated service on other boards; marginalization by the secretary of the gatekeepers (general counsel and inspector general), who were kept from reporting concerns directly to the board; inadequate internal controls and audit functions; and insufficient oversight by the board and management over the business ventures unit.

The Smithsonian crisis, which was subsequently addressed, was not a case where the organization lacked a general counsel or policies and procedures to detect and stop the chief executive from taking advantage of board inattention. Rather, the Independent Review Committee found, the governance structures were badly out of date and the procedures were not fully followed:

> The root cause of the Smithsonian's current problems can be found in failures of governance and management. The governance structure of the Institution is antiquated and in need of reform. The relationship between the Board of Regents and Mr. [Lawrence] Small, as Secretary, was contrary to effective oversight. At a time when organizations are expected to operate with increasing transparency, the operation of the Smithsonian, and especially the actions of Mr. Small and those who reported directly to him, had become increasingly secretive. Mr. Small created an imperialistic and insular culture in the Office of the Secretary in which the Secretary, rather than the Board, dominated the setting of policy and strategic direction for the Smithsonian. The Board of Regents allowed this culture to prevail by failing to provide badly needed oversight of Mr. Small and the operations of the Smithsonian. The Board did not look behind the tightly controlled data provided by Mr. Small. Nor did it engage in the active inquiry of Mr. Small and Smithsonian management that would have alerted the Board to problems.[3]

These matters culminated in a crisis that led to the resignation of the secretary and correction of the underlying structural deficiencies and controls.

A word about terminology: This book uses the terms board member, director, and trustee interchangeably to refer to members of the organization's governing body. In some organizations they have other names, such as regents, overseers, or others, depending on the history of the organization and its bylaws, its state of incorporation, its organizational form, and other factors. This book uses the term board of directors generically to refer to an organization's core governing body, which in some states or organizations may variously be called board of trustees, board of governors, board of regents, board of overseers, or other titles.[4] Plenty of confusion can abound in organizations with artistic boards, honorary boards, advisory boards, junior boards, and the like. These other bodies may be useful to the organization for a variety of purposes, but they should not be confused with the governing body, the one that has the powers and liabilities conferred upon it according to state law.

In Sum/Coming Up Next

Taking an overview of the sector and learning from these examples will enable counsel—knowledgeable, independent, and fully empowered—to act together with institutional leadership to protect nonprofit organizations and promote their missions.

Let's explore the wide variety of areas of law that apply to nonprofits, and find out what the *general* in General Counsel really means.

PART

I

AN OVERVIEW OF NONPROFITS' LEGAL NEEDS

What Good Counsel Can Do for Nonprofits

This chapter surveys the broad landscape of nonprofit organizations, clarifying often-confusing terminology and pinpointing what differentiates nonprofits from for-profits (hint: it's not whether or not the entity makes a profit). The chapter then introduces the main legal concerns that set nonprofits apart from other kinds of business entities. Different from most other books about nonprofit law, it goes on to describe other kinds of business laws that apply to all entities—whether nonprofit or for-profit—much to the surprise of many nonprofit executives, who may have the erroneous impression that their organizations are not only tax exempt but law exempt! The wide array of laws applicable to nonprofits, the similarities and differences between how business laws apply to nonprofits and other kinds of business entities, and how compliance with applicable laws can help the organization make good on its mission, are recurring themes throughout the book.

Board members, management and incoming counsel may benefit from reading together the three chapters in Part I.

Because of the broad sweep of the nonprofit sector, generalizations about legal needs are hard to make. The sector encompasses large institutions and smaller ones; some that predate the founding of our nation and some that are still in the process of being formed; some that attract nationwide attention and others that labor in relative anonymity; some with an international footprint and some that operate out of the founder's living room.

What Legal Needs Do Nonprofits Have in Common?

The primary focus of this book, and the largest category of non-profit organizations, is the million or so public charities that are tax exempt under Section 501(c)(3) of the United States Internal Revenue Code. These organizations include hospitals, museums, private schools, religious congregations, orchestras, public television and radio stations, soup kitchens, and certain types of foundations, such as organizations that prevent cruelty to children or animals or foster a cleaner environment. (Although private foundations and some other types of nonprofit organizations under Section 501(c) of the Internal Revenue Code face legal issues that are similar in many respects to public charities, there are enough differences that it would not be practical to identify each one in this book.) For convenience, this book will use the term nonprofit organizations, or nonprofits, to refer to Section 501(c)(3) public charities.[1]

Other kinds of nonprofit organizations, such as chambers of commerce, fraternal organizations, or civic and athletic leagues, may be tax exempt, but contributions to them are not tax-deductible.

Figure 1.1 may help readers visualize these various categories.

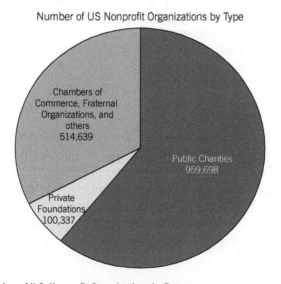

Number of US Nonprofit Organizations by Type

Chambers of Commerce, Fraternal Organizations, and others 514,639

Public Charities 959,698

Private Foundations 100,337

Figure 1.1   Number of U.S. Nonprofit Organizations by Type
Source: National Center for Nonprofit Statistics Business Master File, August 2011.

▭▷ **PRACTICE POINTER**

This volume is aimed at Section 501(c)(3) organizations that qualify as public charities.

Confusion abounds regarding terminology. Tax-exempt organizations, nonprofit organizations, and not-for-profits are often used interchangeably but, technically speaking, these terms have different meanings. The term tax-exempt organization refers to organizations that are exempted from certain kinds of taxes by the federal, state, and local governments. The term nonprofit organization is broader, and may refer to all kinds of entities that exist not to make profits for owners but for a broader purpose. State laws, under which nonprofits are organized, generally prohibit the organizations from making distributions to their founders or insiders, or otherwise operating primarily for the financial benefit of any private party. Instead of paying dividends to shareholders or creating other economic value for private persons, nonprofit organizations plow the net proceeds (that is, profits) from their operations back into their mission-related activities, in furtherance of their stated public purpose.

Different states use different terminology—some use nonprofit, some use not-for-profit, and others use other terminology and different criteria for organizations to qualify as nonprofit corporations. Further confusing matters, experts in the field often use the word charity to refer to all kinds of 501(c)(3) organizations, including organizations with scientific research, culture, or the advancement of religion as their mission, even though the word charity, in common parlance, connotes an organization that primarily serves the poor.

For purposes of this book, the words nonprofit or nonprofit organization refer to organizations that are recognized by their states' laws as nonprofits, that are publicly supported, and that have obtained recognition of tax exempt status by the federal government under Section 501(c)(3) of the Internal Revenue Code.

The public charities that are the subjects of this book fall into eight major areas of focus:

1. *Arts, culture, and humanities*—such as museums, symphonies and orchestras, and community theatres. These may include everything from the renowned Metropolitan Museum of Art

in New York to the tiny Tidewater Classic Guitar Society in Norfolk, VA.

2. *Education and research*—such as private colleges and universities, independent elementary and secondary schools, and noncommercial research institutions. This category includes multi-billion dollar Ivy League universities as well as small local or regional high school dropout prevention programs such as Seven Lakes High School's Project Graduation in Cut Off, Louisiana.

3. *Environmental and animals*—such as zoos, bird sanctuaries, wildlife organizations, and land protection groups. The National Geographic Society in Washington, DC falls into this category, as do local organizations such as Friends of the Verona Street Animal Shelter Inc. in Pittsford, NY.

4. *Health services*—such as hospitals, public clinics, and nursing facilities, mental health and crisis intervention clinics. Examples abound, large and small, from the enormous Kaiser Foundation in Portland, OR to the Trinity Group Homes for addiction treatment in Coeur d'Alene, ID.

5. *Human services*—such as housing and shelter, organizers of sport and recreation programs, and youth programs. Nonprofits in this category include the mighty Legal Services Corporation of Washington, DC, which takes in and expends some $350 million a year providing legal services to indigent people, and the local food pantries that feed the hungry throughout our nation.

6. *International and foreign affairs*—such as overseas relief and development assistance, including Feed the Children (Oklahoma City, OK) and the Hands Across the Border Foundation, a small nonprofit in Boulder, CO dedicated to improving cultural understanding among citizens of the border states of Mexico, Canada, and the United States.

7. *Public and societal benefit* organizations—such as private and community foundations, and civil rights organizations. The ACLU, is one example; the Special Equestrians of Vero Beach, FL, which provides educational and therapeutic horseback riding for the physically and mentally challenged is another.

8. *Religion-related charities*—this includes faith-based programs and congregations large and small.[2]

Clearly these organizations are serving a tremendous range of interests. What do they have in common by way of legal needs? The common threads are their *missions*, their *fiduciary duties*, and their *tax-exempt status*. Let's examine each of these common elements in turn.

Laws About Mission

A nonprofit's mission is its reason for being. Charitable nonprofit organizations are intended to serve a public purpose rather than provide a private benefit to individuals, corporations, industries and others. It follows that the organization's assets and activities must be devoted to the public purpose for which it was incorporated. Everyone in a leadership role must deeply understand that the purpose of the organization is charitable, and that it must engage primarily in activities that accomplish one or more of its public purposes. Deviating from its mission can expose the organization and the people within it to serious consequences: possible personal liability for directors and officers for breach of fiduciary duty; possible removal of board members from service; state Attorney General's action to restrain the organization from carrying on unauthorized activities; reputational and monetary costs to the organization; and, in extreme cases, revocation of tax exempt status or even revocation of charter.

Many organizations, their boards, and their staff are confused about what the mission is and how to identify it. Technically the mission is what the organization has told the IRS its mission is in its application for tax-exempt status, as well as what is reflected in the organization's governing documents (its articles of incorporation and bylaws). The organization may well have updated or amplified its mission statement at board meetings or in publications, but if these updates are inconsistent with the original statement of mission, the changes do not officially change the federal tax-exempt purposes unless the IRS is formally notified. Some organizations have evolved to the point where their stated mission may be unrecognizable; such organizations would do well to consult with qualified counsel to help them update IRS filings to redefine the mission. They may also need to amend their certificate of incorporation, or bylaws, if the purpose clause included there is not written broadly enough to encompass the current activities of the organization.

In all cases, a critical job of an organization's general counsel is to continuously remind trustees and management of the centrality of the organization's mission in all decisions affecting the expenditure of organizational resources.

Laws About Fiduciary Duties

Leaders of the organization—whether they are trustees, officers, or other key players—must know and observe their fiduciary duties under state law, including:

1. The *duty of care*, which requires familiarity with the organization's finances and activities and regular participation in its governance.
2. The *duty of loyalty*, which requires directors and officers to act in the interest of the corporation and to avoid or disclose conflicts of interest or transactions that might appear to create conflicts of interest.
3. The *duty of obedience*, which requires directors and officers to be faithful to the organization's purpose and to the law.[3]

These duties may be expressed somewhat differently in different states, and may be supplemented by other fiduciary duties in various jurisdictions. But at their heart they express the oldest and most fundamental obligations of directors—and also of officers—to the organizations they run.

To translate the somewhat theoretical fiduciary duty of care into more practical terms: Does the board actively and knowledgeably participate in the oversight of the organization, through board meetings and activities between meetings? Or, on the other hand, are board meetings occasional and desultory affairs, with management making most or all of the presentations (or providing scripts for the board members to read), and the board acting largely as a rubber stamp?[4]

The fiduciary duty of loyalty underlies much of the discussion that follows regarding conflicts of interest. Officers' and directors' primary loyalties should lie with the organization, and not with their own personal or business interests, when they are enmeshed with the activities of governing the organization. The duty of loyalty requires the leadership to act in good faith and in, or not opposed to, the best interests of the organization.

The fiduciary duty of obedience is also straightforward: Officers and directors should act in a way that is consistent with the central goals of the organization and with the law.

Here are some ways to tell whether the organization's board members are discharging their duties:

Fiduciary Duty Checklist

❑ Do board members regularly attend meetings?
❑ Do those in attendance carefully review the minutes and correct any errors?
❑ Does the board keep track of what duties are delegated to which committees, and receive follow-up reports?
❑ Do board members periodically meet with senior management to ascertain that organizational policies are followed and the board's vision is being carried out?
❑ Do they have access to, and ask questions of, outside experts such as lawyers, accountants, and investment advisors?
❑ Does the board genuinely debate and deliberate proposals and make informed decisions?
❑ Does the meeting schedule allow time for information gathering and consideration about how comparable institutions deal with similar problems?
❑ Does the board annually evaluate the chief executive officer and set compensation in light of comparable institutions and the work of this particular CEO?
❑ Does the organization have—and follow—policies and procedures for considering the fairness to the organization of proposed business transactions with insiders, such as directors or officers?
❑ Does the leadership know the organization's mission and keep it front and center in its decision-making?
❑ Does the leadership know and understand how to follow applicable laws?

Using this checklist, counsel can help leadership apply the somewhat theoretical principles of fiduciary duties to the real business of governing and running their organization.

Laws About the Tax Exemption

Notwithstanding the breadth of missions and range of sizes, nonprofit organizations face common issues relating to the tax exemption.

Tax-exempt status is a privileged status; the organization performs good works that have been deemed valuable by society, and in exchange they are free from paying most kinds of taxes. In practice, the exemption provides welcome relief from what could be significant additional lines of expense in the organization's operating statement.

Organizations can save on many kinds of taxes:

- Federal and state income taxes
- State/municipal real estate/property taxes
- State sales tax for goods sold
- Taxes on goods purchased from vendors
- Federal and some state unemployment taxes

Section 501(c)(3) organizations benefit also from the deductibility allowed to individuals, corporations, and others, of gifts to the organization. That is, gifts to charities are deductible from both income taxes and inheritance/estate taxes. Exempt organizations may also enjoy nonprofit postage rates, the ability to issue tax-exempt bonds to pay for capital construction or improvements, and other benefits large and small. Other indirect benefits may arise from undertaking activities encouraged by other incentives in the tax code.[5] All told, the value to the sector of the tax exemption plus the tax-deductibility to donors of contributions probably tops $125 billion a year.[6]

Make no mistake: Relieving these organizations from the burden of paying most taxes and providing a tax write-off to donors results in a higher tax burden on everyone else—taxable business entities as well as individuals. The cost borne by the taxpaying community reflects a longstanding and deeply held belief that nonprofits are of critical importance, providing nothing less than the foundation and fabric of a good, decent, and evolved society.

The tax advantages are premised on the notion that these organizations provide important benefits for society; society in turn imposes responsibilities and constraints to hold the sector accountable. Nonprofit organizations face special legal requirements not imposed on taxable, for-profit entities or individuals: restrictions on how they may accumulate, spend, and invest funds; rules about how they may use volunteers; scrutiny of those with whom they may do business and on what terms; and exacting public reporting and disclosure requirements. These matters and others are covered in subsequent chapters.

Beyond Laws about Nonprofits: Complying with Business Laws, Too

Law is not one substantive subject; it is many. Besides complying with laws relating both to their nonprofit and exempt status (such as nonprofit corporations law, nonprofit tax law, and fundraising laws), nonprofits must also comply with laws generally applicable to other kinds of businesses, such as contract law, copyright and trademark, labor and employment, consumer protection, premises liability and more.

And the general counsel of a nonprofit organization is not just practicing law; he or she is also managing the organization's legal function by:

- Ensuring the corporation's compliance with all laws and regulations, including bylaws and organizational policies.
- Monitoring the changing legislative and regulatory environment.
- Overseeing and approving contracts, creating and updating form agreements/purchase orders; establishing and enforcing approved contracting procedures.
- Handling and coordinating any litigation and regulatory scrutiny (inquiries, investigations).
- Selecting, supervising and coordinating outside counsel where necessary.
- Advising on legal aspects of all other operational, policy, and governance matters.

The array of legal responsibilities is breathtaking. The need for competent legal advice is great. The risks of being wrong are significant. And yet most nonprofits, particularly the smaller ones with limited resources, lack regular access to legal advice.[7] Who should carry out these duties? A board member who happens to be a law-yer, although perhaps not trained in the legal needs of nonprofits? The CEO's best friend who is a lawyer? Other professionals on the staff who may be generally conversant with legal matters affecting their functional area?

None of these is a good solution. Clearly the nation's lawyers need to gear up to meet the vast and burgeoning legal needs of nonprofits. Just as clearly, the nation's nonprofits need to become more sophisticated in seeking out competent legal advice and tak-ing responsibility for addressing their legal needs.

First Stop for Legal Advice: CYA (Consult Your Attorney)

Beyond doing what they do best—carrying out their missions with excellence—nonprofit organizations have a wide range of legal responsibilities, from protecting and preserving the nonprofit cor-porate status, mission, and tax exemption, to attending to a vast array of business law and other matters. The role of qualified coun-sel is to help the organization successfully navigate these challenges so that it may most effectively pursue and achieve its mission.

Organizations, their trustees, and managers should beware of seeking legal advice on behalf of the organization from nearby people who happen to be lawyers such as board mem-bers, friends, acquaintances, and others, if such persons are not equipped and empowered to act as counsel to the organization. Board members who are lawyers may experience some role strain— or worse—when asked to provide legal advice to the organization.

⇨ PRACTICE POINTER

An attorney who advises the board on a legal issue upon which he or she may then have to vote as a trustee creates an ethical problem for the lawyer, and may even pose a professional conflict of interest.

Asking a trustee who happens to have a law degree for legal advice makes the boardroom an awkward place when the lawyer gives counsel that the board chooses not to follow. Aside from the ethical quandary, it is rare that a board member who is also a lawyer has formally taken on the organization as a client and properly assumed full ownership and responsibility for a non-profit legal matter in a way necessary for proper client representation, characterized by focused and zealous representation of the nonprofit's legal needs. Indeed, some law firms or their malpractice insurance carriers will not even allow one of their lawyers to serve simultaneously as a board member and as counsel to an organization.

That is not to say that organizations should not bring on lawyers as board members, or that they should not use those lawyers as a sounding board on legal matters for which they are receiving qualified advice from an independent, expert counsel. They just should avoid relying on the trustee-lawyer alone to make legal decisions or render legal advice to the organization.

Another common pitfall is the passing along of received legal wisdom by various non-attorneys within the organization. Fundraisers, finance, human resources, or marketing managers may have just enough legal knowledge based on their experience in the field or in business to be dangerous, but they should not try to perform legal duties. Regardless of how savvy they may feel, those lacking legal training and a license to practice law in their state are not an adequate substitute for retaining independent and knowledgeable counsel.

On the other hand, seasoned nonprofit managers who are attuned to legal issues can be great allies to the lawyer who is officially charged with providing legal advice to the organization.

Nonprofit trustees and managers can be excellent issue-spotters, reliably identifying legal issues at an early stage and bringing in counsel to advise them through the situation.

Legal Education for Non-Lawyers

Counsel's job is to make sure that the organization's trustees and managers are familiar with the kinds of legal issues that may affect each function or department. The lawyer should work closely and regularly with those charged with each function of the organization to sensitize them to the legal issues likely to arise. Once sensitized, these individuals should promptly bring such matters to the attention of counsel—earlier is better so that minor or latent issues do not turn into big problems. Non-legal colleagues should also be educated about how to take and implement legal advice, and how to preserve its privileged character.

Even if the organization is fortunate to have in-house counsel or regular access to outside counsel, a generalist counsel may not be enough. If the matter is specialized, counsel should seek expert legal advice. In the same way a family doctor refers a patient with heart problems to a cardiologist, the general counsel refers specialized matters to legal experts.

⇨ PRACTICE POINTER

The close working relationship between counsel and trustees or managers of an organization should not be misconstrued as an attorney/client relationship between the lawyer and any one individual. The client is the organization; the attorney/client relationship pertains to the counsel's advice to the trustees and managers in their roles on behalf of the organization, and not as individuals.

In Sum/Coming Up Next

Nonprofits bear some similarities and some striking differences to their for-profit counterparts. In both contexts, legal issues are myriad. An organization's counsel, whether paid or pro bono (volunteer), must maintain a high profile within the organization, reaching out to members of the board, especially on governance issues, and to staff in every functional area, so that they are fully conversant with the range of legal matters likely to arise. An attorney who is attuned to good governance and focused on legal compliance is a firm pillar of the organization's fulfillment of its mission.

How counsel can best achieve these ends is the subject of the next and later chapters. In the meantime, the following series of Focus Questions helps to underscore the points raised in this chapter.

The Chapter 1 Work Plan helps users understand the organization's overall legal context and begin to formulate plans to meet the organization's legal needs.

Focus Questions for Chapter 1: The Legal Context of Nonprofits in the United States

1. What distinguishes a nonprofit organization from a for-profit organization?
2. What happens if a nonprofit organization deviates from its mission? If it is used primarily for the benefit of select private individuals?
3. List and describe the three basic fiduciary duties of directors and officers under most states' laws. What consequences result from breach of these duties?
4. List several kinds of taxes that tax-exempt organizations save on, and other kinds of benefits from being tax-exempt. From what kinds of taxes are tax-exempt organizations *not* exempt?
5. What is a tax-exempt organization? Are contributions to all tax-exempt organizations tax deductible to the donor?
6. What are some key areas of nonprofit organizations' legal needs?
7. Besides providing substantive advice, what are some of the other law practice management duties a nonprofit's lawyer may be called upon to perform?
8. What are some common forms of lawyering outside an established client relationship in the nonprofit organization context? Why should it be avoided?
9. What are some risks and opportunities when a lawyer serves on a nonprofit board?

Chapter 1 Work Plan

Understanding an Organization's Basic Legal Context and Setting Goals

This work plan assists users in understanding the organization's overall legal context and begins to formulate plans to meet the organization's legal needs.

❑ Become familiar with the organization's mission, its programmatic functions, and activities.
❑ Understand who are the organization's key stakeholders: What are their interests in the organization, and how are those interests being served?
❑ Obtain and review the following key documents (guidance about what to look for in each of these documents appears in subsequent chapters' work plans):
   • Certificate of incorporation, and any amendments filed.
   • Current bylaws.
   • IRS tax exemption letter.

(*continued*)

- List of members of the board or governing body, including length of service, committee assignments, and any other board or corporate affiliations of each member.
- List of senior managers (direct reports to the CEO/Executive Director), their experience in their functional area, length of service, and current job descriptions; ascertain who is responsible for core managerial functions.
- Current operating budget.
- Financial statement.
- Business or strategic plan (if applicable).
- Most recent IRS Informational Returns (Form 990) and state charities office annual filings.

❏ Take a legal history of the organization:
- Who incorporated the organization, and when? Obtain copies of the founding documents.
- Does the organization currently have legal counsel?
- What was the nature of any legal services rendered over the past several years, and by whom were they rendered?
- Is the organization aware of local legal services groups that provide free or low-cost legal advice to qualifying nonprofits?
- Who interacts with outside legal counsel on behalf of the organization?

❏ Does the board conduct orientation and training of members? What materials does it use?

❏ Is the organization considering a major structural change, such as a merger, joint venture, strategic alliance, partnership, dissolution, bankruptcy filing/restructuring of debts, or a change of mission, name, location, or service area?
- Similarly, determine whether the organization wishes to terminate, modify, or renegotiate the terms of such a joint arrangement.

❏ Ascertain whether there are any current or recent interactions with government regulators.
- Pending, threatened or imminent litigations, investigations, or governmental audits?

❏ Find out whether the organization is undergoing or anticipating a major change in leadership or governance.

❏ Are there any other overarching, pressing legal needs or concerns? Who has primary responsibility for identifying and addressing current and imminent legal needs or concerns?

❑ What are the organization's expectations coming out of this legal review, and what time and resources are available?
  • Short term (over the course of a calendar quarter or school semester): Conduct a function-by-function review of the organization's legal needs; locate resources to help address the most pressing questions.
  • Medium term (over the next one to three years): Prioritize and address non-urgent items that surfaced in the initial review; implement measures for ongoing assessment and education; formalize legal relationships and improvements.
  • Longer term (over the next three to five years): Review impact of legal and governance improvements on achievement of mission; flow positive results through to new initiatives, new grant applications, and new sources of funding; continually improve systems for detecting and addressing legal matters; develop and strengthen ongoing ties to knowledgeable members of legal community.
❑ What would the organization consider to be a good outcome of this legal overview? Are board, senior management and other important stakeholders aligned?

2

Nonprofit Legal Basics: Corporate Law and the Requirements of the Tax Exemption

This chapter covers the basics of nonprofit corporate law: the benefits of incorporating, how to incorporate, what responsibilities come with incorporation, and what's different about a nonprofit corporation than for-profit businesses. The chapter then discusses the basics of tax-exempt status: how to achieve it and how to maintain it in good standing. It wraps up with a discussion of policies that tax-exempt nonprofits establish to protect their interests and meet regulatory expectations.

As a reminder, for purposes of this book, the words nonprofit or nonprofit organization refer to public charities under Section 501(c)(3) of the Internal Revenue Code.

Most Section 501(c)(3) organizations are set up as *corporations*, although some take other forms, such as trusts, unincorporated associations, and limited liability companies. Corporations, whether for-profit or nonprofit, are regarded as legal entities separate from their directors, officers, and employees. They have their own legal existence—in fact, the law treats them as persons—not natural persons, but corporate persons.

The Benefits of Incorporating

The benefits of incorporating are many. Corporate law varies from one state to another, but there are some thematic similarities.

Separate Corporate Existence

The corporation is a legal entity separate from the individuals that form or operate it. Corporations can have employees, bank accounts, real estate, and other assets, and can conduct their business in their own names. A corporation is empowered to enter into leases, borrow money, buy goods and services on credit—all without imposing personal *liability* upon the individuals who carry out these activities on behalf of the organization. To keep this separate corporate existence, individuals within a corporation should maintain and respect corporate formalities such as keeping separate bank account(s) for the company, not commingling (mixing) personal assets with corporate assets, having adequate insurance coverage for the business, signing all agreements in the name of the company, and conducting all company business through the company.

Limited Liability

Incorporating an organization limits the liability of insiders, such as directors, officers, and employees. In other words, incorporating an organization may shield the individuals within the organization from personal liability if a problem arises in the course of business. The only recourse an aggrieved party has is against the legal entity, not the individuals operating it. Similarly, if anyone were to file a lawsuit for the actions or inactions of the business entity, the complaining person could not go after the personal assets (homes, cars, bank accounts) of those operating the organization, as long as they have caused the corporation to comply with law. The insiders must treat the corporation as an entity distinct from themselves and they must act in good faith to reap the benefit of limited liability.

Business Judgment Rule

Directors and officers of corporations generally enjoy deference from courts about matters of business judgment. Although corporate law varies state-to-state, the business judgment rule generally applies to shield corporate directors and officers (in both the for-profit and nonprofit contexts) from liability when their actions or business decisions are made in good faith, with due inquiry, without conflict of interest, and with a reasonable belief that they are in the best interests of the corporation. So long as these criteria are met, the courts will not second-guess the business decision and impose liability on the individual directors and insiders. Thus, when a court reviews the reasonableness of board decisions, absent fraud, self-dealing, unconscionability, or other misconduct, the court will limit its inquiry to whether the action was authorized and whether it was taken in good faith and furthering of the legitimate interests of the corporation. The business judgment rule is a valuable benefit of incorporating.

Credit Score and Bankruptcy Protection

A corporation can establish credit in its name and build up a credit score. Those operating the corporation will not have to rely on their personal credit when seeking credit and loans in the name of the corporation. In the event of a business failure, incorporated entities can file for bankruptcy protection separate from the individuals that operate them.

Intellectual Property Ownership

For creative or educational endeavors, incorporating the organization makes it easier to manage the intellectual property (copyrights, trademarks, patents) created under the organization's auspices. For example, under the simplest case, a corporation can require project participants to work on a work-for-hire basis, or alternatively require the participants to assign copyrights to the company. Incorporating also makes it convenient for the organization to own its trade names and marks, safe against the competing claims of the founder or any other individual. (More about copyrights, trademarks, patents, and the work-made-for-hire doctrine appears in Chapters 4 and 8.)

Perpetual Life

Corporations continue to exist even if the founder leaves or dies.

Evolution of Mission

Corporations can restate their missions, so long as they remain within their authorized purpose (or amend their governing documents to broaden the purpose). By contrast, other types of organizations, such as trusts, are bound to a greater extent by the intent of the founder as expressed in the founding trust document.

These benefits of incorporating apply to for-profit and non-profit corporations alike.

Getting Organized as a Nonprofit Corporation

Corporations are the most common organizational form for entities that wish to become tax-exempt.[1]

Although each state has different procedures,, the following steps outline a common pattern for incorporating a nonprofit.

Create Articles of Incorporation

The articles of incorporation must articulate a nonprofit public purpose—for example, a charitable, educational, religious, scientific, literary, cultural, or humanitarian purpose that will benefit the public. The prospective nonprofit corporation should assure that no individual will profit from the services rendered. The purpose of the corporation as stated in the articles of incorporation may list one or more specific nonprofit corporate purposes and/or a general statement of nonprofit corporate purpose. It should at least be broad enough to embrace a large array of both present and future organizational activities. Note that for a corporation eventually to be recognized as tax-exempt under federal law, its charter or articles of incorporation must also contain certain language.[2]

Choose a Name for the Organization

Make sure the chosen name is available by conducting a name search in the state's corporate and business entity database. It is also a good idea to check the database of trademarks kept by the U.S. Patent and Trademark Office, www.uspto.gov, and check a reliable domain name registry to make sure that an appropriate URL is available. (More information about naming nonprofits appears in Chapter 8.) It is best not to name the organization after an individual; if it does bear an individual's name, be sure a written agreement is in place specifying what happens to the name when the individual dies or leaves. The official corporate name should include a suffix Corp. or Inc. to signify that liability is limited to the assets of the corporation. Many organizations choose to reserve a corporate name by filling out an application for reservation.

File a Certificate of Incorporation

Prepare and file a certificate of incorporation with the state's Secretary of State. The certificate should recite the organization's intent to engage in tax-exempt business activities; to provide reasonable compensation to its employees; to limit political activities and not interfere with political campaigns; and to distribute any remaining assets after debts upon dissolution for charitable purposes.

Depending on the organization's purposes and activities, it may need to obtain state agency approvals (such as with the Department of Health for a health care organization) prior to filing the certificate of incorporation with the Secretary of State.

Choose Founding Directors

Select at least the minimum number of required founding directors/ incorporators willing to take fiduciary and legal responsibility for the corporation being formed.[3]

Although processing times may vary, the process of incorporating takes several weeks to a month in many places.

Establish Bylaws

A nonprofit in the corporate form also needs a set of *bylaws*: rules governing the operations of the board. The *bylaws* establish important facts including how board members are designated, whether members have term limits, and whether there must be one or more members representing specific interests. (Membership on the board is not to be confused with other types of membership in the organization, such as being a member of a museum or a Girl Scout troop.)

Requirements for nonprofit corporations' *bylaws* also vary state by state, but common provisions include:

- A method for electing board of directors, officers and committees.
- An allocation of responsibility for decision making.

- A stated number of directors.
- Requirements for meetings of the board, quorum and voting.
- Statement of the number and power of officers.
- Establishment of committees.
- Indemnification of directors and officers (and sometimes employees and volunteers).
- Other matters, such as conflict of interest policies, check-signing authority, and establishment of bank accounts.
- A mechanism for amending the bylaws.[4]

A sample set of bylaws is available by searching the Web, but be sure to include the name of the organization's state of incorporation in the search terms to get the most appropriate examples.[5]

Bylaws can be amended if they become out of date.

Following Good Corporate Law Practices

Although specific requirements of maintaining corporate form vary from state to state, here is a checklist of the basic kinds of documents a nonprofit corporation should keep close at hand:

- ❑ Certificate of Incorporation, including the statement of corporate purpose.
- ❑ Corporate bylaws.
- ❑ Corporate resolutions.
- ❑ Minutes and other records of board meetings.
- ❑ Copies of other government filings, such as tax filings and annual reports.
- ❑ Copies of other legal documents (for example, leases, deeds, mortgages, joint venture agreements, intellectual property documents, policies and procedures documents, and insurance).

Continuous attention to corporate form is key to keeping the valuable protection of limited liability for the personal assets of the individuals in and around the organization. Maintaining good corporate form—assisting the board in holding regular meetings, providing adequate notice of those meetings, assisting the chair or chief executive in setting forth the agenda, preparing and circulating resolutions, and documenting actions taken and discussions held through a set of minutes which is then circulated in draft for review and revision by those present—are fundamental good corporate law practices.

The board (or a governance committee), together with counsel, should make it a habit periodically to review the organization's bylaws and resolutions pertaining to each director's and officer's role, function, and scope of authority.

Act within the Scope of Authority

As a matter of state law, the corporation must not use its assets for purposes beyond those that are authorized. It follows that persons acting on behalf of the corporation should confine their activities to acts within the purposes of the corporation and within the scope of their authority within the corporation. Everything an officer, director, or key employee does on behalf of the corporation may be imputed to the corporation as an official act. Even actions taken beyond someone's actual job description or capacity could conceivably be imputed to the organization, if it appears to the reasonable outsider that the person had apparent authority to bind the organization. If a person closely associated with an organization blurs the line between his personal identity and the corporate entity (e.g., by commingling his funds with corporate funds; ignoring corporate formalities such as meetings, minutes, and resolutions; undermining the board's oversight role over management; violating its purpose or taking steps to benefit private persons with corporate assets or activities), he could jeopardize the corporation *and* the limitation of liability it provides for his own assets.

Activities that are undertaken beyond the authorized scope of powers are called *ultra vires*, a Latin term meaning beyond powers. Such acts may run afoul of state law and could subject the organization to a court order prohibiting it from undertaking the intended actions or, if they have already occurred, an order unwinding or voiding them.

In addition to specific acts required or proscribed by law, many organizations have codes of ethics requiring officers, directors, and employees to adhere to a high degree of personal integrity in their dealings in the name of the corporation. Such codes may have been taken on by the organization voluntarily; sometimes they are required as a condition of receiving certain governmental funding or other benefits.

Respect the Corporation's Separate Identity

Failure to comply with corporate law—ignoring corporate form, blurring the assets, activities or identity of the organization with those of the individuals within it, undertaking activities outside of the stated corporate purpose, or engaging in self-dealing—can lead a court to look behind the corporation and hold responsible the individuals in charge. A court determination to disregard the corporate entity and strip the organizers and managers of the corporation of the limitation of personal liability that they otherwise would have enjoyed is known as piercing the corporate veil. In effect, the law is willing to respect the separate identity of the corporation— and allow the protection against personal liability exposure for the individuals involved—so long as those individuals themselves respect the separate existence of and adhere to the formalities of the corporate entity.

The musicians of the Audubon String Quartet (summarized as Case Study 1 in the Introduction; also available in longer form at www.wiley.com/go/goodcounsel) learned this lesson the hard way. The individuals behind the Quartet Corporation failed to observe many corporate formalities, most importantly maintaining the distinction between the founder's assets and corporate assets. Corporate assets belong to the corporation alone and must be applied and spent exclusively toward proper corporate activities and goals, not for the personal benefit of founders or directors. The three quartet members failed to include the embattled first violinist in notice of meetings at which corporate decisions were taken—firing a director, retaining counsel for the corporation, establishing new bank accounts, and removing a director's signatory power from existing accounts. The court, examining the circumstances using corporate law, analyzed the majority's actions as akin to a corporate squeeze out of a minority shareholder interest. The judge awarded $611,000 to the ousted first violinist, against both the corporation *and* the other three musicians in their personal capacities. In essence, the three directors who acted together were found to have used corporate assets for their own personal ends, and they paid dearly.

Directors' and officers' liability insurance (D&O) can help defend against such allegations, but if the allegations are found to be meritorious, insurance won't help to satisfy a judgment against wrong-doing individuals.

The following checklist helps an organization assess its compliance with corporate law:

- ❏ Does the board have the requisite number of directors called for in the relevant state laws and the organization's bylaws, and have they been duly appointed?
- ❏ Have the officer and leadership posts specified in the bylaws or by state law been filled, and are those persons carrying out the duties prescribed?
- ❏ Does the board membership consist of representatives or designees of various interest groups, constituents, community groups, and affiliates if required by the bylaws?
- ❏ Do board members commonly serve for specific periods of time (terms), and if so, has the organization renewed or discharged the members whose terms have expired?
- ❏ Does the board meet regularly?
- ❏ Is proper notice given of meetings?
- ❏ Is the quorum requirement met for business to be conducted?
- ❏ Are minutes of the proceedings kept?
- ❏ Are votes taken (in person, including by conference call or by written consent), and are resolutions moved, seconded, and voted upon for the conduct of important pieces of business, in keeping with state law, bylaws, and good practices?
- ❏ Is the corporation up-to-date with its annual filings with the federal and state governments, and does it follow proper procedures in disseminating and reviewing forms before filing?

To summarize, the benefits of incorporating are significant. But the protections of corporate law only apply to those who abide by its requirements.

Incorporating as a Nonprofit: What's Different?   Unlike for-profit corporations, nonprofits are mission-driven rather than profit-driven. Any surplus revenue over expense must be reinvested in the organization to further meet its mission. No one owns a tax-exempt charity, not even those who founded it or who contributed substantial assets to it at inception. Although nonprofit corporate law varies state by state, in general nonprofit corporations may never distribute those assets to individual directors, officers or other private entities, not even when the organization is dissolved.[6] Typically, the state attorney general is charged with monitoring and enforcing compliance with this strict principle.

Tax-exempt nonprofits also must disclose a great deal of information about their operations and finances to the public.

Once the organization is incorporated (or has formed a *charitable trust* or *unincorporated association*) under state law as a nonprofit, it then files for recognition of federal tax-exempt status. (There may be benefits to organizing in one of these alternative forms of nonprofit organizations that are eligible for the tax exemption— charitable trusts and unincorporated associations—depending on the nonprofit's size, scope of activities, sources of funding, and the local state's laws. But if the organization is planning to apply for federal recognition of tax-exempt status, some of the advantages of the alternative forms may disappear.)

Obtaining Recognition of Tax-Exempt Status

Donors to tax-exempt Section 501(c)(3) organizations may receive charitable deductions for their donations. Donations to other types of nonprofits—for example, non-charitable nonprofits such as civic or business leagues, chambers of commerce, and social or recreation clubs—are not tax deductible.

To be *tax-exempt* under Section 501(c)(3) of the Internal Revenue Code, the organization must be organized and operated exclusively for exempt purposes set forth in Section 501(c)(3), and none of its earnings may inure to any private shareholder or individual. In addition, the corporation may not be a political action organization, that is, it may not attempt to influence legislation as anything more than an insubstantial part of its activities, and it may not participate in any campaign activity for or against political candidates.[7]

The U.S. Internal Revenue Service is the body of the federal government that recognizes tax-exempt status. It is also the body that can audit tax-exempt organizations and revoke their tax-exempt status for noncompliance.

Filing IRS Form 1023

To apply for federal recognition of *tax-exempt* status by the Internal Revenue Service, the organization must complete IRS Form 1023, the Application for Recognition of Exemption Under Section 501(c)(3) of the Internal Revenue Code, and pay a filing fee.[8] Form 1023 requires fairly extensive detail covering just about every aspect of the organization's governance, its background and its planned activities. Among other things, this application requires the organization to:

- State its exempt purpose (consistent with the charitable purpose set forth in its articles of incorporation).
- Establish that the organization operates on behalf of one of the listed exempt purposes.
- Outline compensation and other financial arrangements with officers, directors, trustees.
- Affirm that private parties will not incur more than incidental benefit from the operations of the organization.
- Ascertain the independence of board members.
- Disclose any political lobbying or fundraising activities.
- Describe any involvements with foreign countries or foreign organizations, or other closely connected organizations.
- Set forth financial data and other information.
- Affirm that upon dissolution of the organization, its remaining assets must be used exclusively for exempt purposes.
- Provide information regarding public charity status—the public support test.

As part of the process of filing for recognition of federal tax exemption, the organization should obtain a federal employer ID number if it has not already done so.

Filing for federal recognition of tax-exempt status can take anywhere from three to nine months. The organization should use a qualified attorney or accountant for this purpose.

Once the organization is recognized as tax-exempt, the exemption is retroactive to the date of organization's formation if the application is filed within 27 months of the date of the incorporation. This means that donors who contributed in the interim are entitled to tax deductions retroactively.

State Recognition Following Federal Tax-Exempt Status

After receiving federal recognition of tax-exempt status, the organization should file for recognition of its tax-exempt status with state and local governments. Only a few states require a separate application for recognition of income tax exemption, but many states and localities require application for exemption from sales and use taxes, property taxes, and others.

Under most states' and municipalities' laws, a tax-exempt organization is exempt from property taxes to the extent the organization owns and uses its real property for exempt purposes or ancillary purposes, or if it rents out property to other nonprofits with a similar exempt purpose and does not charge rent in excess of carrying costs. However, state laws in the property tax area vary widely, and this is a rapidly evolving area in many states and municipalities. Organizations considering real estate transactions should certainly consult with tax experts and not make assumptions about property tax exemption.

Tax-exempt organizations are not exempt from federal income tax withholding, Social Security and Medicare taxes (FICA), and some excise taxes.

Tax-exempt nonprofits are well advised to keep a copy of their Form 1023, as well as the IRS determination letter and state tax-exemption documentation. Grantor organizations, incoming board members, new counsel, and others may request copies from time to time.

⇨ PRACTICE POINTER

The organization must conform its activities to representations made to the IRS when it first secured recognition of the exempt status. The organization should update these representations from time to time as the organization's activities evolve.

More details pertaining to the tax exemption appear later in this chapter, as well as in Chapter 6.

Maintaining Tax-Exempt Status

Once the organization receives the IRS's recognition of its exempt status, referred to as a *determination letter,* one of the organization's most solemn duties is to make sure that it maintains its tax-exempt status in good standing. The following sections set forth important ongoing requirements.

Make Required Public Disclosures

Tax-exempt nonprofit corporations are required to publicly disclose a great deal of information about their operations—even more than public companies subject to the rigorous securities disclosure laws. Most of these disclosures come through an annual federal informational return called the IRS Form 990.[9] Information that tax-exempt nonprofits are required to disclose to the IRS—and onward from there to state regulators, watchdog agencies, and ultimately the general public—include salaries paid to officers or directors and to the highest-paid employees and contractors. The form also requires many organizations to disclose their expenses according to functional categories—program, administration, and fund-raising—and report the totals for each, along with the amounts expended on each program activity.

Avoid Private Inurement

The earnings from a nonprofit's activities should be dedicated to benefiting the public in accordance with the organization's purposes, not enriching individuals in a position of control over the organization such as its directors and officers. The assets of the nonprofit are held in trust by the organization for the benefit of the public, not for private persons.

The tax exemption under Section 501(c)(3) is granted and sustained only if *"no part of the net earnings of* [the organization] *inures to the benefit of any private shareholder or individual."*[10] The word inure means to gravitate toward or flow to something. The word private, in this sense, means personal benefits, and is the opposite of tax-exempt uses and purposes. Thus, *private inurement* is the phrase used to describe transactions whose benefits flow to private individuals, to the detriment of the organization and its charitable purposes. Private inurement is prohibited under federal law.

Private inurement can arise in several different ways, including:

- Through *business transactions* between the organization and its insiders that provide the insiders with the better end of the deal, such as sales of goods, services, or real property by an insider to the organization on terms unreasonably favorable to the seller.
- Through *low- or no-interest loans* from the organization to an insider (which may also be prohibited under state law).
- Through *excessive salaries* above the fair market value of the insider's work for the organization.

By way of negative examples:

- A nonprofit housing company that operates rooms for college students should not buy millions of dollars worth of Internet, cable and phone service for the dormitories from a company owned by the president's wife. [11]
- A nonprofit institution should not make low-interest loans to its president so that he can buy vacation homes.

As a general matter, officers, directors, key employees and other insiders should refrain from conducting business with the organization, or having any relationship with a company or firm conducting business with the organization that would create a conflict or even the appearance of a conflict of interest, unless that relationship has been cleared by the governing board under the organization's policies for reviewing such transactions.[12] The organization can enter into a transaction with a related party—an officer, director, or other insiders—only when it is fully disclosed, approved, and continuously reviewed by the governing board (or, if there is one, the audit committee) to ensure that the transaction is in the best interests of the organization. (See the section "Conflict of Interest Policy" further on.)

The ban on private inurement does not preclude those who manage a nonprofit organization from receiving fair compensation for their work for the organization. The private inurement ban does mean that their compensation must not exceed the value of the services they provide. If compensation exceeds market value, the IRS may determine that they have received an *excess benefit*. Executive compensation is receiving greater regulatory scrutiny by the IRS, journalists, state charities officials, and the public than ever before. To protect the organization against charges of excessive compensation, the board should periodically review executive salaries and compare them with compensation paid at similar organizations for similar functions. The review should be done by disinterested directors, that is, neither by the people receiving the compensation nor by their relatives. (See the discussion of compensation policies in Chapter 3.)

What happens if a nonprofit is found to have engaged in *excess benefit transactions* with its insiders? Until 1996, the answer was simple: revocation of exempt status. However, federal tax law has added to its arsenal an intermediate step before revocation. *Intermediate sanctions* rules, a step in severity below revocation of the tax exemption, allow penalties to be imposed on the insider who received the excess benefit from the organization, and also on each person who participated in the decision to provide the excess benefit!

Limit Private Benefit Transactions

Unlike the prohibition on private inurement, which is found in the Internal Revenue Code, the limitation on private benefit transactions is derived primarily from U.S. Treasury Department regulations, which provide that an organization is not organized and operated exclusively for one or more charitable purposes "unless it serves a public rather than a private interest."[13] The prohibition on private benefit transactions is broader than private inurement; it restricts organizations from providing inordinate benefits to any private persons, including those who are not related in any way to the organization. Although private persons not in control of the organization may enter into transactions with the organization that benefit the outsider, such private benefit must be purely incidental to the organization's tax-exempt purposes. A private benefit is considered incidental only if (a) the benefit is a necessary circumstance of the activity that benefits to the public at large, that is, the activity can be accomplished only by benefiting certain private individuals, and (b) the private benefit is not substantial after considering the overall public benefit conferred by the activity.

> **Example:** An academy trained individuals for careers as political campaign professionals. Almost all of its graduates worked as consultants for candidates of the Republican Party. Although the primary beneficiaries of the private benefit were the students, the U.S. Tax Court held that the Republican Party and its candidates were secondary private beneficiaries, and on that basis revoked the school's exemption.[14]

The penalty for violating the private benefit rule is revocation of tax-exempt status.

Limit Lobbying Activity and Avoid Prohibited Political Activity

Strict rules limit Section 501(c)(3) nonprofit organizations' ability to participate in legislative activity (lobbying) and require certain public disclosures to the extent they do lobby. Federal law prohibits outright the intervention in political campaigns by Section 501(c)(3) charities, such as making contributions or endorsing candidates for elected office. Employees may of course participate in political activities in their individual capacities and on their own time, but they must not do so in the organization's name or using organizational resources, e-mail or letterhead. (More information about the political and lobbying activity limitations appears in Chapter 10.)

Meeting Additional IRS Expectations

In addition to the legal requirements set forth above, the IRS also expects that organizations will maintain independence of a majority of the governing board. The IRS also believes that organizations should maintain policies and procedures that bespeak a well-governed organization. We turn to these matters next.

Assess Trustee Independence

The IRS views board independence as a hallmark of good nonprofit governance. An organization with an independent board is more likely to avoid private inurement transactions, which inappropriately benefit the people in control of the organization. While not a strict legal requirement for compliance with the tax exemption, the IRS does scrutinize nonprofit boards for lack of independence.

Whether a director is independent depends on whether he or she has a financial or familial relationship with the organization, or with another insider of the organization. The IRS defines an *independent director* as one who is not related to another director, officer or key employee; who is not compensated as an officer or other employee of the organization; who did not receive total compensation or other payments exceeding $10,000 in a year from the organization as an independent contractor; and who was not (nor has had a family member who was) involved in an insider transaction with the organization as discussed above. (The IRS has a specific list of which family relationships count for these purposes.) Insider transactions include excess benefit transactions, where the insider received a benefit in excess of fair market value; loans to and from insiders; grants or assistance such as a scholarship, internship, prize or award from the organization; and other business transactions affecting interested persons.

Adopt and Maintain Good Governance Policies and Procedures

Although nonprofits are not yet subject to quite the same array and degree of statutory and regulatory rules and constraints about corporate governance now in place for their for-profit counterparts, there is certainly a higher degree of scrutiny now than there was before the spate of nonprofit governance scandals of the early 2000s.[15]

IRS officials believe that an independent governing board using well-crafted governance and management policies and procedures is likelier to comply with the requirements of tax exemption.[16] Such policies include:

❑ Conflict of interest policy
❑ Whistleblower policy
❑ Document retention and destruction policy
❑ Gift acceptance policy
❑ Joint venture policy

Not all of these policies and procedures are appropriate for every nonprofit organization. Much depends on the size of the organization. If the organization is sizable enough to be required to file the full-length IRS Form 990 annual informational return (rather than one of the abbreviated forms for smaller organizations), the IRS believes that the organization should have and implement these policies.[17] Failure by an organization of this magnitude to have or implement many of these policies, without indicating good reason for that failure, may lead to a higher likelihood of audit. Let's examine them in turn.

Conflict of Interest Policy   A *conflict of interest policy* assists the organization in analyzing the benefits of entering into a potential transaction or arrangement that might also benefit the private interest of an insider to the organization. Conflict of interest policies help support compliance with the fiduciary duty of loyalty.

Insiders, or interested parties, who are typically covered by the policy include:

- Officers, directors, and key employees.
- Former officers, directors, and key employees.
- Businesses or people who are related to the organization's directors, officers, employees, and controlled corporations and other entities.[18]

A conflict of interest policy generally requires insiders to disclose, before a transaction occurs, the existence of his or her financial interest in an ongoing or proposed transaction with the organization to the members of the governing body charged with considering the transaction or arrangement. After disclosure of the financial interest and all material facts, and after any discussion with the interested person, that person should recuse himself, that is, refrain from voting on the proposed transaction. The governing board or committee should determine whether the organization could obtain, with reasonable effort, a more advantageous transaction or arrangement from a person or entity that would not give rise to a conflict of interest. If a more advantageous transaction or arrangement with a non-insider is not reasonably possible, the organization may approve the transaction or arrangement as in the organization's best interest, for its own benefit, and as fair and reasonable. In all events, approved transactions should conform to the organization's written policies, should be properly recorded, should reflect reasonable investment or payments for goods and services, should further charitable purposes, and should not result in impermissible private inurement, private benefit, or an excess benefit transaction.[19]

If approved, such transactions are reportable to the IRS on the Form 990.

The conflict of interest policy should also provide for ongoing review of continuing transactions or relationships on a regular basis (annually or more often if appropriate). The policy should further empower the governing body to take appropriate disciplinary and corrective action if an insider engages in a transaction without proper disclosure under the conflicts of interest policy. Records should be kept of disclosures and dispositions of such matters.

A well-written conflict of interest policy defines who is in charge of its administration and enforcement. The duty often falls to counsel, the corporate secretary, the comptroller, or other compliance officer to distribute and collect conflict of interest questionnaires on an annual or other periodic basis from directors, officers, senior management/key employees, and anyone who assists with the investment of institutional funds. They may then assist the board or audit committee in analyzing the questionnaires. By way of negative example, the failure of the general counsel/chief ethics officer, in the Smithsonian case study, to insist that the CEO fill out and turn in his conflict of interest questionnaire was considered a factor in that institution's failure of governance.

⇨ PRACTICE POINTER

Directors, officers and key employees should periodically affirm in writing that they have received and reviewed the conflict of interest policy and agree to comply with it.

When Is an Insider Transaction Too Small to Report?   The IRS considers a board member to lack independence if she (or her family member or business) enters into a transaction or compensation arrangement with the organization exceeding $10,000 in a year (other than reasonable compensation for board service). But short of a transaction of a magnitude that would jeopardize her status as an independent director, at what point are transactions with insiders so small that they are not even worth reporting or disclosing on a questionnaire? It is hard to say—it is a case-by-case determination that depends on many factors, including the size of the transaction compared to the size of the organization's annual operating budget. If, for example, the organization's largest customer is a company in which the founder owns a significant interest, that is clearly a disclosable transaction. Or if a major supplier of the organization is owned by the sister of the board chair—disclosable again. On the other hand, if an organization with $100 million in annual operating expenses buys a $30 printer cartridge from the dollar store down the street that happens to be owned by the chief of staff's brother-in-law, that is highly unlikely to be a reportable transaction. But for the moment no guidelines exist—neither in dollar terms nor percentage of budget terms— for determining materiality. Most organizations err on the side of over-disclosure. At the same time organizations should be mindful of the sensibilities of their board members and the time constraints of their key employees, perhaps providing a list of the top 10 to 20 vendor relationships together with the blank questionnaires to speed along responses and reviews. In all events the organization must make reasonable efforts to inquire of and ascertain the existence of such transactions. Counsel should be sure to document those efforts in case their reasonableness is later questioned.

Whistleblower Policy for Accounting Matters   Organizations must establish procedures for receiving, retaining, and handling complaints regarding accounting, internal accounting controls, or auditing matters. The complaint procedure for accounting matters is sometimes called a *whistleblower policy*.[20] It provides employees or others inside the organization who have complaints about accounting or auditing matters with an avenue for submitting such complaints to management without fear of dismissal or reprisal. Generally speaking, the organization's board (or audit committee, if there is one) oversees treatment of concerns in this area.

Accounting, controls, and auditing matters that may be addressed by a whistleblower policy could include:

- Allegations of fraud.
- Deliberate error in the preparation, evaluation, review, or audit of financial statements.
- Fraud or deliberate error in the recording and maintaining of financial records.
- Deficiencies in or non-compliance with internal auditing controls.
- Misrepresentation or false statement in financial records, financial reports, or audit reports.
- Deviation from full and fair reporting of the organization's financial condition.

Issues arising under other organizational policies, such as discrimination, harassment, or other employment or personnel matters, are generally excluded from the accounting matters whistleblower policy, although they may be handled under other types of whistleblower policies.

The accounting matters policy should set forth procedures for the confidential, anonymous (if the complainant wishes) report of concerns. Typically the report would go to the audit committee chair, if there is one, or otherwise to the board chair. Such matters may be reported in person, in writing, over the telephone, via e-mail, or through an anonymous lock box located on the premises. Some larger, for-profit corporations or nonprofit organizations with a history of difficulty with such matters may choose to use an outside hotline service for this purpose.

In all events, matters should be kept confidential to the fullest extent possible, consistent with the need to conduct an adequate investigation and review.

The complaint should be reviewed under the direction and oversight of the audit committee, which may also designate outside

experts such as independent counsel and/or independent foren-
sic accountants. A summary of the findings of such investigations
should be reported to the audit committee, and prompt and appropriate corrective action should be taken if warranted in the judgment of the audit committee.

The whistleblower policy should be distributed to all employees
and other persons likely to come into contact with accounting matters, and it should be reviewed with counsel and the audit committee from time to time.[21]

Document Retention and Destruction Policy   Organizations must have a written policy governing the management and disposal of documents.
Document management policies provide for the proper and efficient management of records. Properly drafted, they also shield
those within it from accusations of improperly destroying records
with the intent to impede a lawsuit or investigation. Knowledgeable
counsel or CPAs can help prepare a document management policy that adequately addresses the types of documents and electronic records of the organization, and advise regarding specific
retention times for various categories of documents.[22] Most document management policies call for cyclic or periodic destruction
of documents no longer needed for business purposes (including electronic, paper, or any other medium). Such policies must
also provide for *litigation holds,* that is, suspension of such destruction cycles for documents pertinent to a pending or threatened
legal claim.[23]

Gift Acceptance Policy   Where relevant, organizations should have policies for handling proposed contributions of assets other than liquid
assets (cash or marketable securities). If the proposed gift item is
illiquid (such as shares in a closely held company), and if the gift
item is not readily usable by the organization in pursuit of its charitable mission (such as the donation of a time-share in Maui to a
humane society in Maine), tax difficulties can arise for both the
donor and the organization. Raising funds for the organization is
challenging business, and its success is greatly enhanced by a gift
acceptance policy that has been adopted by the board and that
stipulates what kinds of assets will and will not be accepted, and on

what terms. (More information about gift acceptance policies is in Chapter 5.)

Joint Venture Policy   A *joint venture* is an arrangement under which an organization jointly undertakes a business enterprise, investment, or even a mission-related activity with another entity. Of particular concern from the point of view of avoiding impermissible private benefits are joint ventures with for-profit business partners. A joint venture is distinguishable from a vendor relationship in that, generally, the organization and its co-venturer share profits, losses, and risks of the venture. They may even form a separate business unit or entity for these activities.

Necessity is the mother of invention in the nonprofit world, as elsewhere; as program revenues, contributed income, and governmental sources shrink in difficult economic times, proactive nonprofits are becoming more entrepreneurial. They may expand their lines of business and their encounters with commercial entities in an effort to improve and diversify their sources of earned income.

Some of these ventures can be a tremendous boon to the organization—a joint venture between a for-profit and a nonprofit could run a gift shop for a museum or digitize a nonprofit's rare film archive for commercial distribution. In the best of all worlds, such ventures hit a sweet spot, benefiting both the mission and the bottom line for the nonprofit while avoiding an impermissibly generous private benefit to the for-profit venture partner.[24]

Nonprofit organizations engaging in joint ventures with others should bear in mind that running the joint venture must be consistent with operating the charity primarily for tax-exempt purposes. Also, the operation of the joint venture must not result in any prohibited private benefit or private inurement.[25]

Another increasingly common variety of collaboration between commercial companies and nonprofits is the *commercial co-venture*, where, for example, a retailer or bookstore contributes a percentage of sales revenues on a given day to the local elementary school PTA or literacy group; or a local restaurant dedicates a portion of every meal check or leftover food to a nearby food bank or anti-hunger organization. Such joint activities, also known as *cause-related marketing*, can boost sales and prestige for the for-profit business while providing financial support and visibility for the nonprofit.

IRS rules state that a Section 501(c)(3) organization may form and participate in a partnership if its participation in the partnership "furthers a charitable purpose," and if the partnership arrangement permits the exempt organization to act exclusively in furtherance of its exempt purpose and only "incidentally" for the benefit of the for-profit partners.[26] Key to analyzing such arrangements is control: the tax-exempt entity must control the exempt elements of the relationship.

Counsel should also review such proposed transactions for fairness and reasonableness. Unscrupulous prospective partners are out there—businesses who lure in new customers with offers to share proceeds of sales with their favorite charities, but who never make good with the charity in the end, or fail to open their books for an accounting. Some states have passed strict regulations and procedures for businesses and organizations to disclose and document such deals.[27] Nonprofit watchdog groups such as the Better Business Bureau also set standards for disclosing how charities benefit from the sale of products or services, the duration of the campaign, and any maximum contribution amount.

Unless carefully structured, the income from such arrangements may be taxable to the organization. Tax exposure can be managed by making these deals as a licensing arrangement, limiting the organization's involvement in the arrangement to just an acknowledgement of the sponsor, and carefully tracking and limiting any return benefits provided to the commercial entity. (More about unrelated business income tax (UBIT) appears in Chapter 6.)

In addition to guarding against private benefit transactions, financial exploitation, and undesirable tax exposure, nonprofits should also be mindful of trademark consequences. Seemingly straightforward and benign-sounding co-ventures, like a grocery store offering shoppers a ten-cent contribution to an ecological charity for each customer reusing shopping bags, nonetheless require review from a trademark perspective. Such ventures can go awry, or the product or service may prove to be faulty. The organization will want to ensure that its valuable name is not being misused, tarnished, or diluted, eroding goodwill toward the organization.

Even a seasoned organization like the Smithsonian Institution can err in its dealings with for-profit partners. Before the governance crisis was resolved, Smithsonian Business Ventures entered into a semi-exclusive television contract with Showtime Networks, Inc., tying up certain museum assets under the deal for a 30-year period. The deal was questioned in congressional hearings as being potentially unfair to institutional interests as well as researchers and scholars.

Before embarking on such ventures, organizations should solicit the advice of legal counsel, both to look out for the corporate, tax, trademark, and other legal interests of the nonprofit and also to school the prospective business partner, who may be unaccustomed to doing deals with nonprofits and may not fully understand the organization's legal restrictions or motivations.

If the organization plans to undertake such ventures on a regular basis, counsel should assist by drafting a joint venture policy. Joint venture policies generally provide safeguards for the organization's tax-exempt status during its participation in the endeavor. Counsel should also assist the board in understanding why adoption of such a policy may be advisable.

In Sum/Coming Up Next

Trustees, executives and counsel should have a common understanding of applicable corporate law and the requirements for tax exemption. Counsel can help analyze the organization's current or proposed activities in light of state corporation laws, the organization's bylaws, IRS expectations, and ongoing policy initiatives to make sure the organization's activities are compliant and consistent with protection of its valuable exempt status.

A glossary of corporate and tax terms appears on the companion web site to this book at www.wiley.com/go/goodcounsel.

The following Focus Questions reflect on the material covered in this chapter, and the Chapter 2 Work Plan assists users in achieving a working understanding of the organization's corporate law context and its compliance with the requirements of tax-exempt status.

The next step is to examine the board's role and discuss how counsel can support the board and the chief executive in good corporate governance. We turn to these matters in Chapter 3.

Focus Questions for Chapter 2: Nonprofit Legal Basics

1. Does anyone own a nonprofit corporation?
2. What are some of the advantages of incorporation?
3. What steps are required to (a) incorporate and (b) obtain tax-exempt status?
4. Once incorporated and exempted from taxes, what formalities should corporations observe? Which ones were omitted in the Audubon String Quartet case, and what was the result?
5. Define terms:
   a. What is private inurement?
   b. What is an independent director?
   c. What is recusal?
6. What are the key terms of a whistleblower policy?
7. What are the key terms of a conflict of interest policy?
8. What are the most important elements of a document management policy?
9. What are some of the other policies and procedures that help support a tax-exempt organization's continuing tax-exempt status?

Chapter 2 Work Plan

Corporate Law and the Requirements of the Tax Exemption

This work plan assists users in understanding the organization's corporate law context and its compliance with the requirements of the tax exemption.

❑ Ascertain form of organization, gather and review organizing documents.
  • Corporate charter, trust instrument, or association document.
  • Examine and understand agreements or understandings with member organizations, affiliates.
  • If the organization is a corporation, study bylaws.
❑ Determine whether the board has the requisite number of directors under applicable law and the bylaws, and whether they have been duly appointed.
❑ Determine whether the officer/leadership posts specified in the bylaws and/or by state law have been filled, and whether those persons are carrying out the duties prescribed.
❑ Ascertain whether the board membership consists of the number of representatives or designees of various interest groups, constituents, community groups, or affiliates, required by the bylaws.

- ❑ Determine whether board members are under term limitations; if so, ascertain whether the organization has renewed or discharged the members whose terms have expired.
- ❑ Review tax-exempt application (Form 1023) and determination letter.
  - Including any IRS letter rulings specific to the organization.
  - Study current mission statement(s) and activities; determine whether organization's activities are within the authorized scope of the Purposes clause of organizing document and an IRS determination letter.
  - Find out when was the last time the board reviewed the mission and assist in determining whether IRS disclosure should be updated.
- ❑ Determine whether the organization has registered with the appropriate state charities officials.
  - Has the organization taken appropriate steps to be exempt from state taxes, property taxes, and sales tax?
  - Has the organization taken appropriate steps to fundraise in the various states where it is active?
- ❑ Determine whether the organization is up-to-date with its filings of federal and state informational returns, and what role the board or its committees play in reviewing documentation before filing.
- ❑ Determine how many trustees meet the definition of independence established by the IRS.
- ❑ Review conflict of interest policies, procedures, and questionnaires.
  - Who is responsible for enforcement?
  - Ascertain whether there are circumstances likely to give rise to concerns regarding private inurement of insiders.
- ❑ Inquire about transactions or relationships that may confer substantial private benefits.
- ❑ Ascertain existence, implementation, and enforcement of other key policies, in conformity with IRS expectations.
  - Document management (retention and destruction) policy.
  - Whistleblower policy for accounting matters.
  - Gift acceptance policy.
  - Joint venture policy.

CHAPTER 3

Good Counsel about
Corporate Governance

This chapter tackles the question: Who governs a nonprofit organization? The obvious answer is, the governing board. Frequently, though, the
board's role is anything but clear. Are board members primarily fundraisers? Cheerleaders? A rubber stamp to legitimize the actions and decisions of
the executives? Do they run the organization to the extent staff is unable?
Are they window-dressing to spruce up the organization's letterhead? If they
are rich or famous, must they attend board meetings? The duties of the
governing board are a matter of law. This chapter discusses the legal
precepts and describes what can happen when they are not followed.

What Does the Board Do?

Good governance starts with the board of directors. It is the board's
role and legal obligation under most states' law to *oversee* the
administration (management) of the organization and ensure that
the organization fulfills its mission. The board does not execute the
day-to-day management of the organization; that role is reserved
for its executives or managers. It would be contrary to its oversight
and visionary role for non-executive board members to get into the
business of running the organization. Good board members monitor, guide, and enable good management; they do not do it themselves. The board generally has decision-making powers regarding

matters of policy, direction, strategy, and governance of the organization. Encapsulating its role, the board:

- Formulates key corporate policies and strategic goals, focusing both on near-term and longer-term challenges and opportunities.
- Authorizes major transactions or other actions.
- Oversees matters critical to the health of the organization— not decisions or approvals about specific matters, which is management's role—but instead those involving fundamental matters such as the viability of its business model, the integrity of its internal systems and controls, and the accuracy of its financial statements.
- Evaluates and helps manage risk.
- Stewards the resources of the organization for the longer run, not just by carefully reviewing annual budgets and evaluating operations but also by encouraging foresight through several budget cycles, considering investments in light of future programmatic evolution, and planning for future capital needs.
- Mentors senior management, providing resources, advice and introductions to help facilitate operations and fundraising.

The power to control and oversee the management of the affairs and concerns of the organization is set forth in most organizations' charters. As described in Chapter 2, the charter is given life through a set of bylaws or other governing instruments, which are in turn given the force of law under state law. Generally speaking, state law permits the organization to self-direct significant allocations of power and responsibility, and then requires the organizations to follow their own corporate governance and operational policies. The *fiduciary duties* set forth in Chapter 1—generally, duties of care, loyalty, and obedience—undergird these requirements.

Board Composition

There is no best number of board members (as long as the state minimum is met); nor is there a best definition of trustee leadership roles; nor is there a perfect arrangement of membership slots to represent the various stakeholders; nor is there an ideal committee structure. These matters depend on the structure, size, needs, and history of the organization.

Where the board has enough members to warrant committees, or particular activities of the organization would benefit from oversight by committees of the board, the board may determine to organize committees. Common types of standing committees include an executive committee; a finance and/or budget committee; a nominating, governance and/or membership committee; an audit committee; an investment committee; a program committee; and a human resources and/or executive compensation committee. For passing or short-term needs, *ad hoc committees* may be appointed, such as a capital campaign committee, an executive search committee, or a strategic planning committee.[1]

The governing board should meet regularly—in most organizations of any significant size, no less than once every other month, although reasonable practices differ—or there should be a robust executive committee that is empowered, within legal limits, to discharge the duties of the board between meetings. Where there is such an executive committee, its deliberations and actions should be promptly reported to the full board for review. Although the actions of the executive committee may be binding, and do not need ratification from the board to be effective, they must be reported to the full board.

Board Handbook

New board members should receive board orientation materials (handbook), key organizational documents, and pertinent policies and procedures. Counsel can help by regularly reviewing these materials each time they are issued. Key documents that are often included in the board handbook are:

- Charter/certificate of incorporation.
- Tax-exempt determination letters.
- Mission statement (if different from that stated in charter).
- Bylaws.
- Board policies, including conflict of interest policy.
- Organization chart of board and key staff.
- List of board members, with contact information.
- Current strategic plan.
- Recent and/or key resolutions.
- Minutes from recent and/or key meetings.
- Fundraising information and expectations.

- Current annual budget and long-term capital plan.
- Most recent annual report.
- Most recent Form 990 filing.
- Media relations policy.

Having these documents neatly assembled and close at hand helps incoming and ongoing board members fulfill their responsibilities.

Counsel can serve the board's fulfillment of its oversight responsibilities and fiduciary duties by providing information, analysis, and advice. Where the organization has in-house counsel, the board should make sure that counsel is a strong, independent, and essential part of the organization's controls and governance. If the organization has both a general counsel and outside counsel and/ or other in-house attorneys, there should be a direct line of report between all outside and inside counsel to the general counsel, and through him or her directly to the board, its chair, and the chair of such key committees as may exist, such as the executive committee and the finance and/or audit committee.

A Minute About Minutes

The minute-taking function is not merely a ministerial or house-keeping matter. It is a substantive responsibility that must be discharged with care and discretion. Many states' nonprofit laws require the organization to maintain books and records of account and minutes of the proceedings of the board and its committees. Those statutes, however, may be inadequate in assisting a board member in understanding how that responsibility is satisfied.

Minutes are the official record of what occurred at a meeting. Through meeting minutes, the organization can record its conscientious review and approval of the budget, financial statements, auditing matters, insurance coverages, personnel performance and compensation, and the performance of the organization as a whole. One of the most important functions of the minutes is to memorialize and serve as evidence that the board (or a committee) properly and fully considered and decided organizational matters and, thereby, properly and fully discharged its duties. Through minutes, the organization can document the board's exercise of its oversight function, whether discharged directly by the board or through delegation of its authority and monitoring of the results.

▭▷ PRACTICE POINTER

Properly drafted, minutes can demonstrate that the board is fulfilling its fiduciary duties and complying with other corporate law requirements.

Minutes are not a transcript of what is stated at a meeting. Their function is to address those matters raised on the meeting agenda (as amended at the meeting), state the salient points considered by the board, and set forth the conclusion of the board's actions.

Matters commonly covered by minutes include discussion and outcome of decisions by the board: approval or disapproval of a matter, delegation of the matter to a committee or agent for later reporting back to the board, or tabling of the matter for another meeting. Other activities that occur at board meetings that should be reported in minutes include reports by committees to the board in full.

Because the board acts as a whole, in accord with corporate bylaws, it is important to note the existence of a quorum and a proper vote on any actions of the board, including how many voted in favor of (or against) a particular measure (along with any abstentions, whether due to conflicts of otherwise).

Generally the corporate secretary takes minutes at meetings of the board and its committees. The secretary need not be a lawyer; but there is enough overlap in the skills and judgment required to prepare a good set of minutes that it is advisable for the organization's general counsel, if there is one, to be (or oversee) its corporate secretary. A worthy corporate secretary carries out this important, yet often underestimated, task with diligence: taking accurate and complete minutes of the deliberations and actions taken at board meetings and meetings of board committees, soliciting corrections from those in attendance, and distributing the minutes to all those entitled to know what transpired.[2]

Taking minutes is an art; a good corporate secretary exercises judgment in deciding what to leave out and what to include. For example, while it is important to note who attended and whether a quorum was present for board actions, there is no obligation to record an ending time or duration of a meeting. There is no obligation to attribute particular points of view to board members by name. While the minutes must record the board's consideration of important organizational matters, they should not be so detailed as to chill board discussions or needlessly embarrass donors or others.

Minutes are not private to board members. They are provided annually to the organization's auditors. They may be called for by regulators and even by the media or the general public. Some states have open meetings laws that require nonprofit organizations to open board meetings to the public and provide minutes to anyone who asks for them. Even in states without open meeting laws applicable to nonprofits, if government officials serve on the nonprofit's board (for example, in an *ex officio* capacity), the minutes may be subject to freedom-of-information requests made upon that official's office. Accordingly, the secretary may take the opportunity to share the minutes in draft with the organization's public relations professionals, coordinating its contents and wording with the overall PR strategy, before the minutes are made final.

Nominating and Assessment

The board is ultimately responsible for reviewing the corporation's effectiveness in satisfying its charitable mission. Without fail it should undertake periodic self-evaluation, assessment of the organization's fulfillment of its charitable mission, and oversight of management efforts to identify and address any shortcomings.

Large organizations or boards may consider delegating this function to a *governance* or *nominating committee*. Such committees may be responsible for reviewing the performance of existing directors and the board as a whole, as well as considering new candidates for directors. They may also periodically reconsider committee assignments and call for rotation of membership to keep fresh eyes on the various areas of committee oversight. They should initiate discussions about succession planning for senior leadership of the organization, even if no one is planning an imminent departure. Indeed, waiting until someone is leaving to start succession planning is a signal of poor governance. The organization never knows when there may be a call to the bullpen, and well-governed organizations are ready for anything.

Decisions about whom to elect (or re-elect) to the board of directors is not a process prudently undertaken at a single meeting. A well-functioning nominating committee keeps an evolving list of potential board candidates, with different degrees of relationship to the organization. It also regularly evaluates the performance of existing board members. At the point of election or re-election, candidates occupy a particular position on the list of governance needs of the organization—a list maintained and modified by the nominating function as new candidates present themselves, board members grow or stagnate in their roles, and organizational needs change.

Some organizations have board members designated by a specific constituency to represent their interests. Nevertheless, all board members owe fiduciary duties to the organization when rendering decisions about that organization. The board chair's role in such circumstances is to galvanize the board to act together as one *corpus*, or body.

Counsel can support all of these efforts by educating members about their legal duties and assisting with board trainings and materials.

Finance, Budget, Investment, and Audit

Many nonprofit boards have established one or more committees to oversee financial matters. There may be a finance/budget committee, an audit committee, an investment committee, or some combination of these. (A discussion of finance and investment committee roles appears in Chapter 6.)

Not every nonprofit has an outside auditing firm, but if it does, counsel may recommend that the board consider forming an audit committee and separating the audit committee from the finance committee.[3] Outside auditors generally report directly to the audit committee, and counsel should make sure that their engagement letter is addressed to and signed by the audit committee chair.

What is an Audit Committee? An *audit committee* (or smaller boards acting in fulfillment of the audit committee function) oversees policies and practices for accounting, financial reporting, and disclosure; systems of internal financial control; compliance with applicable laws and regulations and with the organization's own policies, including those concerning conflicts of interest; and awareness of management procedures to monitor and control major exposures to financial risk.

Counsel should take a leading role in ensuring that these critical oversight functions are performed regularly and documented well, by individuals of suitable independence.

If there is an audit committee, its composition is a matter of utmost importance. The committee, whose members are appointed by the board, should include at least two or three members, each of whom is independent, meaning that the member is not compensated by the organization, neither as an employee nor as a contractor, nor as a party to a business transaction with the organization (including a loan or grant). Members of a well-composed audit committee have a working familiarity with finance and accounting practices (a CPA, for example, is a good candidate for the audit committee). Optimally, at least one member of the committee should have expertise in financial, management, accounting or audit practices, although such persons are in high demand and may be difficult to find.

The committee meets with the organization's auditors and management regularly, discussing the effectiveness of the auditors and of management, each outside the presence of the other. It also evaluates and discusses with the auditor its independence, effectiveness, and performance, including any relationships that may impact its objectivity and independence. The audit committee should evaluate any major changes to the auditing and accounting principles and practices that are suggested by the auditors or management, assess internal controls, and review any significant disagreement between or among management, the independent auditors, and an internal auditor in connection with the preparation of the organization's financial statements. The audit committee often is charged with reviewing and approving the contents of the organization's Form 990 informational return each year prior to filing with the IRS. It may also hold management accountable for distributing the return to the full board before filing.

The committee's activities should be recorded in a set of minutes and reported from time to time to the board.

If there is an audit committee, its functions should be spelled out either in the organization's bylaws or in a committee charter, setting forth the duties, eligibility requirements for service, and the frequency of meetings deemed necessary to fulfill the responsibilities of the committee. The committee (or if there is none, the board discharging its audit oversight functions) may also be charged with maintaining effective controls with regard to the prevention of fraud or misappropriation of funds and adherence to the organization's policies, including those concerning conflicts of interest.

The organization's counsel should review directly with the audit committee or board chair any legal matter that could have a significant impact on its financial statements. Many organizations distribute annual financial disclosure questionnaires to identify and evaluate potential or actual conflicts of interest. The board or audit committee reviews the answers to these questionnaires for conformity with the organization's policies.

The audit oversight function also includes reviewing benefits, pension, deferred compensation, any low- or no-interest loans, and travel and entertainment expense reports by members of management, as these are all part of total compensation and may represent a disguised form of prohibited private benefits or excessive compensation.

Fees paid to firms associated with members of the board or their relatives should be regularly reviewed. In larger organizations with high-profile chief executive officers, the executive's significant outside activities, particularly time-consuming and ongoing paid engagements such as service on for-profit boards also should be carefully and continuously monitored because of:

1. The time commitments that may be involved.
2. The impact of compensated service, particularly where such compensation may be sizable relative to the executive's compensation at the nonprofit institution.
3. Business relationships between the outside organization and the institution that may involve, or appear to involve, a conflict of interest.

Gatekeepers of the organization—general counsel and corporate secretary, chief financial officer, outside auditors, and if the organization is large enough to warrant it or has a history to suggest it, an inspector general or internal auditor—must be assured independence. They should have direct access to the audit committee and board chair even if their formal reporting is to the chief executive.

Setting Compensation

The board or a compensation committee should regularly review the compensation and expenses of senior management, in accordance with pre-determined policies and procedures. As a general matter, compensation policies should adhere to and reflect state law and tax law constraints imposed on the organization because of its charitable, tax-exempt status. Adequate procedures include comparison with compensation and performance of similarly situated executives at other organizations.

An organization's executive compensation practices are now specifically a part of the organization's reporting to the IRS through the informational return Form 990 (for organizations sizable enough to file the full-length form).[4]

Compensation data disclosed on Form 990 is available for public inspection. State charities officials are also attentive to nonprofit compensation matters, particularly for organizations that receive state contracts, grants, or other public funding. As executive compensation issues have heated up in both the for-profit and nonprofit sectors, journalists, donors and other commentators are getting much savvier about locating and reporting on this information.

With so much riding on the results of compensation decision-making, many organizations' boards have overhauled compensation review procedures, and larger boards may consider establishing a compensation committee to oversee this review. Trustees charged with this important oversight function may engage outside independent compensation and legal advisors to assist with the compensation study. Such advisors should report directly to the chair of the board (or compensation committee, if there is one) and not to any executive who is the subject of the study. The executives whose compensation is being discussed should not be present for, or participate in, committee deliberations or the vote on their own compensation. If such executives are present at the meeting, they should exit the room for the compensation discussion, and their departure should be noted in the minutes. According to the Independent Review Committee in the Smithsonian situation (see Case 3 in the Introduction; full details are available on the companion web site to this book at www.wiley.com/go/goodcounsel), the chief executive allegedly got involved directly with the comparability study of the compensation experts and the discussion of their results to such an extent that the experts' work may have been compromised.[5]

The Rebuttable Presumption of Reasonable Compensation   If an organization follows three simple steps, its compensation arrangements with its executives will fall safely within the IRS's *rebuttable presumption of reasonableness*,[6] entitling it to a level of protection from federal intermediate sanctions. Those steps are:

1. A compensation committee of independent directors to approve the compensation arrangements.
2. Before making its determination, the committee must obtain and rely upon appropriate data as to comparability.
3. Committee minutes must be documented to show the basis for its determination concurrently with making that determination. The documentation should include:
   a. The names of committee members present during debate on the transaction that was approved and those who voted on it.
   b. A list of the comparability data obtained and relied upon by the committee and how the data was obtained, as well as the nature and scope of the deliberations and the decision-making process.
   c. The terms of the approved transaction and the date approved.

State law may impose other criteria as well.

Other Compensation Matters   The board or an authorized body such as the audit committee should also regularly review senior management's outside business and professional involvements and transactions with interested parties. If a key employee has extensive, paid outside involvements, they may compromise his or her attentiveness to the organization and/or tempt him or her to place the other entity's interests above those of the employer. A key employee who has financially significant entanglements with interested parties such as board members may also pose problems. The board or audit committee should review such matters on an ongoing basis to ensure the manager's primary loyalty and attention reside with the organization.[7]

⇨ PRACTICE POINTER

High-quality documentation is an important companion to the informed, independent judgments and decision-making of the board. The quality of the records of compensation discussions is of particular importance.

Advocacy and Independent Judgment: Counsel in Relation to the Chief Executive

The managerial leadership of the organization (sometimes called the president, the chief executive officer, the executive director, the managing director or the general manager) reports directly to the board of directors. The CEO's primary function is to manage the organization and implement the mission and the board's vision. He or she may work with the board and staff to create a strategic plan for the organization, as well as supervise and coordinate the programmatic, financial management, marketing, fundraising, human resources, communications and other functions. The CEO is also often the public face of the organization, through whose voice the organization's message is communicated.

Counsel can be a critical part of the chief executive's operational success. During a particularly active period of innovation, the chief executive of Lincoln Center, Reynold Levy, described the organization's progress and the role of in-house counsel in facilitating that work, as follows:

> When a nonprofit like Lincoln Center enters new territory, having a resourceful and entrepreneurial lawyer at one's side is indispensable. In an environment that is highly regulated, how to support a nonprofit's freedom of action, to promote its managerial drive and to protect the institution, its employees, volunteers and trustees from liability is a huge challenge.

Sound counsel gives the CEO the courage of his conviction to blaze new trails. Yes, add a facility charge on to the ticket price. Yes, explore vigorously the transfer of air rights to an adjacent site. Yes, place new 21st century technology appliances onto the cityscape. Yes, rent space to a public television station and create a brand new destination restaurant on a 16-acre campus. Yes, negotiate a 99-year lease with an adjacent condominium, allowing for the total modernization of a virtually abandoned and non-code compliant, privately owned public space to be converted into a civic asset and to a Lincoln Center commons.

To every one of these steps and dozens like them, there were cautions, caveats, protective language, negotiations, full disclosure and the like. But the best counsels lead with a simple phrase: "Yes, we can do that. Let me show you several ways to get there."

Language is a powerful communication tool. Well-trained lawyers can craft a position, summarize a meeting, advance a theory of the case and compose an action-forcing memorandum with ease. These are invaluable skills that can move an organization forward, and they are very scarce.

Terrific attorneys possess clear vision: long distance, close-up and peripheral. They enjoy excellent listening skills. They acquire pertinent information rapidly and offer the CEO many alternatives to consider.

As such, a solid general counsel is, by turns advocate, safety net, superb advisor and excellent team member.[8]

A relationship of trust between CEO and counsel, who can provide confidential advice, act as a sounding board, and supply a wealth of good judgment while maintaining objectivity, makes the hard job of leadership a little easier.

When Governance Fails: Learning by Negative Example

In a well-governed organization, the board does not permit executives to run and dominate board meetings, set agendas, or determine what information will be provided to board members. Under the leadership of an active and functioning board chair, there is adequate opportunity at board meetings for members to receive and discuss reports from not only the chief executive, but also, as appropriate, directly from program executives, other in-house and outside professionals, and independent consultants if necessary. Time should be reserved for executive sessions, at which management should be excluded so that its performance may be fully and freely discussed.

One common shortcoming of nonprofit boards is that they are too small, too insular, or too deferential to the founder or chief executive. Another common error is inviting people to sit on the board because of their marquee name within a certain field of endeavor (e.g., a famous dancer on the board of a dance organization) without due consideration to the person's ability and availability to fulfill fiduciary duties, providing the critical oversight function. Board attention is crucial to good governance. The Smithsonian Institution case is instructive. Notwithstanding the breathtaking scope and scale of the institution—the world's largest museum and research complex—at the time of its 2007 crisis, its Board of Regents (the institution's governing board) was composed of just seventeen persons. And not just seventeen ordinary persons, but seventeen of the busiest people in the nation: by law, the board consisted of the vice president of the United States, the chief justice of the United States, three members of the Senate, three members of the House of Representatives, and nine other persons selected by joint resolution of Congress.[9] The chief justice of the U.S. Supreme Court served as chancellor.

Despite regular attendance by most regents and active participation in meetings, the independent review committee appointed to assess the institution's failures following its crisis concluded that, in the end, the regents did not provide the level of leadership and oversight that the regents had intended. Contributing to the situation was an agenda and information flow tightly controlled by the CEO's office. Information leading to difficult and critical decisions was at times prepared and presented in a summary fashion that did not encourage full and complete discussion. As a result, the regents were at times unable to thoroughly consider the major and strategic issues facing the Institution.

Moreover, the Smithsonian is a complex institution, including not only mission-related entities such as leading museums, research centers, and a zoo, but also business ventures such as retail shops, restaurants, and buildings. To provide proper oversight and strategic guidance for all of these various functions, board candidates should possess expertise in financial management, investment strategies, audit functions, governance, compensation, and facilities management, as well as an interest in and a devotion to the arts and sciences. Prominent persons—donors, artists, scientists, public officials, and others—with an interest in the organization's program but lacking the time, availability, or expertise to provide meaningful oversight may serve the organization in a non-fiduciary capacity, such as an honorary or advisory board, or on professional councils.

The governing body of a nonprofit must be made up entirely of people in a position to govern it—setting the strategic direction of the organization and overseeing management's execution of the mission.

In Sum/Coming Up Next

As this Part I has described, nonprofit leaders and the lawyers who counsel organizations should know about corporate and tax laws and the principles of good governance. These laws provide a foundation for organizations to do their best work in the public's interest.

The following Focus Questions for Chapter 3 reinforce the elements of good governance and its role in nonprofit success. The Chapter 3 Work Plan helps strengthen institutional leadership's understanding of their role in the organization, and the legal basis for that role.

Although nonprofit organizations may be tax-exempt, they are not law-exempt! Part II takes a department-by-department look at the business law issues that arise across all parts of the organization. For lawyers, Chapters 4 through 10 may refresh their knowledge of familiar business law topics and translate it to the nonprofit context. For nonprofit executives and trustees without legal background, these chapters provide an introduction to many of the legal issues that commonly arise. By the end Part II, the leaders and attorneys will be poised to work together to take advantage of opportunities and address risks.

Focus Questions for Chapter 3: Good Counsel about Corporate Governance

1. What is the board of directors' role, and how does it differ from management?
2. What key documents should every board member have?
3. What are meeting minutes, and why are they important?
4. What does a governance or nominating committee do?
5. What are some key audit-related functions of the board, and what are the important qualifications of its members who fulfill these functions?
6. List the most important considerations for trustees setting or reviewing executive compensation.
7. How can counsel most effectively serve the chief executive?
8. What were some of the corporate governance failures alleged in the Smithsonian and Stevens case studies, and what are some of the lessons learned?

Chapter 3 Work Plan

Good Counsel about Corporate Governance

This work plan can help strengthen institutional leadership's understanding of the somewhat theoretical principles of fiduciary duties—care, loyalty, and obedience—and apply them to the real business of governing the organization.

❑ Obtain a copy of the board training/orientation materials or handbook.
  • Ascertain the board's understanding of the mission of the organization.
  • Understand how the board of directors discharges its oversight role.
  • Understand how well the boundary is observed between oversight (a board function) and day-to-day execution and management (a management function).

❑ Ascertain whether the board meets regularly—when were its last several meetings?
  • Understand periodicity of board meetings and committee meetings, ascertain whether the board (or executive committee) meets frequently enough to meet legal requirements and to assure good governance.
  • Review notice of meetings to ascertain whether it is properly given.

❑ Review attendance at recent meetings.
  • Is the quorum requirement met for business to be conducted?
  • Are there members who have missed several meetings consecutively or persistently?

❑ Determine whether votes are taken (in person, including by conference call or by written consent), and whether resolutions are moved, seconded, and voted upon for the conduct of important pieces of business, in keeping with state law, bylaws, and good practices.

❑ Review minutes going back three to five years, including resolutions passed or other actions taken.

- Do the minutes record the board's consideration of important organizational matters, properly record votes, appear to be accurate and complete without being so detailed as to chill or obfuscate board discussions?
- Are they timely distributed to and reviewed by members in attendance, with the opportunity to propose corrections?

❑ Ascertain the extent to which the board genuinely debates and deliberates about proposals and makes informed decisions about important matters concerning the organization, its planning, and its execution of mission.

❑ Assess whether materials are timely distributed in advance of board meetings, providing ample opportunity for members to consider new or tabled agenda items and to fully understand draft resolutions and other proposed board actions.

❑ Understand whether the board and committee meeting schedule allows time for information gathering and consideration about how comparable institutions deal with similar problems.

❑ Ascertain whether board members have access to, and are permitted to ask questions of, outside experts such as lawyers, accountants, and investment advisors, as appropriate.

❑ Ascertain what duties have been delegated to committees (e.g., initial review of auditor's report by the audit committee, and/or the budget by the finance committee, and/or executive compensation matters by the personnel committee, etc.).

- Review charters/mandates of committees.
- Ascertain that committees report findings and recommendations to the full board.

❑ Determine whether board members meet periodically with members of senior management as appropriate; for example, the chair of the finance committee with the chief financial officer.

❑ Find out whether the board or its nominating/governance committee undertakes regular self-evaluations, member evaluations and organizational evaluations. Review recent evaluations as well as steps taken to carry out recommendations.

❑ Review executive compensation procedures.

- Obtain minutes from most recent executive compensation review to assess compliance with legal requirements.

PART

II

A GRAND TOUR OF NONPROFITS' BUSINESS LAW NEEDS

CHAPTER

4

Contracts and Intellectual Property: Laws that Matter to Program Staff

Part II, consisting of Chapters 4 to 10, is a grand tour through the legal needs of a nonprofit organization, department by department. We begin with the organization's Program department, that is, the staff in charge of carrying out the organization's primary mission-related activities. Chapter 4 explores two fundamental legal concerns of the organization's Program staff: contracts and intellectual property (copyrights, trademarks and patents). The contract law discussion explains the basic elements of legal agreements. It then shows how all the parts fit together in a simplified sample contract. The intellectual property law discussion in this chapter focuses mainly on copyright law, explaining how an organization can keep legal control of the original works its Program department creates. With a view toward disseminating and monetizing intellectual property assets, it also includes a simplified sample license agreement.

Since intellectual property law questions also arise in the work of marketing and public relations professionals, the discussion continues in that context in Chapter 8.

Understanding the Organization's Program

The organization's program is what it does: Environmental groups address environmental matters, educational organizations educate, health organizations research the causes of disease and/or care for the sick, orchestras perform symphonic repertoire, and more.

An organization's Chief Program Officer, who may carry any of a number of titles depending on the work of the organization—the dean of an educational institution, the chief medical officer of a hospital, the head curator of a museum for example—generally has responsibility for achieving the mission-furthering program work of the organization. The Chief Program Officer, who may work side-by-side with the executive director, may report to him or her, or (in smaller organizations) may also be the executive director, is responsible for ensuring the high-quality implementation, evaluation, and delivery of all programs. This post has a broad and powerful mandate, and this person's efforts must be buttressed by each of the other management functions: finance, administration, fundraising, operations, communications, technology, legal, and so on. The Chief Program Officer may also have direct relations with external stakeholders (the community served by the organization), as well as its board of directors. Larger nonprofit organizations may have several programmatic functions, each a mini-business contributing to the organization's mission. Each of these programs may have a Chief Program Officer.

The lawyer serving a nonprofit must become thoroughly familiar with the programmatic functions of the organization, how it carries out its cultural, educational, health/human services, social, or other mission. It is difficult to generalize about what types of legal issues are likeliest to arise for the programmatic departments of nonprofits because the programmatic functions among the eight different types of charitable organizations differ greatly, and the legal matters involved may be specialized. For instance, the legal issues surrounding the programmatic function of a wildlife refuge are very different from those surrounding the programmatic function of a religious institution, a hospice, a university, or a dropout prevention program.

Although the diversity of missions and programs across the sector makes it difficult to generalize, two areas of law are relevant for just about every nonprofit. They are *contract law* and *intellectual property law*.

We turn first to contract law.

Contracts: At the Heart of the Program's Legal Arrangements

Although every nonprofit organization's program is different, all are concerned with contract law. Contracts enable the organization to procure and provide the goods and services needed to carry out its program-related activities. Depending on the size of the organization and the nature and scope of its programmatic activities, there may be many different kinds of contracts. The following is a discussion of what they have in common.

Contracts are the tie that binds an organization to its clients, vendors, workers, affiliates, facilities, and sources of funding. For program managers at the various types of charitable organizations, contracts may include:

- Artist agreements
- Student, client, or patient enrollment forms (signifying the services for which the client is registering and the organization is promising to deliver)
- Service provider agreements
- Grant agreements
- Institutional affiliation agreements
- Other kinds of contracts

This section explains the basics of contract law as relevant to nonprofit program executives, trustees and counsel.

What Program Executives Need to Know about Contract Law

A contract is the binding exchange of mutual promises. Each party agrees to provide a specific thing or things of value to the other. The valuables thus exchanged are called *consideration*. For example, in a contract for a violinist to play a recital in a nonprofit organization's concert series, the artist agrees to play, and the organization agrees to present him and pay his fee.

Contracts must set forth the consideration with reasonable specificity so that both parties can perform their obligations under the contract. Specifics include who is to perform the obligations (the *parties* to the contract), when or over what period of time the exchange of obligations is to occur (the *term*), and other details that are meaningful to the parties. Without these specifics, a contract may not be valid, as it merely expresses an agreement to agree, rather than a binding agreement.

Establishing a Contract

Contracts are formed by *offer and acceptance*. In our example of the artist contract, the organization offers the artist an opportunity to perform at a particular concert hall on a particular date, for a particular fee, and other terms and conditions, and the artist may accept that offer. Or the artist may counteroffer—proposing a different date, a greater sum of money, or other consideration—and the organization may accept the counteroffer. Once there is offer and acceptance, the parties should render their agreement in *writing* and *sign the writing*, demonstrating their intent to be bound. In a business setting, most contracts are in writing, and signed by authorized representatives of each party, with the intent to be bound. There are rare instances of oral contracts, which under some circumstances are enforceable. However, for the sake of good internal controls and good managerial practice, obligations of the organization should be put in writing so that they can be reviewed and complied with by all who may need to know.

"In writing" doesn't necessarily mean on paper; electronic contracts have been recognized in most jurisdictions as binding upon both parties, so long as they contain all the necessary elements: the exchange of consideration, specificity of terms, and electronic signatures indicating intent to be mutually bound.

These basic principles are applicable to nonprofits, for-profits, individuals, and other types of contracting parties as well.

The parties proceed to perform their obligations under the contract, in accordance with its terms. In the vast majority of cases, they put the contract away and forget about it—until or unless a problem arises, at which time they should call in counsel to help interpret the situation in light of the contract and advise as to next steps.

Living with a Contract

Generally, the contract will remain in effect until it has been fully performed (meaning that consideration has been exchanged and obligations have been fulfilled). If it is time-based, like a lease, service contract, or affiliation agreement, eventually its *term* will expire and if the parties wish the relationship to continue, they will have to renew the agreement. Managers who are responsible for time-based agreements should maintain a calendar, tickler file, or other system to remind them when contracts come due for expiration or renewal. Counsel can help with a back-up system or file, but the responsibility should reside primarily with the program officer who is the keeper of that relationship or function.

Upon *full performance* of all obligations, or upon expiration at the end of the term, the agreement comes to an end, and the parties have no further obligation to one another under the contract. Contracts can also come to an end if one party or the other *terminates* the agreement before all obligations have been fully performed or before the term has expired. Depending on a party's bargaining power, it may be able to negotiate an early termination right, sometimes also called a *termination for convenience*. Termination for convenience allows a party the ability to end the contract even before all contemplated actions and obligations are performed (or before the term has expired), even if there has been no *breach*, as long as the terminating party provides notice and pays for what has transpired to date.

⇨ PRACTICE POINTER

Reserving the right of termination for convenience helps nonprofits undertaking new or experimental ventures, and also provides flexibility in longer-term arrangements for which funding has not been fully secured or budgeted.

Survival clauses spell out any continuing obligations the parties may have to one another even after the contract is completed or terminated. Generally the contract will call out duties that survive termination. Common examples include the duty to keep the terms of an arrangement confidential, the duty not to disclose sensitive information about the organization, its operations or its clients (such as trade secrets), and the obligation to continue a policy of insurance in effect.

Breaches, Terminations, and Damages

Next comes the what-if part. What if one party fails to live up to its obligations? Violating an obligation of a contract is called a *breach*. Generally speaking, if one party breaches a material term of a contract, the other party is entitled to *terminate the contract for cause*. Sometimes, in longer-term contracts with complicated duties to perform, the breaching party is entitled to receive *notice* from the non-breaching party of the breach, and an *opportunity to cure*. If the breaching party nevertheless fails to cure within the stated notice period, the other party is then entitled to terminate for cause. Terminating the contract means neither party has any further obligation to the other: no more payments, no more performance of obligations.

In addition to terminating the contract, the non-breaching party may be entitled to recover the provable financial cost to it of the other party's breach. This cost is called damages. To take our example, if the violinist signs a contract to perform in the arts organization's series and then doesn't show up, the arts organization may have to refund ticket holders' money. If the organization rented out the hall, printed programs, and hired stagehands, ushers, and others to work at the concert, it may be entitled to recover all of those costs from the artist as part of its *measure of damages*. In rare instances where a breaching party lets its intentions be known ahead of time and the cost to the nonbreaching party cannot be calculated, the nonbreaching party may go to court and try to obtain an *injunction*, or court order, stopping the party from breaching or ordering it to take (or refrain from taking) other action to avoid the harm. So, for example, if the artist gets a better-paying gig at the concert hall down the street for the same night, his prospective failure to show up at the planned concert may cause our organization *irreparable harm*, such as reputational harm, that could not be fully compensated by paying money damages after the fact. The organization could go to court as soon as it sees the concert posters in front of the competing concert hall and try to persuade a judge to *enjoin* the artist from performing at the other venue. (It probably cannot get an injunction forcing him to perform at its own venue, however.)

Other Common Contract Provisions

Many contracts contain a *force majeure* clause, explaining what happens if a major disruption outside the control of the parties — for example, an earthquake, fire, flood, widespread power outage, terrorist attack or strike—were to prevent the work from proceeding. In such an event, parties are generally excused from further performance and not liable for damages.

Contracts may also contain *risk-allocation* provisions such as insurance and indemnification. *Insurance provisions* spell out which party or parties is required to procure amounts and types of insurance to cover a variety of mishaps such as a worker injury, injury to a member of the public, or damage to premises or property. The insuring party can prove to the insured party that it has procured the required types and amounts of insurance by presenting a *certificate of insurance.*

Indemnification is a promise to cover another party's loss or harm, regardless of the presence or availability of insurance. It often serves as a backup to the insurance provision, in case the insuring party fails to procure the insurance, or fails to procure enough, or the insurance does not cover the harm. (More about insurance appears in Chapters 6 and 9.)

The *integration clause* is a provision, typically toward the end of a contract, which states that the agreement contains the entire understanding of the parties. The written contract overrides anything said in the course of negotiation, and provides that changes cannot be made except in writing, with the same formality as the original contract.

Sometimes, further explanatory materials are attached to a contract, such as *riders, exhibits, schedules* or *appendices.* It is important to distinguish whether those materials are merely attached there as additional information or samples, or whether those materials contain terms that are intended to be a part of the parties' agreement. If the parties expect these matters to be enforceable, then the main body of the agreement should refer to those materials and state that they are *incorporated by reference* as if fully set forth in the agreement. In case of a conflict or inconsistency between a provision of the main agreement and a provision of a rider, exhibit, schedule or appendix, there should be a statement as to which provision overrides the other.

Retaining, Filing, and Referring to Contracts

Contracts should generally be retained by the organization for a period of time even after the work is completed or otherwise terminated. Past contracts may serve as a useful template, or *precedent,* for a future relationship with that counterparty or a similar arrangement the organization may wish to enter into with someone else—suitably revised, of course, to reflect the new parties, dates, and other terms. Contracts also serve as a useful record of the organization's obligations for the year-end closing of the books, when auditors may wish to review them.

Finally, some untoward consequence of the contract may arise long after its performance—a lawsuit, for example, or a claim of copyright infringement by someone whose work was allegedly performed without permission—and the contract serves as the definitive statement of the parties' rights and responsibilities. State law varies as to how long after the term such claims may be brought—for example, the statute of limitations for contract claims in New York is six years. Copyright claims expire under federal law three years after the date of the last infringement. It is sensible to keep contracts on file for at least the duration of the state's statute of limitations, plus a year just to be safe. Of course if there is an ongoing dispute or threatened lawsuit about the subject of a contract, the contract and all documents pertaining to it should be retained until the matter is concluded and counsel gives clearance to discard them.

A Simplified Sample Contract, Dissected

Let's give some life to these concepts by looking at a simplified sample contract. The definitions, concepts and observations in the preceding section are noted throughout Figure 4.1.

Sign on the Dotted Line

In legal terms, a person authorized to act on behalf of an organization when dealing with third parties is called an *agent*. The organization is considered the *principal.* An agent is authorized to enter into binding agreements on the principal's behalf. An organization should continuously consider which people within the organization are its authorized agents, empowered to sign contracts on its behalf as a principal. It is important that these duties be delegated consciously and carefully, and that frequent reminders are provided to those who are and are not authorized to bind the organization and at what dollar levels.

What can go wrong? A contract law doctrine known as *apparent authority* gives a counterparty the right to assume that the person speaking (or signing) for the organization is empowered to

SIMPLIFIED SAMPLE ARTIST AGREEMENT

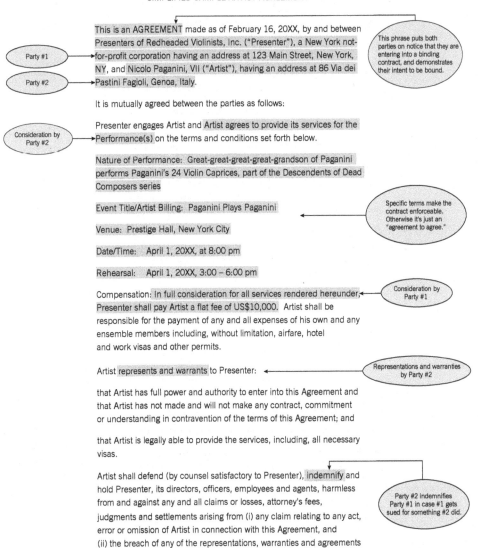

This is an AGREEMENT made as of February 16, 20XX, by and between Presenters of Redheaded Violinists, Inc. ("Presenter"), a New York not-for-profit corporation having an address at 123 Main Street, New York, NY, and Nicolo Paganini, VII ("Artist"), having an address at 86 Via dei Pastini Fagioli, Genoa, Italy.

Party #1

Party #2

This phrase puts both parties on notice that they are entering into a binding contract, and demonstrates their intent to be bound.

It is mutually agreed between the parties as follows:

Presenter engages Artist and Artist agrees to provide its services for the Performance(s) on the terms and conditions set forth below.

Consideration by Party #2

Nature of Performance: Great-great-great-great-grandson of Paganini performs Paganini's 24 Violin Caprices, part of the Descendents of Dead Composers series

Event Title/Artist Billing: Paganini Plays Paganini

Venue: Prestige Hall, New York City

Date/Time: April 1, 20XX, at 8:00 pm

Rehearsal: April 1, 20XX, 3:00 – 6:00 pm

Specific terms make the contract enforceable. Otherwise it's just an "agreement to agree."

Compensation: In full consideration for all services rendered hereunder, Presenter shall pay Artist a flat fee of US$10,000. Artist shall be responsible for the payment of any and all expenses of his own and any ensemble members including, without limitation, airfare, hotel and work visas and other permits.

Consideration by Party #1

Artist represents and warrants to Presenter:

Representations and warranties by Party #2

that Artist has full power and authority to enter into this Agreement and that Artist has not made and will not make any contract, commitment or understanding in contravention of the terms of this Agreement; and

that Artist is legally able to provide the services, including, all necessary visas.

Artist shall defend (by counsel satisfactory to Presenter), indemnify and hold Presenter, its directors, officers, employees and agents, harmless from and against any and all claims or losses, attorney's fees, judgments and settlements arising from (i) any claim relating to any act, error or omission of Artist in connection with this Agreement, and (ii) the breach of any of the representations, warranties and agreements set forth herein.

Party #2 indemnifies Party #1 in case #1 gets sued for something #2 did.

Figure 4.1   Simplified Sample Agreement (continued)

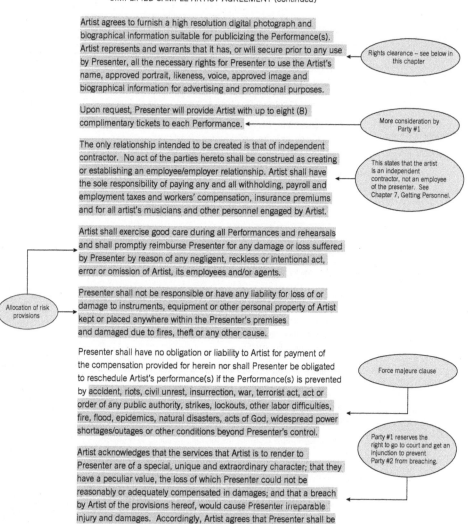

SIMPLIFIED SAMPLE ARTIST AGREEMENT (continued)

Artist agrees to furnish a high resolution digital photograph and biographical information suitable for publicizing the Performance(s). Artist represents and warrants that it has, or will secure prior to any use by Presenter, all the necessary rights for Presenter to use the Artist's name, approved portrait, likeness, voice, approved image and biographical information for advertising and promotional purposes.

Rights clearance – see below in this chapter

Upon request, Presenter will provide Artist with up to eight (8) complimentary tickets to each Performance.

More consideration by Party #1

The only relationship intended to be created is that of independent contractor. No act of the parties hereto shall be construed as creating or establishing an employee/employer relationship. Artist shall have the sole responsibility of paying any and all withholding, payroll and employment taxes and workers' compensation, insurance premiums and for all artist's musicians and other personnel engaged by Artist.

This states that the artist is an independent contractor, not an employee of the presenter. See Chapter 7, Getting Personnel.

Artist shall exercise good care during all Performances and rehearsals and shall promptly reimburse Presenter for any damage or loss suffered by Presenter by reason of any negligent, reckless or intentional act, error or omission of Artist, its employees and/or agents.

Presenter shall not be responsible or have any liability for loss of or damage to instruments, equipment or other personal property of Artist kept or placed anywhere within the Presenter's premises and damaged due to fires, theft or any other cause.

Allocation of risk provisions

Presenter shall have no obligation or liability to Artist for payment of the compensation provided for herein nor shall Presenter be obligated to reschedule Artist's performance(s) if the Performance(s) is prevented by accident, riots, civil unrest, insurrection, war, terrorist act, act or order of any public authority, strikes, lockouts, other labor difficulties, fire, flood, epidemics, natural disasters, acts of God, widespread power shortages/outages or other conditions beyond Presenter's control.

Force majeure clause

Artist acknowledges that the services that Artist is to render to Presenter are of a special, unique and extraordinary character; that they have a peculiar value, the loss of which Presenter could not be reasonably or adequately compensated in damages; and that a breach by Artist of the provisions hereof, would cause Presenter irreparable injury and damages. Accordingly, Artist agrees that Presenter shall be entitled to injunctive relief to prevent any such breach.

Party #1 reserves the right to go to court and get an injunction to prevent Party #2 from breaching.

Figure 4.1

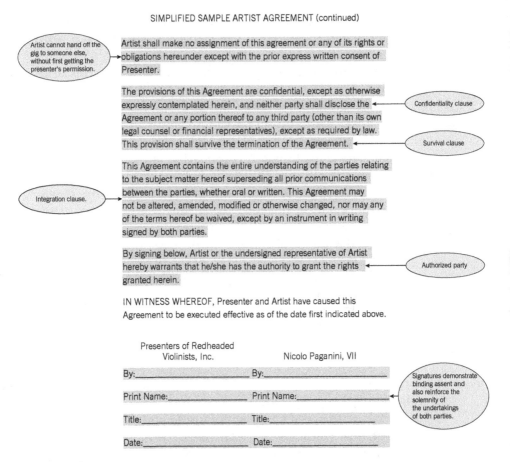

SIMPLIFIED SAMPLE ARTIST AGREEMENT (continued)

Artist cannot hand off the gig to someone else, without first getting the presenter's permission.

Artist shall make no assignment of this agreement or any of its rights or obligations hereunder except with the prior express written consent of Presenter.

The provisions of this Agreement are confidential, except as otherwise expressly contemplated herein, and neither party shall disclose the Agreement or any portion thereof to any third party (other than its own legal counsel or financial representatives), except as required by law. This provision shall survive the termination of the Agreement.

Confidentiality clause

Survival clause

Integration clause.

This Agreement contains the entire understanding of the parties relating to the subject matter hereof superseding all prior communications between the parties, whether oral or written. This Agreement may not be altered, amended, modified or otherwise changed, nor may any of the terms hereof be waived, except by an instrument in writing signed by both parties.

By signing below, Artist or the undersigned representative of Artist hereby warrants that he/she has the authority to grant the rights granted herein.

Authorized party

IN WITNESS WHEREOF, Presenter and Artist have caused this Agreement to be executed effective as of the date first indicated above.

Presenters of Redheaded Violinists, Inc.   Nicolo Paganini, VII

By:_____   By:_____

Print Name:_____   Print Name:_____

Title:_____   Title:_____

Date:_____   Date:_____

Signatures demonstrate binding assent and also reinforce the solemnity of the undertakings of both parties.

Figure 4.1

do so, if such assumption appears reasonable under the circumstances. This means the organization could be held fiscally and legally liable for a contract signed by someone purporting to act on behalf of the organization, even if that person in fact lacks the designated authority, if it was reasonable for the outsider to believe that the person had the authority. In addition, all persons dealing with contracting matters—even those not authorized to sign on the organization's behalf—should be trained to understand the basic elements of contract formation, so that they do not inadvertently form contracts in the name of the organization without authorization.

Suppose a nonprofit concert hall has a policy that only someone at the level of manager or higher can sign contracts. Mary, a manager at the nonprofit, asks her subordinate Sally to negotiate with an artist to perform on Saturday night. Sally Subordinate calls Artie Artist, identifies herself as working for the hall, and offers him $500 to appear at the nonprofit's venue on Saturday night at 8 P.M. to play two sets of jazz standards on his violin. Sally writes a confirming note to Artie from her work e-mail account, setting forth the details of the gig, with her digital signature appearing at the bottom of the screen. Artie writes back that he'll be delighted to play, and he too has a digital signature block at the end of his e-mail. In the meantime Mary, half-forgetting that she asked Sally to engage an artist, heard a great marimba player at a local restaurant and offered her the gig for Saturday night at the hall. Both Artie and the marimba player show up on Saturday night, expecting to play and be paid. Mary thinks that because no one has signed anything with Artie, and because Sally doesn't have signing authority anyway, the organization is not bound and doesn't owe him anything. She is probably wrong on both counts. Sally's interaction with Artie had all the earmarks of an enforceable agreement—offer, acceptance, consideration, and evidence of an intent to be bound—and moreover he had no reason to know that she was not authorized to negotiate a deal on behalf of the organization.

The moral of this story is that nonprofit employees who are unclear about how contracts are formed—or who do not observe limitations on signing authority—may create vulnerability for the organization. They may subject the organization to obligations it did not realize it was undertaking, did not set aside funding for, and has not taken into account in its insurance and other arrangements.

Likewise, the organization should be sure that the person signing the agreement for the counterparty is authorized. In the example of the artist contract, it would be unfortunate if the organization received a signed contract back from a person holding himself out as the agent, manager, or bandleader of the artistic act, when in fact the artist has fired the agent or the band has broken up. In addition to inquiring (are you authorized to make this contract on behalf of this artist?), well-counseled organizations will also include *representations and warranties* in their written form agreements to protect themselves. (See either of the sample contracts in this chapter for reference.)

The Wide Variety of Contracts

Beyond the Program department, kinds of contracts commonly encountered by nonprofit organizations include:

- Leases
- Venue rental/catering agreements for galas
- Retainer agreements with accountants, investment advisors, outside counsel, or other professionals
- Employment agreements
- Contracts spelling out the terms and conditions of outsourced functions such as maintenance, security, executive search, temporary staffing, and public relations

Although these kinds of contracts contain different terms, they all have the basic contractual elements described here. Qualified counsel can help an organization's executives devise, negotiate, and interpret contracts.

A contract is much more than a piece of paper with the word Agreement across the top and signature lines at the bottom. Contracts can take a number of forms, some of which might be surprising to the layperson. These can include the following.

Bank, Trust Account, and Credit Application Forms   With this variety of contract, a financial institution offers to provide certain services for a fee, subject to the various terms stated on the forms (the fine print). The organization accepts those terms by filling out and signing those forms. The consideration is the fees paid by the organization and the services provided by the financial institution.

Enrollment Forms   Enrollment forms, for example, for educational or rehabilitation services offered by the organization, are a form of contract with the organization's clients or students. In this case it is the organization making the offer to provide these services to the applicant, subject to payment of fees and other terms; and the client, student, or enrollee who fills out the form and signs at the bottom signifies his or her acceptance of those terms. The consideration is the fees paid by the participant and the services provided by the organization.

Entry Tickets   Entry tickets, for example, into a bird sanctuary or sporting event, permit the holder to enter the premises at the date and time specified. They are a variant of a contract, subject to revocation by the owner, known as a revocable *license.*

Web site Terms of Use   Terms of use are also a form of contract with users of the organization's web site. Even though it is all electronic, it is still a contract. Where's the assent? It resides in those checkboxes that only .01 percent of people read before clicking YES, I ACCEPT. (More on the subject of web site terms of use and privacy policies appears in Chapter 8.)

Pledge Forms   Pledge forms are often used with donors who spread out their promised payments over time. Although generally gift promises are not enforceable, there are some words the organization can include in its pledge forms to increase the chances of collecting on the gift. (Find out more in Chapter 5.)

Other Kinds of Contracts   Insurance policies are a type of contract. (More about insurance appears in Chapter 6.) Collective bargaining agreements between the organization and labor unions are another special kind of contract. (Collective bargaining agreements are discussed in Chapter 7.)

Contract Law in Sum

Clearly the organization's program officials, as well as many others carrying out other functions, should be familiar with the rudiments of contract law; just as clearly, they should have the opportunity to consult with counsel for guidance before entering into key contractual relationships. Counsel can also help establish systems for the efficient administration of contracts: the flow of contracts from initiation to signature and performance, storage, and use of past contracts as precedents for future arrangements. Counsel can also make sure that the variety of contractual relations are internally consistent and do not set up conflicting obligations that the organization cannot meet, or leave gaps between what it has promised one party and what it can reasonably expect another party to provide in order to effectuate that promise. Sound contract coordination and administration are critically important ways that counsel can support the organization's programmatic functions. Chapter 11 discusses contract management in detail.

As we conclude the discussion of contract law for nonprofits, note that a glossary of contract law terms is available on the companion web site to this book at www.wiley.com/go/goodcounsel. A contract law Work Plan appears at the end of this chapter.

What Is Intellectual Property (and What Does It Have to Do with Nonprofits?)

Intellectual property, or IP, refers to "creations of the mind": inventions, literary and artistic works, and symbols, names, images, and designs used in commerce.[1] Intellectual property includes *copyrights, trademarks, patents, trade secrets,* and other rights. Intellectual property is a common legal concern for an organizations' program leadership and staff. Among other things the organization may do, it may create intellectual property and it may use the intellectual property of others. IP can take various forms including:

Copyrights

Copyrights protect original literary, musical, pictorial, and graphic works fixed in a tangible medium of expression. For example, a nonprofit may have copyright protection in materials prepared by its employees in the scope of their duties, such as lesson plans, educational films, or descriptive materials surrounding its collections or presentations.

Trademarks

Trademarks are an identifying word, name, or symbol (e.g., a brand name or slogan). Some famous nonprofit trademarks are "Autism Speaks" and its puzzle piece logo; "WWF" (World Wide Fund for Nature) and its panda logo, and Susan G. Komen Race for the Cure and its pink ribbon logo.

Patents

Patents are legal monopolies that give the owner protection for its inventions. If, for example, a disaster relief charity invents a better and cheaper kind of tarpaulin for use in harsh climates, it may file for patent protection of the new kind of tarp. If others want to manufacture or distribute that new kind of tarp, they have to get a license from the organization, which may charge a license fee and/ or collect royalties.

Famous Nonprofit Trademarks

Other Kinds of Intellectual Property

Other kinds of intellectual property include *rights of publicity*, trade secrets (formulas, processes, devices, or other business information that is kept confidential to maintain an advantage over competitors), and the rights of trade unions.

Copyright Law for Nonprofits: An Introduction

The rest of this chapter describes how an organization's intellectual property, particularly its copyrighted works, come into being, how copyrighted works can be protected, and how they can be exploited (in a good way). (Chapter 8 discusses how the organization can legally use the intellectual property of others, and also how the organization's trademarks can be used to good effect, in Chapter 8.)

Copyright law protects literary works, musical works (including any accompanying words), dramatic works (including any accompanying music), choreographic works (dances), pantomimes, motion pictures (films, videos) and other audiovisual works, sound recordings, and architectural works. It also protects training materials, educational curricula and other written works. Copyright law derives from the Copyright Clause of the United States Constitution, which enables Congress to pass laws protecting original works in order to promote creative innovation.[2] The idea behind copyright law is that if content creators are fairly compensated for their creative labors, they will be incentivized to create new work for the public good.

Copyright law generally gives the creator of an original work the right to control how that work is used. The rights granted by copyright are intended to ensure that authors receive a fair return for their labors. Owning the copyright to a work provides the creator with important benefits, protections, and economic opportunities. It means that he or she has the exclusive right (monopoly) in that work. The owner of a copyrighted work is the only one who can reproduce the work; adapt the work; make copies and distribute the work; and publicly perform or display the work.[3] In order to use a copyrighted work, the user must obtain a license for such use from the copyright owner, unless the use is fair use. (The fair use doctrine is defined and discussed in Chapter 8.)

A work achieves copyright status once it is fixed in a tangible medium, whether it is in writing, in a data file (such as computer code), on canvas (such as a painting), on film, or other media. The owner of the work should affix the internationally recognized copyright symbol (©) together with the year and the owner's name, in order to put the world on notice that the work belongs to that owner.

In past years (prior to 1976), under U.S. law the creator of a work had to register that work in order to benefit from copyright protection—but not anymore. Once the work has been created and fixed in a tangible medium, it is automatically copyrighted. However, registering the work with the United States Copyright Office is a prerequisite to enforcing the owner's rights and obtaining certain types of relief from infringement. Registering also facilitates licensing of the copyrighted work. The U.S. Copyright Office's web site provides a user-friendly interface called Electronic Copyright Office, or eCO, that can be used with or without the help of a lawyer.[4] The electronic *registration* process requires logging in, uploading the work, answering some questions about the work, and paying a modest fee. The process can also be carried out in hard copy through the mail.

Copyright law protects original works of authorship. Works that may not be copyrighted include works that lack originality,

U.S. government works, or works that are strictly informational, such as the phone book.

Duration of Copyright Protection and Licensing

Ascertaining the duration of copyright protection is complicated. Under U.S. law, copyright protection for works created after 1978 lasts for the life of the author plus 70 years. (If joint authors create the work, the copyright lasts for the life of the longest surviving author plus 70 years.) *Works-made-for-hire* (defined in the next section) are protected for 95 years from publication or 120 years from creation, whichever is shorter. Works published between 1923 and 1978 are subject to several renewal terms of copyright, and if properly renewed, are protected for 95 years.[5] Works published prior to 1923 are no longer protected by copyright.[6]

The duration of copyright protection varies even further outside of U.S. borders. Countries that have signed on to the Berne Convention for the Protection of Literary and Artistic Works, including the United Kingdom, Spain, France, China and Japan, have agreed that the term of copyright protection must be at least the life of the author plus 50 years. A country may choose to extend the duration.[7]

Works that are no longer protected, or were not copyrightable to begin with, are said to be in the *public domain*, that is, they are not owned by anyone and can be freely used, posted, and repurposed without permission.

An organization can get permission to use the copyrighted work owned by someone else by obtaining a *license*. A license is a type of contract permitting the *licensee* to use the *licensor*'s work, sometimes for a fee, known as a *license fee*. A license is like renting the work (as opposed to owning it). The licensee's right to use the work may be limited in time or in scope by the terms of the license, and the licensee may or may not have the right to *sublicense* (akin to subleasing) the work to someone else, depending on what the license agreement says.

License agreements may be written on paper and signed by the two parties, as contracts often are. (A sample simplified license agreement appears later in this chapter.) Another common type of licenses is a *click-through license*, which gives users permission to use software by clicking a box agreeing to license terms as part of the installation process.

A *derivative work* is a work based upon one or more pre-existing works, such as a film adaptation of a novel, or posters depicting characters from a play.[8] The right to create and license derivative works belongs to the copyright holder.[9] Thus, a derivative work cannot be made without permission from the copyright holder of the original work.

The right to license derivative works can often be a source of valuable income to an organization.

> **Example**: The nonprofit Birdwatchers Society owns a drawing of a bird that a greeting card company finds attractive for a Christmas card. The greeting card company obtains a license from the Society and pays a fee.

> **Example**: A Hollywood film studio wishes to use a musical work commissioned and owned by a local chamber orchestra as the soundtrack for its next blockbuster. The chamber orchestra licenses out the work and reaps not only a license fee but royalties (a percentage of revenue form the film).

Organizations should take a detailed inventory of all works in which it has copyright ownership in order to ascertain what works it can license, whether directly or derivatively, and also in order to facilitate the identification (and either licensing or stopping the use) of unlicensed derivative works.

Taking Stock of Copyrighted Works Owned by the Organization

Many nonprofit organizations own copyrighted works. The works may have been created by the organization, such as articles in its newsletter, photographs it takes of its activities, web pages, training manuals and even specialty computer programs written by the organization.

Works created by an organization's workers in the course of doing their jobs on company time are generally considered to be owned by the organization—even if the person creating the works within the scope of his employment is the founder or principal employee of the organization.[10] These relationships are called *work-made-for-hire* relationships. The organization may also establish work-made-for-hire relationships with its volunteers or contractors who may be creating material within the scope of their duties for the organization. The organization's policies, including employee handbooks, should make clear that works created for the organization on company time and using company resources belong to the organization.

Nonprofits may also acquire copyrighted works by buying the works and the copyright, such as a painting, sculpture, or piece of choreography that has been written down. The contract or agreement under which the organization acquires the work should specify that the organization is acquiring the copyright in the work and not just the work itself.

⇨ **PRACTICE POINTER**

It is critically important that the organization keep track of how it creates, uses, licenses, and stores its intellectual property, and how it uses intellectual property belonging to others.

Nonprofit executives registering work on behalf of the organization should be sure to do so in the organization's name and not their own.

Unlocking the Treasure Trove: Licensing the Organization's Copyrighted Works for Others to Use

If an organization believes that its copyrighted works would be valuable for others to use, it should register those works and establish a standard license agreement under which to license its works to third parties. The license agreement often establishes a fee to be paid by the licensee, or other consideration. If the agreement ordinarily would involve a fee, the organization may decide to waive it if there is a reasonable business justification to do so. For example, a nonprofit may decide to waive a fee if the organization will receive valuable promotion from the use, or if the licensee is a fellow nonprofit that reciprocates with *gratis* (free) licenses of its own. The opportunity to license an organization's copyrighted works may also put the work in front of new and larger audiences, building the organization's visibility and credibility. The license agreement should specify what uses the copyrighted works may be put to, and should also state any limitations on use, such as no derivative works or no sublicensing to third parties without prior written approval by the owner.

(The tax treatment of license fees and royalties generated by non-profit organizations' licensing activities is discussed in Chapter 6.)

Figure 4.2 offers insight into some sample provisions of a letter agreement licensing an organization's copyrighted work.

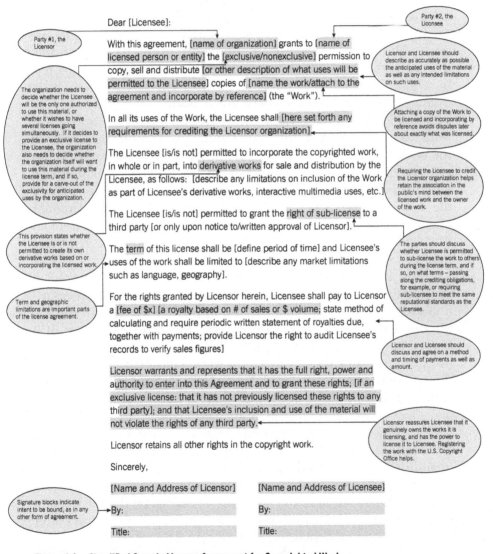

SIMPLIFIED SAMPLE LICENSE AGREEMENT
FOR COPYRIGHTED WORK

Figure 4.2   Simplified Sample License Agreement for Copyrighted Work

Protecting and Enforcing the Organization's Copyrights

To maintain the integrity of its copyrighted works (and to achieve the full potential of its licensing business), the organization should establish a means of monitoring, or policing, unauthorized uses of its copyrighted material. Policing of copyrighted works includes periodically searching the Internet, perusing like material published by others, and generally maintaining in the organization's employees a sense of alertness about the organization's rights in the work.

Upon discovering an unauthorized use, the organization should work with counsel to investigate the nature of the use. Specifically, the organization should determine how the material is being used, by whom, and for what purpose, such as commercial, nonprofit, derivative use, or fair use. There are reasons both in favor of and against allowing unauthorized use of an organization's copyrighted work to continue. On the one hand, the unauthorized use of the work may provide a window into the market for the work and can generate publicity. On the other hand, allowing the unauthorized use to persist may anger donors whose funding made the creation of the work possible, and also may reduce the value and desirability of potential licenses of the work. However, the unauthorized use may actually be a fair use, which cannot be prevented by the copyright holder.

After investigating the unauthorized use, the organization, in consultation with counsel, should make a preliminary determination as to whether to permit the use with a license, permit the use without a license, or try to stop the use. Before taking action, it is a good practice for counsel and/or at least one other authoritative person within the organization to be consulted as to whether the recommendation is sound. Some organizations choose to have committees review the recommendation. While an organization may elect to monitor the use and re-evaluate its action plan at a later date, a copyright infringement action must be commenced within three years of the infringing activity.[11] However, each new unauthorized use restarts the clock as to that use; for example, if an infringer posts an unauthorized copy of the organization's training video to a video sharing site, each day it remains on display is a new infringement, and thus the owner can sue up to three years after the last day it is on display.[12]

In Sum/Coming Up Next

This chapter has discussed two areas of law vitally important to the program staff: contract law and intellectual property law. The contract law discussion examined each element of contract formation, documentation, and administration. The intellectual property law discussion focused mainly on protecting the copyrighted works created by the program professionals of the organization. Other elements of intellectual property laws, such as licensing the works of others for the organization's use, protecting the organization's trade name, and the fair use defense, are discussed in Chapter 8.

A glossary of contract law and intellectual property law terms is available on the companion web site to this book at www.wiley .com/go/goodcounsel. A Work Plan for surveying an organization's contract law and intellectual property law needs appears after this chapter's Focus Questions.

After reviewing the following Focus Questions and Work Plans for Chapter 4, let's step down the hall as we leave the Program department and enter the Fundraising department. Chapter 5 offers an overview of the legal issues most commonly encountered by those who raise charitable funds for the organization.

Focus Questions for Chapter 4: Contracts and Intellectual Property: Laws that Matter to Program Staff

1. What is an organization's program? Name some examples of the program(s) of one or more nonprofits.
2. What is a contract, and what are the necessary elements to form one?
3. What are some kinds of contracts typically encountered by nonprofit organizations, no matter what their program?
4. Why should an organization have written policies and procedures about who is authorized to make and sign contracts on behalf of the organization?
5. What types of contractual provisions may survive termination?
6. Name some examples of contracts other than the kind written on a piece of paper and signed by both parties.
7. What is a force majeure? What typically happens to the parties' obligations to perform under the contract in case of a force majeure event?

(continued)

8. What are the differences between copyrights, trademarks, and patents?
9. When does a work achieve copyright status?
10. Why should an organization take stock of its copyrighted assets?
11. How can an organization allow another entity to use its copyrighted materials?
12. What are some of the advantages and disadvantages to allowing another entity to use an organization's copyrighted materials:
    a. Through a license?
    b. Without a license?

Chapter 4 Work Plans

Contracts and Intellectual Property: Laws that Matter to the Program Department

These two work plans can assist counsel or supervised law students in surveying an organization's contract and copyright law contexts.

Work Plan 1: Contract Administration

This work plan can assist counsel or supervised law students to survey an organization's contracting procedures.

❑ Understand contracting procedures and how they differ throughout the organization.
- How are contracts created, reviewed, and signed?
- Who is responsible for overseeing compliance with contractual rights and duties?
- Who keeps track of deadlines, renewal dates, expirations, and milestones toward completion?
- Does the answer differ department to department?

❑ Determine whether there are particular contracts that the organization would like assistance with negotiating/renegotiating, drafting, reviewing, or understanding.
- Vendors, funders, partners, others.

❑ Determine whether contract law presentations would help non-legal staff members become more conversant with the many and sometimes surprising forms that contracts can take.
- Examples include contractor work orders, donor pledge forms, enrollment forms, insurance policies, banking and credit application forms, intellectual property licenses, venue rental agreements, and click-through software licenses.

❑ Ascertain how legal review of contracts is sought and provided.
  • Is there a notification system to initiate review of a new contract?
  • Would it strengthen and streamline contracting procedures to have law-yers assist in pre-approving certain standard form contracts?
  • Do non-lawyers receive training to administer form contracts?
  • Is there clarity about when counsel should be consulted in connection with contract review?
  • Is there a database of executed contracts for current and future reference?
  • Are signed contracts, invoices and payments coordinated with Finance and subject to the organization's internal control system?
  • Are contract matters such as legal notices, breaches, opportunities to cure, amendments, renewals, and terminations referred for legal advice and handling?
❑ Obtain a copy of signing authorizations (if applicable) and ascertain the extent to which they are written, understood and enforced.
  • Who is responsible for enforcing and updating signing authorizations?
  • Are there gaps between apparent authority and actual authority to bind the organization?
  • Would non-legal staff benefit from a presentation about authorization to bind the organization, and the dangers of apparent authority?

Work Plan 2: Copyright Administration

This work plan can assist counsel or supervised law students in surveying an organization's management of its copyrights.
❑ Ascertain what steps are taken to ensure that copyrightable works created by employees in the course of their jobs belong to the company.
  • Review employment contracts, offer letters, employee handbooks, poli-cies, and procedures under the work-made-for-hire doctrine.
❑ Ascertain whether the organization has a protocol for registering its copyrighted works for license to others.
  • Take stock of any copyrighted works owned by the organization.
  • Determine whether there are other works that are good candidates for registration.
❑ Determine whether the organization is currently licensing out any of its copyrighted works.
  • Gather and examine license agreements.
  • Understand what steps it takes to enforce terms of licenses.
❑ Ascertain the organization's means of monitoring, investigating, and handling unauthorized uses of its copyrighted works.
  • Formulate recommendations for any unauthorized uses that this process uncovers.

CHAPTER

5

Counseling the Rainmakers:
Legal Aspects of Raising Money

Attracting contributions is important for charities whose earned revenue does not cover expenses—which is to say, just about all of them. When the organization's board approves an annual budget and/or budgets for special purposes, such as capital needs or major new initiatives, it sets targets for the amount of fundraising that will be required. In well-governed and well-run organizations, funds are not raised haphazardly or wishfully; they are raised with particular targets in mind and metrics for success.

Charitable fundraising has become more varied and pitches have become more creative. Regulatory scrutiny of the various fundraising tools and techniques has increased accordingly. This chapter discusses the legal aspects of charitable fundraising: who regulates fundraising activity, and what steps organizations must follow to comply. It talks about the laws and regulations governing routine kinds of fundraising, such as annual gift solicitations, as well as special kinds of fundraising such as major gifts, pledges, bequests, and other types of planned giving. The chapter provides legal perspectives on gifts other than cash, such as gifts of real estate, closely held stock, in-kind giving and appreciated investments. It also touches upon joint fundraising campaigns among cooperating nonprofits, and discusses the legal elements of fundraising from corporations. The chapter provides some perspectives on disputes with donors, which are rare but potentially high-stakes affairs, with legal and governance implications for the institution. The chapter also discusses ways in which lawyers can help their favorite charities in the fundraising effort. It closes with some observations about the ways in which good governance and compliance supports the efforts of the fundraisers.

A Lawyer's Introduction to Fundraising

Fundraising is critical, particularly in charities where earned income is substantially less than expenses. *Earned income* is money the organization receives in exchange for goods it sells or services it renders—for example, fees paid by or for patients treated in a health care facility, tuition paid by students at an educational institution, or admission tickets purchased by visitors at a zoo or wildlife habitat. *Contributed income*, or *unearned income*, by contrast, is money the organization receives through charitable donations. Simply put, the organization's program services provide earned income, while the fundraising generates contributed income.

In smaller nonprofits, fundraising may be primarily the executive director's job, with the help and support of the board, while at larger organizations, a separate person, or even a whole department, may be dedicated to raising monies to help support the organization.

Generally speaking, the responsibility of the fundraiser(s) is to develop, manage, implement, and evaluate the organization's fundraising program. The head of fundraising, as (or reporting to) the CEO, interacts frequently with the board in its fundraising capacity. The job title or function sometimes includes the words development, institutional advancement or external affairs. The work includes responsibility for planning and executing a wide variety of fundraising activities, such as:

- Organizing annual fund drives.
- Producing special benefit events, such as walk-a-thons and golf tournaments.
- Soliciting corporate sponsorships.
- Planning and executing capital and endowment campaigns.
- Establishing and publicizing planned giving programs.
- Running periodic membership drives.
- Writing public and private grant applications.
- Activating board members and their contacts.

Development professionals harness the energies of trustees and volunteers, as well as paid staff (and sometimes outside consultants and fundraisers), to plan and execute these activities. They also oversee the solicitation and acknowledgment process, maintain records, establish and disclose donor benefits in accordance with IRS requirements, research and cultivate new prospects, and seek out new funding opportunities of all kinds.

Charities are subject to regulations governing the solicitation and collection of donations under the laws of each state. Charitable organizations intending to solicit contributions in such states must generally register with the charity regulators in each state's Attorney General's office or with the Secretary of State, and then comply with ongoing reporting and other requirements. Such laws, of course, prohibit false statements in registration, fraudulent or illegal acts in connection with solicitations, failure to use contributions in a manner consistent with the purposes stated in the solicitation efforts, and/or failure to maintain books and records. Violations can result in an action by the state Attorney General to turn over ill-gotten gains to the state and/or make restitution.

With this background in mind, counsel can begin thinking about how they can support this crucial function of every nonprofit organization.

How Do Fundraisers Raise Money?

Donated funds are the lifeblood of many nonprofit organizations. To fully grasp the types, characteristics, and orders of magnitude of an organization's fundraising activities, counsel should know and understand the different ways that charitable dollars are raised.

General Operating Fundraising   General operating fundraising is the money raised to carry out the organization's ordinary operations. These funds may be raised through annual or periodic appeals, through mailings, web site solicitations, social media pages, fundraising events, and benefits. Unless otherwise described to the public, these funds are generally unrestricted, meaning that the monies can be used to pay the bills of the organization and need not be set aside for any specific purpose or use.

Restricted Gifts   A *restricted gift* is a gift made to the organization for a specific use. The restrictions are generally specified in a written agreement between the organization and the donor, although the organization's statements—in brochures or web site appeals for example—about how certain monies will be used are generally considered binding on the organization. A donation to a special hurricane fund of the American Red Cross or a contribution to the capital campaign of a local public radio station to build a new studio are examples of restricted gifts. The organization must track such monies in a separate accounting line and spend them only for the purpose intended by the donor.

Endowment Funds *Endowment funds* are monies—generally larger gifts—that are raised and kept by the organization as a nest egg. Endowment funds form the permanent assets of the organization and are not ordinarily spent down, although the income or appreciated value may be spent to support annual operations. It is desirable for organizations of any size to set up an endowment because of the budgetary stability it provides: a relatively constant source of annual funding for operations, even in years where earned revenues and contributed income may vary due to changes in the national economy or other reasons. An endowment helps diversify the organization's funding base.

Counsel's advice may be useful on many topics relating to the endowment:

- Advising the board on setting up restrictions for the use of endowment funds that are consistent with the organization's nonprofit, tax-exempt purposes, donor intent, and state law.
- Counseling the board, in consultation with finance and investment professionals, as it sets guidelines for how much (what percentage or other measure) of the interest income or growth can be used yearly (the *spending rate*, or *draw*).
- Helping the board establish and review policies for deciding when the endowment principal can be invaded, if needed under extraordinary circumstances, subject to state law and donor intent.
- Setting up the endowment within the organization's books, spinning it off into a separate entity, or enlisting the help of a community foundation to hold the endowment for the organization.

- Establishing form agreements, bequest language, and other documents to be used with prospective endowment donors.
- Working closely with finance and audit professionals for continued compliance with legal requirements and donor intent.

(More information about the legal aspects of endowment funds appears in Chapter 6.)

Other Kinds of Gifts   Donations may take different forms, depending on the means of the donor, the needs of the organization, and the expected duration of the support. The simplest is a gift of cash or marketable securities (*liquids*). Donors also may donate goods or services (*in-kind support*). Individuals also may make charitable giving part of their estate plan through *bequests* (gifts made through a will), charitable remainder trusts and annuities, gifts of life insurance, and other forms of *planned giving* or *legacy giving*. Donors also may make *pledges*, or installment payments (or ongoing payments), of larger gifts over a period of time.

About Charitable Receipts   Section 501(c)(3) organizations are unique in that contributions to them are tax deductible to the donor. A charity receiving a donation worth $250 or more must provide the donor with a written *receipt*. Although there is no standard format for contribution receipts, they should include the donor's name; the date of the gift; the amount of money given; and a statement as to whether goods or services were received in exchange for the gift.

The rules for in-kind donations (gifts of goods or services) are different. The organization provides a receipt for a gift of goods (for example, donating used clothes to the Salvation Army) worth over $75. The receipt (called a disclosure statement) includes a description of the item donated and a good-faith estimate of its value. It is the donor's responsibility, not the charity's, to provide the estimated value of an in-kind donation.

Note that in most cases, the donation of in-kind *services* is not tax-deductible to the donor.

Quid pro quo (a Latin phrase meaning this for that) contributions are monetary contributions to an organization for which the donor receives services or goods in return. Quid pro quo contributions commonly arise in the context of special fundraising events, such as galas or charity auctions.

> **Example:** A parent pays $100 to attend a PTA dinner and student concert. The market value of the dinner and the concert ticket is $40. The charitable contribution portion of the payment is $60. The PTA provides the donor with a disclosure statement, even though his contribution portion is less than $75, because the quid pro quo contribution is greater than $75.[1]
>
> The donor may claim a charitable contribution of $60 for the price paid above the fair market value of the items received.[2] If he also bid and paid $500 for a watch at the PTA's silent auction, knowing that the watch's fair market value was only $150, he may also claim a charitable contribution of $350.[3] He may not, however, claim as a charitable contribution the cost of the raffles, lotteries, or bingo games he played that night.[4]

Because many donations are given near the end of the calendar year in anticipation of the donor obtaining a tax write-off, it is helpful to know that donations are deemed given on the date the check is mailed, or the credit card is charged. Donations of stock are deemed completed on the date of the transfer into the nonprofit's brokerage account, or if stock certificates are mailed, on the date of postmark.

Dues are generally not considered contributions if the member receives benefits in return for his or her payment (the benefits of membership generally are deemed to be equal in value to the *membership fees or dues*). Likewise, tuition or fees-for-service paid to nonprofit educational or health organizations are not deductible to the extent the amounts paid are commensurate with the value of the services received (e.g., YMCA gym membership, summer sports camp for disabled youth). Some organizations incorporate a voluntary element of charitable giving on their invoices; if the member responds by checking the box and paying the additional amount, she gets a charitable receipt just for the excess amount of the gift over the value of the services or other benefits received in return.

Individuals, foundations, or corporations may contribute funds. Rules pertaining to contributions by corporations, often as corporate sponsorships, are set forth later in this chapter.

The organization may have different personnel who steward these different types of donors, and may have somewhat differing procedures for soliciting, recording, and acknowledging gifts, depending on the source.

Laws That Matter to Fundraisers

Governments regulate the processes by which organizations solicit, record, invest, expend, disclose, and provide receipts for charitable donations. Each of the 50 states plus the District of Columbia regulates these activities, and some states have a specific bureau or office for this purpose. By periodically navigating the charity bureau's web site, attending public speeches of its leadership, and reviewing bureau publications, counsel and fundraising staff can become acquainted with the bureau's priorities and key personnel.[5]

In addition to state regulation, through the IRS the federal government has greatly expanded its oversight of the sector, requiring much more information about a charity's fundraising practices in the annual information return (IRS Form 990) than ever before—with more changes coming. Accordingly, counsel should visit the IRS web site often and become familiar with the public statements of the IRS' Exempt Organizations leadership. Several valuable IRS annual conferences and continuing education programs, along with free weekly IRS newsletters, help counsel and organizations keep abreast of these developments. The IRS web site contains a wealth of information on its Exempt Organizations page.[6]

Donor Privacy and Security

Privacy is important to many donors and regulators. Counsel should become familiar with how donors' personally identifiable information (names, contact information, amount and frequency of gifts, bank account numbers, and credit card information) is stored, used, and purged by the nonprofit, how donors can remove or change their information from the organization's database, how donors may request that they be contacted by some means but not others (e.g., by e-mail or postal mail but not by telephone), and what steps are taken periodically to ensure that the organization follows applicable law as well as any voluntarily promised privacy protections (such as that the organization will not sell or rent its donor list to third parties). Even absent legal considerations, from a donor relations and consumer relations perspective, it is far better not to make such promises than to make them and not keep them.

Interestingly, the Federal Trade Commission's National Do Not Call Registry exempts calls that solicit contributions for a charity, even if a for-profit agent makes the calls on the charity's behalf. However, for-profit organizations soliciting contributions must honor a call recipient's request to be placed on an entity-specific do not call list.[7]

The federal informational return Form 990 does not require organizations to publicly disclose information about specific donors and gifts. This information is reported to the government on Schedule B of the form but is removed before posting for public view. However, some states are examining whether certain nonprofit institutions should be forced to disclose the identity of their donors. In such cases, any promises by the organization to maintain donors' privacy should be made subject to applicable law.

Data security concerns also figure into nonprofit fundraising; the last thing a nonprofit needs is for its clients' or donors' bank account numbers or credit card information to be stolen and used for improper purposes because the organization carelessly handles this information. An organization should ensure that there are proper protocols in place for:

- Handling checks, making photocopies, and storing and shredding paper records with confidential information, such as bank account numbers or credit card numbers.
- Protecting data stored in password-protected databases, limiting access, and implementing other security measures.
- Training employees on protocols and enforcing the protocols.

Especially when advising smaller nonprofits with limited staff, counsel should encourage the creation of written procedures for daily tasks, including mail handling, cash handling, gift processing, tax acknowledgment processing, and banking deposit reconciliation. Counsel should work with the Finance team in scanning for vulnerabilities in the cash and credit card handling systems, and eliminate opportunities for theft and fraud.

Registration Requirements for Charitable Solicitations

Many charities hire outside fundraising consultants to help raise funds because the charities lack the time, expertise or sufficient staff to raise funds themselves. Due diligence in selecting outside fundraisers is critical, because they represent the organization to its prospective donors and may even handle the organization's money or incur expenses in its name. Most states have adopted charitable solicitation laws that require charities and their outside fundraisers to register with the state, describe their fundraising activities, file financial and other disclosure documents, and pay a fee that covers the administrative expenses of monitoring charities. The purpose of these registration laws is to enhance transparency and facilitate state charities officers' efforts to protect donors, the general public, and the charities themselves from fraud and deception.

Fortunately for organizations that fundraise in more than one state, registration has been simplified and made more uniform among various cooperating states. Thanks to the National Association of State Charities Officials and the National Association of Attorneys General, most U.S. states accept a uniform registration form. Just a few states that require registration do not accept the uniform registration form; registrations must be done separately for these states.[8]

The purpose of the Unified Registration Statement (URS) is to consolidate the information requirements, making the data gathering and filing process more efficient for the organizations and more standardized for the regulators.

The uniform forms are helpful, and their goals are laudable, but they do not eliminate all of the hassles of registering. Annual reporting must be done every year. Oftentimes the various states' renewal dates and deadlines do not coincide with one another—nor with the organization's fiscal year or other reporting cycles—adding the burden of producing off-cycle financial information. Some states require organizations to file supplemental information along with the uniform registration form. Organizations in the midst of a capital or endowment campaign along with ordinary annual operating fundraising may wish to seek further advice about how such information should be reflected on these forms.

Organizations using paid outside fundraising solicitors must be sure that the providers are also properly registered in states that require it. A key element of interest to state charities regulators as well as to donors is the cost of fundraising. This cost is typically tracked as the percentage of funds solicited that is retained by the outside fundraiser. The average amount retained by the charity after the outside fundraiser is paid can be frighteningly low: in recent studies in New York State, the average has been found to be less than 40 percent to the charity, 60 percent to the fundraisers![9] Certain state laws require particular provisions in agreements between charities and outside solicitors, such as a cooling off period within which the charity may cancel the relationship without penalty.

▭⇨ PRACTICE POINTER

Counsel should consult applicable state laws before the organization enters into agreements with outside fundraisers, and check their registration status before awarding contracts to them.[10]

State trade commissions and a handful of counties and municipalities have also set up regulatory schemes to prevent misleading charitable fundraising. Counsel should be sure to consult the charitable solicitation laws governing the organization's locality.

Compliance with Grant Terms

Government grants are funds provided to nonprofit organizations for programs and services that benefit specific causes, the community or the public at large. The grant application may request certain legal information about the organization, such as information about the nonprofit's state of incorporation, mission, bylaws, board composition, conflict of interest rules, and a summary of pending litigations (lawsuits, regulatory matters), among other information. Counsel should review any responses on a grant application that summarize or provide legal information.

Once the grant is awarded, the organization may be asked to sign a funding agreement stipulating the terms and conditions of the funding. Counsel should review this agreement with relevant staff so that the personnel responsible for fulfilling grant terms understand their commitments. At the end of the grant, and sometimes periodically during the course of a longer grant, the organization will be asked to provide additional information and documentation of its compliance with grant terms. Often these forms require the sworn (and possibly notarized) signature of an official of the organization. Because documents relating to government grants are usually available to the public, and because the signed forms may carry significant penalties if they contain misinformation, they should be reviewed with care by counsel.

Here's how *not* to comply with the requirements of a government grant:

> **Example:** A nonprofit CEO got a 10-year jail term and an order to repay $65 million to the government after lying to the government about the number of blind or severely disabled workers employed by his organization. The misrepresentations enabled the organization to qualify for no-bid government contracts set aside for nonprofits that employed such workers. The organization was raided by federal officials and is now defunct.[11]

Needless to say the organization would have benefited from counsel's review of the application forms and ongoing review of compliance with contract terms.

Grants often require that the funds and associated expenses be segregated within the organization's accounting system and separately tracked. Counsel can double-check the finance and fundraising teams' compliance with this requirement. Many nonprofits, especially smaller nonprofits, may be tempted to deposit grant funding in their general accounts for immediate use for urgent needs, and then some time later go back to reconstruct the expenditures for tracking and reporting purposes. This practice is extremely risky and should be avoided.

Planned Giving

Planned gifts, as contrasted to annual donations of cash, are the various ways that donors can support the organization in the longer term through their financial plans or estate plans. Common planned-giving techniques include:

- Bequests (gifts made at the time of death, usually through a will but sometimes through a trust).

- Gifts made through a trust or other instrument that returns income or other financial benefits to the donor while he or she is still alive, with the remainder going to the charity after the donor (and sometimes one other beneficiary) passes away.
- Gifts of appreciated assets, such as stock, real estate, artwork, partnership interests, life insurance, or a retirement plan.

Many planned gifts use estate and tax planning techniques that provide valuable tax benefits to donors (or their heirs) while also providing for the charity in the long term.

Fundraising staff, in consultation with counsel, should enlist an attorney with expertise in trusts and estate law to help set up or periodically review the organization's planned giving programs and policies.

⇨ PRACTICE POINTER

Most planned giving donors have counsel of their own. The organization should not mistake this attorney for the organization's attorney, but should retain its own counsel to review the arrangements from the organization's point of view.

In reviewing the organization's policies, counsel should take note of the following:

- Who is authorized to discuss, negotiate, and sign planned giving arrangements with prospective donors?
- Who is authorized to receive property? What types of property will the organization accept?
- What methods of planned giving are recognized by the organization, and with what restrictions?

Most organizations place bequest proceeds in an endowment fund, giving the donor a form of perpetual life through their gift. The organization is best served if the bequests are made in the form of cash or readily marketable securities, to avoid some of the delays and potential complications of a sale or liquidation of assets. If a gift is of tangible personal property (such as art, antiques, instruments, or jewelry) or real estate that cannot readily be used by the organization to further its nonprofit purposes, the donor should be encouraged to give instructions to the executor of the will to provide the organization with the option of receiving the property or the net proceeds of a sale.

Many organizations have devised attractive ways of acknowledging bequest donors while they are still alive, for example, in a planned giving circle or a legacy society. However, as an accounting matter bequests are not recorded on the organization's books until the gift is *irrevocable*, meaning that the donor can no longer change his will or other donative instrument. Counsel can help analyze the revocability of the gift and advise when it is appropriate to move it to the financial books. Counsel can also help review a will in probate to make sure the organization receives its due.

Larger charities will be equipped to receive *charitable gift annuities*, a form of deferred gift. A charitable gift annuity is a contract under which a charity receives a gift from a donor and agrees in turn to pay a fixed amount of money to one or two individuals, for their lifetime. A portion of the payments is tax-deductible to the donor, and the contributed property (the gift) becomes a part of the charity's assets. Many states regulate gift annuities, often under the state's insurance or securities laws, requiring registration and segregation of gift annuity funds and subjecting them to periodic audit. The board should know the results of such audits.

For their own convenience, charities also may impose restrictions on such charitable gift annuities, such as:

- Placing a minimum amount (e.g., $10,000) and a minimum age for an individual donor (such as 50 years old), otherwise the costs of administering the annuity over time may outweigh its benefit to the organization.
- Rejecting real estate, tangible personal property, or other illiquid assets in exchange for current charitable gift annuities.
- Requiring that the gift to the organization exceeds 10 percent of the amount donated for the annuity—otherwise a large part of the gift may be taxable to the organization.
- Appointing a custodian, investment advisor, and administrator to hold the funds.

Qualified trusts and estate counsel should advise an organization on charitable gift annuity matters.

Gift Acceptance Policies

Not all gifts are created equal, and some are considerably less valuable than others. In rare instances a gift may even be detrimental to an organization's interests.

Gift acceptance policies are board-approved policies that stipulate what types of gifts the organization will accept. (Gift acceptance policies are introduced in Chapter 2.) Commonly, gift acceptance policies provide that:

- Cash and cash equivalents are the most desirable form of gift (e.g., CDs, money market accounts, payments by credit card).
- Gifts of securities (stocks and bonds listed on major exchanges and over-the-counter) are also to be encouraged. Generally, organizations receiving gifts of securities will sell them immediately and reinvest the proceeds in accordance with their investment policies (see Chapter 6).
- Gifts of life insurance also can be readily accepted and encouraged; like bequests, they should be recorded when they become irrevocable.
- Closely held stock or interests in partnerships should be considered on a case-by-case basis; they are usually accepted only if they can be sold within a reasonable period of time.
- Tangible personal property (e.g., art, antiques, instruments, and jewelry) can be donated, but the donor should acknowledge in the donation documentation that the organization can sell the property. Tax rules may limit the extent to which the value of the gift is deductible to the donor. Donors should have their own counsel or tax advisor review these arrangements.
- If a gift subjects the organization to significant carrying costs (such as boats or planes that need to be stored, maintained, and insured), the gift should be carefully reviewed to ensure prompt marketability.
- A gift of real estate presents similar issues: it should be researched to ascertain potential carrying costs (taxes, mortgage payments, liens, maintenance and repair costs), use restrictions, easements or reservations associated with the property, and the marketability of property. The organization should also examine potential liability under environmental laws and other considerations. In each case, it is the donor, not

the organization, who should obtain the written appraisal of market value.

- Timeshares should be carefully considered before the organization agrees to accept them, as they may pose particular difficulties in valuation, liquidity, and unknown tax or environmental liabilities.

For convenience, the organization may consider setting minimum value limits (e.g., $100,000) on gifts imposing significant cost, administrative burden, or risk. For accounting purposes, the value of the gift is the net amount realized after all costs incurred in the acceptance of the gift have been subtracted. The organization should establish a donor recognition policy so that all donors feel that they have been recognized appropriately—and proportionately—in annual reports and other listings.

Pledge Forms

Organizations raising larger gifts—for example, endowment gifts, capital gifts (funds for a major undertaking such as a large construction project), or multi-year gift pledges for annual support (for example, $100,000 over five years for Life Fellows membership)— may decide to permit such gifts to be paid over a period of time. Promises to donate over time are often written in a pledge agreement or pledge form. Using principles of contract law, counsel can help make sure that these pledge agreements or forms are enforceable. The organization and its builders, lenders, and other funders will be grateful for the assurance that pledge monies will come in when expected. And although no organization would ever wish to bring a donor to court to enforce a pledge, having a legally binding pledge agreement can serve as a potent reminder to those around the well-intentioned donor—potential heirs, creditors, lawyers, accountants, and others—that this obligation is a solemn one.

Although the general rule in contract law is that gift promises are not enforceable because they lack consideration, among other elements, courts may deem them enforceable if the parties follow contract law precepts as described in Chapter 4. Important elements include establishing consideration (and/or detrimental reliance) and an intent to be bound. Figure 5.1 is a simplified form of pledge agreement with the elements tending to support enforceability.

SIMPLIFIED SAMPLE PLEDGE PAYMENT AGREEMENT

In consideration of my/our interest in [briefly describe mission of the organization], I/we, _____, (the "Donor(s)"), agree to make a charitable donation of _____ dollars ($XXXXXX) to [name of organization].

As seen in the contract law section of Chapter 4, reciting the "consideration" increases the likelihood that the promise will be regarded as legally binding.

I/We agree to complete payment of such donation in full no later than [date], with installments to be paid annually according to the following schedule:

[Fill in schedule]

Specific terms help make the contract enforceable.

Whenever the organization recognizes this gift publicly, the Donor(s) would like to be acknowledged as
_____.

Gift recognition serves as a form of consideration.

The concept of detrimental reliance—that the organization will take certain steps to its detriment in reliance on of this pledge—helps reinforce that this is not a mere gift promise but an enforceable obligation.

Donor(s) understand that this Agreement represents a legally binding obligation upon me/us and my/our estate, and Donor(s) acknowledge(s) that by entering into this Agreement, Donor(s) will have caused the organization to rely upon this pledge in securing the pledges of others and in authorizing expenses to be incurred and/or paid in anticipation of the payment of my/our pledge.

This languauge re-emhasizes the solemnity of the obligation and the expectation that it will be enforceable.

This Agreement will be governed by the laws of [State].

This Agreement represents the entire understanding of the undersigned Donor(s) and the organization with respect to the subject matter of this Agreement, and it may not be modified except by written instrument signed by the Donor(s) and an authorized representative of the organization.

Integration clause

Agreed and accepted:

For Donor(s):   For organization:

By:_____   By:_____

Date:_____   Date:_____

As with other kinds of contracts, signing on the dotted line serves to reinforce the solemnity of the obligations, and underscores that the signer's promises are intended to be enforceable.

Figure 5.1   Simplified Sample Pledge Payment Agreement

Inserting these potent phrases into pledge forms—without turning off donors—benefits the organization enormously.

Gaming and Raffles

Raffles and gaming (such as bingo) are a common way for organizations to raise money. Organizations may carry out such activities regularly, such as a bingo game every Wednesday night, or may build a one-off special event around a particularly generous donation of a raffle item of value, such as a car or a vacation package.

State law governs raffles, and each state defines and regulates them somewhat differently. Some states even prohibit them entirely. Most states require the organization to apply for a raffle license or permit. In New York, for example, an organization must register with the New York State Racing and Wagering Board before conducting a raffle. If an organization earns $30,000 or more from raffles per year, it must also apply for a raffle license. An organization may not award more than $100,000 worth of cash or merchandise prizes per year, and may not sell raffle tickets through or to minors. Similarly, California requires all organizations conducting raffles to register, and to submit an annual report of their raffle activities during the previous year.

State gaming boards may be backlogged with applications for weeks or months, so it is a good idea to apply well in advance of the planned event. Counsel may help prepare and file the application and may also advise about how to prepare the tickets, publicize the raffle, collect entry fees, and award the prizes, so that all of these activities comply with applicable laws.

In addition to state laws, federal laws also apply to gaming, which may include bingo, pull-tabs/instant bingo, card games, raffles, scratch-offs, charitable gaming tickets, casino nights, and coin-operated gambling devices. (Special exclusions are made for bingo and for gaming events staffed by volunteer workers.) The federal government may consider income from gaming as unrelated business taxable income (UBTI, as defined in Chapter 6). Organizations that raise more than $15,000 from gaming events must file a Schedule G with their IRS Form 990 informational returns. The IRS has a publication explaining the federal rules for gaming.[12]

Consumer regulatory laws govern charity-originated sweepstakes and contests. Because organizations often undertake these activities to enhance visibility and build mailing lists, a discussion of these elements appears in Chapter 8, on Communications.

Corporate Contributions, Promotional Information, and Product Placements

A basic tenet of nonprofit law is that nonprofits generally should undertake activities that further their missions. When nonprofits regularly undertake activities substantially unrelated to their trade or business, they may be taxed on the net income from these activities. (For a discussion of unrelated business income tax [UBIT] and unrelated business taxable income [UBTI], see Chapter 6). If they engage in too much unrelated activity, they may jeopardize their tax-exempt status.

Soliciting and receiving sponsorship payments is considered related to the nonprofit's trade or business, and therefore exempt from taxes, provided that the sponsorships are "qualified."[13] The IRS distinguishes between acknowledging a sponsor's payment (not taxable) and advertising a sponsor's products or services (taxable). If the payments are not qualified—that is, they are not really acknowledgment but are instead *advertisement*—the organization may owe taxes on this income. A sponsorship is qualified, and the receipt of the money is tax-exempt to the nonprofit, if there is no arrangement or expectation that the sponsor will receive any substantial return benefit.

To maximize the value to the organization of the sponsor's payment, the organization should avoid:

- Promising that the organization will do business with the sponsor, or that anyone else will.
- Guaranteeing any particular degree of public exposure (e.g., the level of attendance at events, particular broadcast ratings).
- Guaranteeing that competing products will not be served or provided (although sponsorships in exclusive categories are okay).

If the benefits provided to a sponsor are less than 2 percent of the value of the contribution, they are by definition not substantial and will be disregarded. The 2 percent rule provides a safe harbor for qualified sponsorship payments.[14]

A corporate sponsor's brand or trade names, logo, established slogans, and description of its lines of products or services can be cited in the *acknowledgment* of the sponsor, if there is no direct message to buy the product or instructions about how to buy the product. In thanking the corporate donor, the organization may display the corporate sponsor's logos and slogans as long as they do not contain qualitative or comparative descriptions of the sponsor's products, services, facilities, or company. Acceptable forms of acknowledgment and sponsor identification include a list of the sponsor's locations, telephone numbers and web site address, value-neutral descriptions including displays or visual depictions of the sponsor's products or services, and display of the sponsor's product, such as a car in the lobby of a performance hall.

By contrast, advertising, or direct messages to buy products or instructions about how to buy a product, likely would go beyond the scope of factual information and potentially cause the sponsor's payment to be reclassified as an advertising buy, causing the organization to likely incur unrelated business taxable income. If the organization's messages about the sponsor contain qualitative or comparative language, price information, other indications of savings or value, an endorsement or inducement to purchase, sell, or use the sponsor's products or services, they will likely be considered an advertisement and not an acknowledgment, and may subject the organization to income tax on the sponsorship payment. The IRS and the U.S. Department of the Treasury offer illustrative examples.[15]

Even if some portion of the arrangement does not fit within the qualified corporate sponsorship exception, other elements of the relationship may be tax exempt, and counsel can help the organization bifurcate the transaction into taxable and tax-free portions. Although a corporate sponsorship arrangement may not be qualified in whole or in part, the income is not automatically taxable; the three-part unrelated business income tax analysis described in Chapter 6 still applies to determine if the income is taxable.

Corporate sponsorships can be an important source of support for an organization, but they require attentiveness to IRS rules. Ongoing and large-scale failure to comply could lead to significant consequences, even threatening the organization's tax-exempt status.

Accounting for Acceptance of Corporate Privileges

A nonprofit may show its appreciation to donors by offering an array of privileges commensurate with giving levels. Under federal tax law, a corporation or firm is entitled to an income tax charitable deduction only to the extent that its donation to a tax-exempt organization exceeds the value of any goods and services provided to it and its employees in return.[16]

The organization should make a good faith effort to determine the value of any benefits being made available to a donor corporation or firm. To the extent the corporation opts to avail itself of these benefits, it can use those valuations to determine how much to deduct from its charitable contribution amount. It can also opt out of those benefits to receive the maximum charitable deduction. The organization can facilitate this option by sending a *privileges acceptance form*.

The text in a simplified sample privileges acceptance form appears in Figure 5.2.

SIMPLIFIED SAMPLE PRIVILEGES ACCEPTANCE FORM

I wish to accept the following benefits: (Please mark all that apply.)

Waiver of the Studio Rental Fee ($X,000)

[Delineate other benefits here and an approximate market value.]

[Corporation] will still be entitled to all other donor benefits
and privileges as described in the donor privileges brochure
according to the level of its gift. I understand that by accepting
the remaining privileges, my corporation and its employees are
receiving goods and services which have an estimated fair
market value as described in the accompanying letter
and therefore my corporation's gift is entitled to an income tax
charitable deduction only to the extent that its donation
exceeds such value.

[Signed]

Authorized representative of the donor corporation.

Date:

Figure 5.2   Simplified Sample Privileges Acceptance Form

In this example, an organization with studio space it generally rents out at market rates may offer free use of the studio to donors at a certain level or above. The value of the foregone rental payment would ordinarily be deducted from the donor's contribution for charitable receipt purposes, unless the donor opts to waive this benefit.

Other Places Where Legal Meets Fundraising

Now that we have covered the basic legal issues pertaining to fundraising—registration laws, grant requirements, planned giving, gift acceptance policies, pledge forms, gaming, corporate sponsorships and more—we turn now to some advanced topics: joint fundraising, handling disputes with donors, and getting counsel involved with fundraising.

Joint Fundraising: Partnering with Other Organizations

Sometimes, like-minded organizations or organizations with complementary missions band together for a *joint fundraising campaign.* Joint fundraising can yield efficiencies in personnel and economies of scale. A combined campaign also may enable smaller organizations to go after larger grant dollars than any one of them could credibly handle standing alone. Joint efforts also can provide mentoring for smaller or newer organizations and access to a new demographic for larger, more well-established organizations. Well-run joint fundraising campaigns operate in accordance with a governing document that has been agreed upon by all participants, spelling out their mutual expectations and responsibilities for obtaining, managing, and disbursing funds, as well as other matters, such as trademark usage and publicity.

Organizations that have not yet obtained recognition of their tax-exempt status from the IRS may decide in the meantime to become a program of a *fiscal sponsor,* a recognized tax-exempt organization that can accept donations on behalf of the sponsored organization and re-grant the contributed funds to the sponsored organization, minus an administrative fee (often from 6 to 10 percent). The fiscal sponsor also provides certain financial oversight to ensure compliance with requirements of the federal tax code. Some organizations are *dedicated sponsors,* meaning that they focus only on providing fiscal sponsorship services, such as Fractured Atlas in New York, The Tides Center in San Francisco, and Nonprofit Central in New Orleans.[17]

Coalitions

Organizations may wish to become involved with a *coalition of organizations,* such as the United Way Campaign or the Combined Federal Campaign. An organization must satisfy numerous requirements to become a member of the coalition. For example, to join the Combined Federal Campaign as a national or international organization, an organization must certify that it:

- Is tax-exempt under IRS § 501(c)(3).
- Is a health and human welfare organization that provides benefits affecting human health and welfare.
- Keeps an accounting of its funds and has an independent audit annually.

- Has submitted IRS Form 990 or is exempt from doing so.
- Has provided its percentage and fundraising rate.
- Has an active governing body.
- Prohibits the sale of donor lists.
- Does not have deceptive advertising campaigns.
- Uses contributed funds for their stated purpose.
- Does not interact with countries with which such interaction is prohibited by law.[18]

Coalitions and other means of joint fundraising can be a very effective and efficient way for organizations to enhance their fundraising. It is an especially good opportunity for start-up organizations that have not yet obtained tax-exempt status or have limited lists, fundraising staff, or expertise.

Handling Disputes with Donors

Notwithstanding the efforts of most organizations to treat donors with the utmost of grace and gratitude, and the best intentions of donors to support the organization's mission through selfless contributions, disputes do occasionally arise.

Under state laws, nonprofits owe a fiduciary duty to their donors to use gifts for the purposes for which the funds are given. Moreover, most of the charitable solicitation registration laws described above require nonprofits to use funds for the purpose for which they are solicited. At the same time, the organization's mission or program may have evolved since the date of the gift.

One area for disputes to arise is the expenditure of funds in a manner different than the donor may have intended. The donor's intent should be spelled out in a written document to avoid future disagreements. Counsel can work with fundraisers to craft solicitations using broad language where possible, so that in case the organization reaps more funding than it can use for the original purpose, or if the project changes, the organization can still use the funds for other (or general) charitable purposes.

On the other hand, organizations should be wary about donors seeking to retain an undue amount of control over the expenditure of their gifts. If the donor means for the gift to benefit a specific individual, it will not be deductible. If the donor intends to exercise decision-making control through the gift, such as dictating the choice of a new coach for a university's baseball team or a Mideast Studies professor with a particular point of view for its political science department, the donor may be improperly usurping control that is reserved to the organization and those charged with fiduciary duties in governing and operating it.

Counsel may help troubleshoot such situations at the outset by carefully reviewing the language of the grant agreement. Counsel may also be called upon to advocate for the organization's interests after a dispute has ripened, by outlining for the donor the legal and policy considerations animating restricted gift rules. In the worst case, the organization may need to consider returning the gift if it comes with so many strings attached that it is not tenable for the organization to meet the imposed requirements without compromising its own mission, independence, and the integrity of its governance.

Lawyers as Fundraisers

Counsel can help an organization tap into a wealth of professional contacts that may be as public-minded as the organization's attorney.

Introduce, Connect, Network   Counsel can become a valuable source of prospects for the fundraisers and the organization. Here's how:

- Open your contact list—provide lists of contacts and permission to reach out.
- Personally solicit prospective donors, particularly from the legal community, to join in supporting the organization.
- Introduce the organization to law firms, corporations, foundations, and others that make charitable contributions, purchase tables at galas, offer donated items for silent auction or as prizes.
- If a corporation or individual is being honored by the organization at an upcoming event, research which law firms serve that corporation's or individual's legal needs and assist in persuading them to donate to the organization in tribute to their client.
- Assemble a list of law firms currently supporting the organization and create a little friendly competition between peer law firms to outdo one another in their giving.

Found Money: The Cy Pres Doctrine   Under an obscure legal doctrine known as *cy pres*, charities can receive leftover amounts of money from recently resolved lawsuits after all known plaintiffs have been made whole. The term *cy pres* (pronounced sigh pray) is derived from the Norman French phrase *cy pres comme possible*, meaning as near as possible. In a class action, mass tort, or regulatory settlement, defendants may allocate large sums of money to resolve the case, but it may not be possible to locate and directly distribute all of the money to the class. The *cy pres* doctrine permits the court to decide what to do with the leftover funds. In conjunction with counsel participating in the lawsuit, the court may order that the residual funds be distributed under the *cy pres* doctrine to a nonprofit charitable organization whose work advances the public interest and indirectly benefits the class members who were never located or did not recover. The *cy pres* remedy can also be used for the entirety of a statutory damage award when the amount of damages to each class member is too small to warrant distribution.

By raising the organization's profile with class-action counsel or judges presiding over class-action lawsuits and major regulatory matters, counsel can help put the organization in line to receive *cy pres* distributions.

Different jurisdictions have different views about how proximate the charity's mission or program needs to be to the underlying cause in order to be eligible to receive *cy pres* funds. Many such awards are limited to organizations providing legal services to the poor. But even other kinds of nonprofits who are savvy about this little-known corner of the legal world can benefit enormously.

> **Example:** A 1993 antitrust class action lawsuit in the glass container industry resulted in $2 million of unclaimed funds. The court published a notice inviting grant applications for *cy pres* funds. Most of the grantees selected by the judge were nonprofit legal groups and law schools; one of them was an art museum specializing in glass objects.[19]

> **Example:** An enterprising and charitable class-action lawyer in the Cleveland area garnered $14 million for 34 Ohio charities addressing hunger, homelessness, disease prevention, education, drug and alcohol treatment, and other matters. The monies arose from a lawsuit filed against an insurer

alleging that motorists were charged twice for the same insurance coverage. The insurer agreed to pay at least $30 million in the settlement, but only $16 million was claimed, so plaintiffs' and defendants' counsel negotiated an arrangement, approved by the court, under which the rest went to charity they selected together.[20]

In addition to class action settlements, settlements of regulatory matters may also provide monies for nonprofits whose work relates to the subject of the enforcement proceeding. For example, in 2005, the New York State Attorney General's office investigated alleged pay-for-play practices by a number of record labels, alleging that they were illegally bribing radio station employees to garner additional airtime for those labels' songs and artists. Ultimately, the matters were settled, and $15 million was earmarked for disbursement to nonprofit organizations associated with music education and appreciation programs in the state.

Dissolution of a charity may occasion the distribution of its remaining assets to a charity with similar mission to continue the work.

By leveraging relationships with lawyers, judges, and corporate leaders, counsel can turn her legal community into a powerful force for the good.

Better Fundraising Through Good Governance and Compliance

Good management, good governance, and good fundraising practices go hand in hand. They attract more donors, who in turn give more funds to carry out more good works. The opposite is true as well: Organizations with weak financial controls, weak governance structures, and/or poor fundraising practices may soon find their sources of donations drying up.

Industry watchdog services, such as Guidestar and Charity Navigator, gather and analyze Form 990 information, calculate the cost of fundraising at charities, and share their findings widely through their web sites with prospective donors, the media, and the general public. Nonprofit divisions of the Better Business Bureau in various states also publish reports for donors and the public summarizing the charity's mission, activities, governance, and key financial information. Traditionally, these watchdog organizations have focused on financial measures, such as the cost of dollars raised and the ratio of administrative costs to overall revenue. However, a trend is emerging to add evaluations of accountability, transparency, governance, and effectiveness to traditional financial measures.[21]

Good legal compliance in the fundraising area helps lessen risk and strengthens the organization. Counsel can also highlight for the fundraisers the good governance and compliance practices occurring across the organization, instilling confidence and further bolstering fundraising efforts.

⇨ PRACTICE POINTER

Paying attention to governance and compliance matters can improve an organization's fundraising prospects, ultimately helping it better fulfill its mission.

In Sum/Coming Up Next

The organization's fundraisers should understand the legal topics that touch upon their important work, including state registration laws, truth-in-advertising laws, and the legal requirements pertaining to restricted gifts, endowment gifts, and special-purpose fundraising. The fundraisers should know where to go for legal advice about pledges, bequests, and other types of planned giving. They should be well counseled on gift receipt practices, both for cash and non-cash gifts. Their pledge agreements should bear the hallmarks of enforceability. When approaching corporations they should be clear what they can and cannot offer in return. For their part, lawyers should be sure to help fundraising professionals spot legal issues and provide resources for resolving questions that arise. Going beyond the strict definition of legal services, lawyers can serve organizations by helping introduce the legal community to worthy charities. Savvy fundraisers leverage good governance and compliance practices into even more successful fundraising.

A glossary of fundraising terms is available on the companion web site to this book at www.wiley.com/go/goodcounsel. A Work Plan for assessing compliance with fundraising laws appears after the Chapter 5 Focus Questions.

The organization's fundraisers are now hard at work and fully compliant with applicable laws. Where does the money go, how does it get managed, and how can counsel help? Let's go over to the finance area to find out.

Focus Questions for Chapter 5: Counseling the Rainmakers

1. What are some common techniques used by organizations to raise funds?
2. Define:
   a. Unrestricted gift
   b. Restricted gift
   c. Endowment gift
3. What are *quid pro quo* contributions and how are they taxed? How are fundraising events, gaming events, and auctions treated from a tax perspective?
4. What information should charitable receipts contain?
5. What are some advisable methods for handling donor information?
6. What are the important legal elements of the relationship between an organization and an outside fundraiser?
7. What is planned giving? May the donor's trusts and estates lawyer advise the receiving organization about legal aspects of a planned gift?
8. What are some important elements of a gift acceptance policy? What types of gifts should organizations think twice about before accepting?
9. What is a pledge, and how does it differ from an outright gift? What are some ways that an organization can make its pledge agreements more likely enforceable?
10. What are qualified corporate sponsorship payments? Why isn't a payment for advertising a qualified corporate sponsorship payment?
11. What are some advantages and disadvantages of joint fundraising?
12. What are *cy pres* awards and how can an organization become eligible to receive them?
13. What is the relationship between good governance and successful fundraising?

Chapter 5 Work Plan

Compliance with Fundraising Laws

This work plan can assist counsel or supervised law students in surveying an organization's compliance with fundraising laws.

❏ Learn about the various ways in which the organization raises money:
  • Annual fundraisers, including general solicitations, galas, walks, runs and auctions.
  • Restricted gift campaigns, including capital campaigns and endowment campaigns.
  • Other fundraising activities.
❏ Research fundraising laws in all states where the organization raises money, and review the organization's compliance with applicable laws.
  • Review agreements with outside fundraisers to ensure they comply with applicable state registration and disclosure requirements.
❏ Gather restricted gift documents and review the organization's procedures for complying with donors' restrictions.
❏ Review the handling of endowment funds, including proper recordkeeping and expenditures of investment income and growth in compliance with the organization's spending policy and law.
  • Ascertain whether the organization has plans to invade principal, and if so, determine whether legal requirements such as donor notification, board and/or government approval have been met.
❏ Ascertain how the organization handles and secures donors' personal information and financial information, such as checks, credit card numbers, and bank account numbers.
❏ Review the organization's practices for providing receipts for donations.
  • Review the form of receipts for donations over $250.
  • Ascertain that receipts subtract the value of return benefits, such as gala meals and entertainment.
  • Be sure membership dues, services rendered, and other non-contribution payments are not included in charitable receipts.
  • Understand procedures for issuing receipts for in-kind gifts.
  • Review the gift acceptance policy for large non-liquid gifts (or consider adopting one if such gifts are commonly made).
❏ Understand procedures for applying for, and certifying compliance with, governmental and private grants and contracts.
❏ Review pledge agreements for larger donations and/or payments over time.
  • Formulate recommendations to achieve greater enforceability, if appropriate.
❏ Review the organization's compliance with state and federal laws governing gaming and raffles.

❏ Understand all corporate sponsorship relationships and ascertain compliance with applicable federal regulations.
  • Rules regarding taxable advertisements.
  • Acceptance of corporate privileges.
❏ Determine who represents the organization when a planned gift is offered.
❏ Review any joint fundraising relationships and fiscal sponsorship agreements.
  • Assess compliance with applicable tax laws and contractual obligations.

6

Laws That Matter to the Finance Department (or Not-for-Profit, but Not-for-Loss Either)

This chapter introduces the legal aspects of a nonprofit organization's finances. It opens with a description of basic financial and planning concepts: business model, strategic plan, budget, cash flow, internal controls, and relationship with the external auditor, with an eye toward legal aspects of each of these matters. The chapter then describes a year in the life of an organization's finance department, describing the annual cycle of activities and alerting counsel to its potential role at each stage.

Additionally, other financial topics that may call for legal advice are covered, including profits and reserves, endowments and trusts, charitable investing, pensions, insurance and risk management, income taxes, and other matters.

Chapter 6 concludes with information about the legal elements of an orderly wind-down when the organization dissolves or merges into another.

The chief financial officer (CFO, Director of Finance, or equivalent title) bears primary responsibility for the financial functions of a nonprofit organization. He or she is responsible for planning annual budgets, generating monthly financial reports, analyzing the organization's finances, and measuring actual performance against budget figures. Members of the finance team also maintain cash flow projections, manage (or oversee the management of) the organization's investments, and negotiate and administer any financing (borrowing and repayment) transactions.

The organization's finance professionals may work with external auditors charged with confirming the validity of the organization's financial statements. The Finance department may also facilitate audits by lenders, regulators, grant-making organizations, and others. In collaboration with facilities and operations staff, the CFO plans capital budgets for major repairs or new building projects. She or he may also negotiate leases and other important business transactions. Working with the chief executive, program staff, and others, the CFO often also plays a pivotal role in fashioning strategic plans and facilitating new initiatives. In carrying out these duties, the CFO interacts with board members and key committees, including the finance, audit, and investment committees.

Counsel should form a strategic alliance with the chief financial officer to support these important functions. While financial matters don't come easily to many lawyers, those who make the effort to learn the language and educate colleagues are likelier to be brought into situations by the CFO at an earlier stage of transactions, negotiations, regulatory matters or problems, materially improving the chances of good outcomes and helping avoid needless losses and risks.

Counsel (and CEOs and board members for that matter) who understand the basic elements of the nonprofit finance function are also of significantly greater value to the organization as a whole—its overall governance and compliance, as well as its execution of mission. Lawyers who make the investment required to understand their nonprofit client's financial picture will earn the trust and respect of the CFO, CEO, and financially savvy members of the board, becoming a key resource for the chairs of the finance and audit committees.[1]

Understand the Big Financial Picture

In order to establish a constructive relationship with the CFO, the organization's lawyer must understand its business model, its strategic plan (if there is one), and its governance processes. As a practical matter, counsel should be able to read the organization's financial statements, understand basic financial tools such as budgeting, planning, and reporting, and appreciate the cyclic nature of the Finance department's work.

The Business Model

As a preliminary matter, counsel (and the trustees and chief executive) should understand the organization's *business model:* how it serves its clients or the public, and how it gets paid for doing so, in a manner that sustains its activities. There may be different business models for different program activities, each of which has a profit and loss statement (P&L). For example, a nonprofit cultural organization devoted to presenting orchestral works may fund its auditorium concerts through sales of tickets, while it pays for its free, outdoor concerts through a combination of government grants and corporate sponsorships. Other kinds of contributions, such as gifts from individuals, may make up the balance of funding for both activities. As another example, a nonprofit nursing home may receive funding for residents' care through government and private payments; but the educational initiative it is piloting in the nearby community to educate the general public about signs of elder abuse may be funded by foundation grants.[2]

Ancillary activities, such as a coffee shop, parking garage, or gift shop, also contribute to the bottom line, although the organization's nonprofit, tax-exempt status depends on not letting non-mission-related activities overshadow the mission-related ones.

Some commentators describe nonprofit business models as having a double bottom line—financial and social. Some nonprofits are even starting to measure performance not in terms of ROI (return on investment) but SROI (social return on investment). For example, a suicide prevention hotline might measure the number of lives saved per dollar spent, or a teen pregnancy awareness initiative might measure the amount of awareness gained per dollar invested. The SROI method of performance measurement can be used by leadership to further refine the model and initiate improvements. SROI figures can also help the organization earn public and private support for its activities.

The Strategic Plan

Strategic planning is an interactive process, generally between the finance and executive staff and the board, to develop the organization's plans and objectives over the long term. Leadership's work on the strategic planning exercise must occur in tandem with the development of a financial and investment plan to accomplish the goals. The organization's plans and objectives have to be realistic in light of its financial resources and surrounding regulatory circumstances. Balancing short-term versus long-term needs presents unique challenges. Counsel should be sure to have a handle on both the status of strategic planning as well as the governance processes surrounding it.

Sources and Uses of Funds

The next step to understanding an organization's financial context is to review the important information summarized in the balance sheets, statement of activities, statement of cash flows, and other elements of the financial statements. Counsel should gain a working understanding of how transactions are recorded and how entries in bookkeeping journals become part of the financial statements; know the organization's accounting methods— does it account on a *cash* or *accrual basis?*—and find out whether it is on a calendar or fiscal year; learn how the organization earns revenue, tracks contributed income, incurs obligations, and spends money through contracts, invoices, and payment requisitions; look at payroll accounts for employees and also become familiar with all outstanding and recently repaid borrowings/debt instruments; and know what variables strongly influence the organization's financial results and when and how their effect is measured—for audit, regulatory, contractual, and internal control purposes.

Once counsel understands these basic financial matters, she can begin to assist finance and accounting staff on legal questions pertaining to their work.

⇨ PRACTICE POINTER

If you are counsel asking finance staff to explain these matters to you, be sure to bring donuts (for finance staff—sugar is scientifically proven to increase patience and goodwill) and coffee (for yourself).

Know Where the Money Comes From   Three main types of income are earned income, unearned (or contributed) income, and investment income. Common examples of earned revenue are tuition payments at an educational organization, ticket proceeds at a museum or cultural center, or payments to a hospital for medical services rendered. Contributed income comes in the form of donations and grants. Investment income arises from dividends, growth, and sales of managed assets.

The ratios of earned income, contributed income, and investment income vary greatly by type of organization. Hospitals, educational organizations, and residential facilities tend to receive a large proportion of their income from fee-for-service payments, such as payments for medical services rendered, tuition billings, or rent. Cultural, humanities, international, environmental, and animal rights organizations tend to rely much more heavily on private contributions. Larger, older organizations are likelier than smaller, newer ones to have endowments that generate enough investment income and growth to fund a material portion of their annual operating budget.[3]

Knowing where the money comes from is an important first step to understanding a nonprofit's financial health. Knowing how the money gets spent is, of course, the other half of the equation.

Know Where the Money Goes   An operating budget is the plan of what it will cost to run the organization's activities for the coming year. Important categories of expense include program, administration, and fundraising. The budget also forecasts what sources will be available to pay for these expenses. Once the finance team, often in collaboration with the program, fundraising, and executive leadership, formulates the operating budget it is then discussed with the board and put to a vote. The budget should be adopted before the start of the organization's fiscal year.

Nonprofits strive for balanced budgets, although there are known instances where organizations acknowledge even in the planning stage that they will run a deficit in the coming year. In the long run, operating deficits are unsustainable, and a frank discussion should be held between management and the board/finance committee about how an anticipated budget deficit will be addressed, especially if it has become an ongoing, structural part of the organization's operations.

An upcoming section on profits and reserves discusses the legal aspects of now nonprofits handle surplus revenues.

Cash Flow

The organization may have a balanced budget throughout the year, but if it hasn't correctly planned its *cash flow*—when the money comes in and when it is likely to go out—it could find itself unable to pay its bills. For example, many charities receive most contributions at the holiday season, but they incur expenses all year round. Regular updating of cash flow reports enables the organization to see into the future and avoid cash crunches.

It is a good practice to budget for a *surplus*. By planning to spend less than the organization anticipates bringing in, the organization can avoid crises, close calls, and maybe even build up a modest reserve cushion for future lean years. Surpluses can also be used to fund new strategic initiatives that are projected to run short-term deficits before they begin providing a return on investment.

Pro forma financial statements can be used for the exercise of plugging "What if . . . ?" scenarios into the organization's financial reports, helping the organization plan, see trouble coming, and make informed decisions for the future.

Some organizations are fortunate enough to have an emergency fund. Organizations with invested assets may see fit to establish an appropriate ratio of cash (or other liquid assets) to invested assets. Finance staff should periodically review those ratios with the board or its finance committee, in relation to the organization's needs, experience in managing cash, and broader market conditions.

Internal Controls

Finance staff, board, counsel and outside auditors should develop a joint understanding of the organization's system of *internal controls*. Internal controls are the processes designed to provide reasonable assurance regarding the reliability of the organization's financial reporting and its compliance with applicable laws and regulations. Internal controls are typically established and overseen by the board (or audit committee) and effectuated by financial management. Counsel should learn the method, purpose, and schedule of these existing controls and should help the finance department consider how adequately they are documented.

Internal controls help minimize the risk of fraud and ensure that the organization's operations work as intended, instilling greater confidence in the integrity of its books and its measures of performance against goals. With a functioning set of internal controls, organizations can reduce their exposure to waste, inefficiency, and dishonesty.

There are two kinds of internal controls. *Preventive controls*, such as segregation of duties and proper authorizations, deter or avoid unwanted events. *Detective controls*, such as inventories and audits, detect whether unwanted events have already occurred.

A good system for segregation of duties provides, for example, that one person within the organization may be allowed to add new vendors to the accounts payable system while a different person is allowed to make payments to the vendors. When responsibilities for authorizing payments and issuing payments are not segregated, opportunities for embezzlement arise.

Here are some examples of weak or circumvented preventive controls:

> **Example:** The former office manager of the Kentucky Big Brothers Big Sisters was responsible for both issuing checks and approving payments. The lack of segregation of duties proved too tempting to resist. Ultimately she pleaded guilty to embezzling over $400,000 from the charity.[4]

> **Example:** A former payroll clerk at a Boston healthcare nonprofit was responsible both for keeping the books and writing the checks. Eventually he was indicted on charges of larceny and making false entries in corporate books after allegedly writing himself bonus checks for over $750,000—at a time when the organization was struggling to pay utility bills.[5]

Both preventive and detective controls are essential to an effective internal-control system.

Embezzlement and Fraud—Snakes in the Nonprofit Garden   As incongruous as it may seem, even mission-driven organizations occasionally are the victims of embezzlement and other frauds. Perhaps it seems unfathomable that an organization could be wronged as it tries to do good, or that, due to poor controls and misplaced trust, its leadership may be somewhat slow to detect and correct wrongs, punish thieves, and recover lost assets. But every so often there is an embezzler or fraudster in the nonprofit's midst. Financial wrongdoing can be an enormous drain on the organization's resources and its reputation—including its ability to raise funds, win contracts, attract clients, and garner public support—all to the ultimate detriment of the mission.

Nonprofit leaders have a fiduciary duty to protect their non-profits' assets and preserve their ability to provide services. If non-profit leaders fail to take action against a wrongdoer, the state attorney general, district attorney's office, taxing authorities, or other law enforcement may step in. Action steps include:[6]

- Make sure that the full facts are known.
- Punish the offender.
- Report the fraud or embezzlement and cooperate with law enforcement authorities and other concerned parties.
- Reclaim stolen property.
- Conduct a post-mortem to determine what went wrong—were fiscal controls or audit processes lacking? Should the personnel manual establish higher expectations? Is the organization the victim of founder's syndrome or otherwise weak in checks-and-balances? (See Chapter 7.)
- Put new safeguards in place.

Confronting and dealing with a fraud is infinitely better than ignoring it, hiding it from auditors, board members, and law enforcement, and otherwise engaging in denial. The crisis is a learning opportunity, and at the very least the organization can help keep other trusting nonprofits from becoming the embezzler's next victim.

While primary responsibility for the control environment rests with the organization's financial staff (CFO, controller, etc.) under the supervision of the board and/or its audit committee, and the independent eye of its outside auditors, counsel should familiarize themselves with those controls and serve as an additional check that proper and effective procedures are in place.

Annual audits focus in part on whether the organization has established and maintained adequate internal controls and procedures for financial reporting. We turn next to the subject of audits and auditors.

External Auditors

External auditors are professionals at an accounting firm who review the work of the organization's finance team in putting together the financial statements. Some smaller organizations may rely on outside accountants to prepare the financial statements based on information supplied in the general ledger at year-end. Chapter 3 discusses when an organization should consider retaining external auditors. Once an organization has made that determination, counsel should become a part of the organization's selection team, providing legal support to the board members, CEO, and CFO for the *request for proposal* process or other procedure for selecting, periodically reassessing, and/or rotating the auditing team. As the external auditors are retained, or their existing engagement is renewed or modified, counsel should review the engagement letter to make sure it conforms to expectation and organizational practices, and to ensure that the auditors are primarily accountable to the board/audit committee, not to finance staff, whose work they are reviewing, in order to maintain their independence.

Counsel may be asked to attend periodic meetings with internal and outside auditors for the purpose of discussing any fraud/embezzlement, reviewing material new legal agreements, and providing a legal perspective on the quality and adherence to internal controls. As part of an external auditors' annual review, they will require counsel to provide a list of pending or threatened lawsuits involving the organization, together with an indication about the extent to which such pending matters may be expected to have a significant impact on the organization's financial statements.

Other Kinds of Audits

In addition to external auditors' audits to certify the organization's financial statements, nonprofit organizations may also be audited by federal or state regulators or funding providers. For example, the organization may be subject to routine, periodic (annual or biannual) governmental audits of specific funds, such as segregated gift annuity accounts and pension funds. The finance or other staffers who first become aware that such audits are impending should be sure to alert counsel. Counsel can often help interface between these outside auditors and the organization's staff. The aim is to provide full reasonable cooperation to facilitate the audit while avoiding disruption to the business and uncontrolled access to organizational records and personnel—otherwise known as a fishing expedition. Counsel is well suited to help control and to document (or to supervise documentation of) this process; his or her involvement will also assure that the organization appreciates the legal significance of any adverse findings prior to completion of the audit. Counsel can assist in reviewing submittals and advising those signing the forms about the importance of making truthful and accurate statements. Counsel should also make sure that the results of such audits are properly reported out to the board and/or audit committee.

From time to time the organization may be subject to a special governmental audit, such as an IRS audit. Counsel, in consultation with financial staff and the board, will be actively involved, and should have a good understanding of who is authorized to meet, report, make statements, offer and enter into settlements, object to findings, and report back to the board or audit committee. Counsel is also likely to oversee document production and testimony if the matter ripens into a lawsuit or regulatory action.

A Year in the Life

The work of an organization's financial staff tends to be cyclical. The elements of an annual cycle include the following:

Budget Season

Counsel should understand the budget planning and prioritization process and become familiar with how the board (and finance committee, if there is one) reviews and approves the budget for the coming year.

Comparing Budget to Actual Year-to-Date

As the year goes along, the board and/or its finance committee should be receiving regular briefings from the CFO comparing the budget to actual year-to-date performance. The CFO may provide to the CEO and trustees a budget *dashboard*, or a short summary statement, benchmarking actual performance against budget and/ or prior years, at these meetings. A dashboard helps trustees, the CEO, and other non-financial experts grasp the big picture and not get lost in a slew of numbers.

Reconciling Budgets and Addressing Variances

Once differences surface between budget and actual performance (also known as *variances*), finance professionals will likely work with other key staffers, the CEO, and the board (or its budget or finance committee) to try to address the variances—by cutting expenditures, increasing revenues, adjusting cash flows, or other efforts. They may also amend the budget, following the same procedures for approving the budget amendment as they did for passing the budget in the first instance. Counsel should follow the process of budget reconciliation and understand the steps being taken to address variances. Counsel should attend meetings of any board committees that receive financial briefings from the CFO team (e.g., finance committee, audit committee) and keep minutes (see Chapter 3 for a discussion of minutes).

Closing the Books

After the fiscal year ends, the finance staff closes the books, that is, makes the final journal entries for the year that are necessary to close the accounts, post balances to the profit and loss account, and ultimately close the profit and loss account by posting its balance to a capital or other account. Any odd or unusual book entries, or accounts with balances that never seem to change over time, should be brought out and discussed during this process. Once the books are closed, finance staff then prepares financial statements accurately setting forth the financial condition of the organization at year-end.

The organization may use outside auditors to provide an independent review of the financial statements; if so, counsel should understand how the organization plans for the external audit process and prepares for the next accounting cycle.

In some organizations the process of closing the books on a fiscal year may significantly influence time demands for a number of employees. It is a good practice for attorneys (and others) to be considerate of financial staffers' time when they are in the midst of this process.

Preparing Financial Statements for Auditors' Certification

Following the closing of the books and the preparation of financial statements by the organization's financial staff, the organization may bring in an external auditing team from an accounting firm. The auditors' job is to verify the accuracy of the financial statements by sampling certain records and transactions, reviewing the internal control environment, and seeking and obtaining management representations about the accuracy of the financial information presented in the statements. Counsel will also have to supply (and gather from outside counsel, if any) letters to the auditors describing legal matters, for example, pending or threatened lawsuits or regulatory actions that may pose a financial or other risk to the organization.

Important information about the organization's financial and legal circumstances may be listed in *notes* accompanying the resulting audited financial statements. Counsel should carefully review the statements and notes as part of the preparation for the auditors to present the audited financials to the board or its audit committee. As part of this same process, the external auditors will also prepare a *management letter* detailing any material weaknesses or significant deficiencies identified by the auditors in the preparation of the audited financial statements. Counsel should follow this process closely and be prepared to support any corrective action that may be recommended by the auditors. Grantors, government contracting agencies, watchdog groups such as the Better Business Bureau and others are likely to request copies of the audited financial statements.

Preparing the IRS Form 990 Informational Return

After the audited financial statements are completed and accepted by the board, finance staff or outside professional advisors prepare the Form 990 informational return and similar state filings. Counsel should take an appropriate role in reviewing any legal and governance matters arising through the process of preparing the Form 990 and other periodic governmental filings, and should ensure that the board (and/or audit committee, if there is one) plays its proper oversight role in reviewing and approving the forms before they are filed. Counsel should also make sure these filings are provided to all board members and made publicly available as required, removing any schedules (such as Form 990 Schedule B, listing significant donors by name and amount) from the versions made available to the public.

Once counsel grasps the cyclic nature of the financial staff's work and understands the key elements that make up the finance department's work, he or she will be well placed to answer the kinds of legal questions that arise in the finance department.

Other Places Where Legal and Finance Meet

The financial circumstances of nonprofits vary enormously, by size of organization and by sub-sector within the nonprofit sector. However, certain legal questions do seem to come up with regularity, regardless of size or mission. These include questions about profits and reserves, endowments and trusts, investments, pensions, insurance and risk management, taxes, and insolvency. The CFO should be sure to seek out the advice of counsel for a legal perspective on these issues.

Profits and Reserves

Nonprofit organizations are not-for-profit, but they are not-for-losses either! The financial staff helps the CEO understand the sources of any deviations from the budget, both on the income and expense side.

Nonprofit does not mean that the organization fails to generate a surplus of revenues over expenses year in and year out. As stated in Chapter 2, the nonprofit designation means that the organization's *profit* (surplus revenue or change in net assets) is not passed on to shareholders (the non-distribution constraint), but instead is plowed back into the organization to fulfill its charitable or public purpose. A nonprofit entity may generate a profit as long as it uses the profit exclusively for attaining the organization's goals.

Surpluses can be put into a rainy day fund, or a *reserve.* However, the organization's reserves should not get too large, because large reserves may indicate that the organization is not doing as much good as it could or should. While public companies are rewarded by rising stock prices and earnings per share when their companies are well-managed, not-for-profit organizations with strong balance sheets are often criticized for generating or carrying surpluses that are too large.[7] Another reason for discouraging nonprofits from building up large reserves is to avoid a mismatch in timing between when the donor gets the tax deduction (immediately) and when the organization performs the resulting benefit to society (deferred), to the detriment of society as a whole.

Not all surpluses are bad; to the contrary, the long-term financial stability of the organization depends on its accumulating surpluses to establish and maintain adequate reserves for the future. Hard times can befall nonprofits, for example in an economic downturn, in case of missing or late funding (government grants that may have slowed down due to budget deficits, shrinkage of donor base, late fulfillment of pledge payments), weaker-than-expected returns on revenue-generating activity, or large, unanticipated losses or expenses.[8] In such lean times, reserves can be used to pay for current program activities.

There is no federal law requiring the organization to spend the surplus within a particular period of time, nor is there a limitation on how much surplus it can accumulate. However, maintaining *excessive reserves* may subject the organization to criticism that it is not doing enough to serve the public's present needs.[9] Exactly what constitutes excessive reserves is a subject of debate—not unlike the question of how much of a rainy day fund you should set aside in your family budget in the event the primary breadwinner is incapacitated. Six months to a year seems to be a common answer to the question, but of course it depends in large measure on how strong, diversified, and resilient the organization's sources of revenue are.

The answer to how much surplus is appropriate involves not only financial matters but also legal matters. Counsel can help by coordinating with finance staff as these decisions are made and documented, including weighing in on the following matters:

- Insurance deductibles: Some organizations may carry insurance policies with sizable *deductibles* (self-insured retentions), where the policy does not cover attorneys' fees or losses until they reach a certain size. Examples of insurance policies available to nonprofits with significant deductibles include public liability, casualty losses, and workers' compensation policies. Counsel should also help the finance team understand whether insurance coverages include or exclude defense costs, and to estimate such costs as necessary. (Chapter 9 includes a further discussion of insurance.)

- Self-insurance: Some larger organizations may *self-insure* for medical, casualty, and workers' compensation claims. Organizations with self-insured exposure must establish liability funds to cover known claims as well as incurred but not reported claims and the costs of defense.

- Pending or threatened litigation: Counsel should be sure to update the finance staff regularly on the status of pending, threatened or other potential litigation matters, particularly matters for which insurance coverage or defense may not be available, and help calculate the material potential financial impact on the organization against which reserves should be held.

- Compliance with matching funding requirements: Counsel should coordinate with finance and fundraising staff about the terms of governmental or foundation grants that require matching funding. Together they should establish appropriate levels of reserves to make sure that matching obligations are met.

- Workforce reductions: The size and complexity of an organization's workforce may also affect the level of reserves that are required. Organizations that are considering workforce reductions or retraining/redeployment actions may need to maintain specific reserves to provide for such efforts. Counsel can work together with finance and human resources personnel to help determine what levels of reserves may be prudent or even required, based on laws governing such reductions or departmental restructurings.

- Pension liabilities: Actuaries, benefits consultants, and counsel with knowledge of pension law should also be consulted about establishing additional reserves to cover pension and post-retirement liabilities.

Other considerations pertinent to the size of reserves are the age, size, and condition of the physical plant (see Chapter 9), which may make it prudent to set aside monies over time to fund expensive future capital repairs. If the organization has long-term debt on its balance sheet with a bullet payment at maturity, it might do well to apply available funds to increase its reserves to provide for this repayment obligation or, in certain instances, to partially prepay it. If it has plans to borrow in the future, it may be prudent to establish and maintain higher reserve levels, depending on the credit of the organization and market conditions.

In sum, many factors inform the size of an organization's reserves, and many of these factors require legal input.

Endowments and Trusts

Endowment funds, including charitable trusts, are an organization's nest egg. As described in Chapter 5, they are funds of cash, securities, or other assets that generally are not spent by the organization but instead are held by it in perpetuity for the purpose of providing income for maintenance and operations of the organization. These funds must be carefully accounted for, prudently invested, and properly handled.

Under generally accepted accounting principles (GAAP), which are applicable to nonprofits,[10] the assets of an organization's endowment are reported as either:

- *Permanently restricted assets*, meaning assets with donor-imposed restrictions requiring that the assets be maintained permanently, but permitting the nonprofit entity to use or spend part or all of the income and/or appreciation derived from the assets.
- *Temporarily restricted assets*, meaning assets with donor-imposed restrictions that expire either by the passage of time or due to certain predetermined events or actions.
- *Unrestricted assets*, meaning assets without permanent or temporary restrictions.
- *Quasi-endowment* or *board restricted funds*, meaning unrestricted assets on which the nonprofit's board has imposed restrictions.

Although states' laws vary, in general the organization is legally prohibited from spending or investing endowment assets in violation of donors' restrictions without getting the donor's permission and/or approval from the state attorney general.

The organization should also establish and comply with a prudent spending rate, or draw, that preserves the endowment's value for future beneficiaries. Common spending rates range from 4 to 6 percent per year; sometimes the denominator (the value of the endowment against which the percentage is calculated) is smoothed out over a five-year period to avoid a rollercoaster ride for the organization's operating budget when the stock market takes sudden turns up or down. The draw then becomes a budgeted income item.

Astute boards periodically review their spending rate in light of recent investment results and other institutional considerations. Counsel should be sure to understand the rationale for the existing rate and the motivation for proposed changes and should take responsibility for making sure that full and informed consideration by the board of the long-term effects of any proposed change (including upon the organization's ability to comply with any financial covenants and regulatory requirements) takes place. Counsel should then document the change in an updated investment policy.

Charitable Investing

As discussed in Chapter 2, the assets of a nonprofit are not owned by any individual person or shareholder, but instead are held by the organization in trust for the benefit of the constituencies and purposes for which the organization exists. The persons at the nonprofit who are responsible for investment decisions are acting in a fiduciary capacity for those constituencies and purposes. As defined in Chapter 3, a *fiduciary* is a person or an entity that holds a trust relationship to another.

The Move from Prudent Man to Prudent Investor Standard   Charitable investing has become very complex. It's not as simple as just investing in CDs and U.S. Government bonds anymore, although many nonprofits still have a legacy of conservatism—a widows-and-orphans, simple fixed-income type of strategy or prudent man investing left over from the common law days. This approach probably no longer complies with the law of prudent investing, which today is more performance-based, requiring sophisticated judgments about asset allocation to maximize returns per unit of risk (i.e., optimize results).[11]

Although legal requirements governing nonprofit investing vary state by state, there is a model state law governing the management of nonprofit funds that has been adopted in one form or another in most states: UPMIFA, or the Uniform Prudential Management of Institutional Funds Act.[12] In states that have adopted UPMIFA, endowment assets can be invested prudently not only for *income* but also for *growth*. Capital appreciation can now prudently be spent for the purposes of any endowment fund held by a charitable institution, replacing the older trust law concept that only income (e.g., interest and dividends) could be spent. Thus, asset growth and income can now be appropriated for program purposes, subject to the rule in a few states that a fund cannot be spent below its historic dollar value—at least not without first notifying the donor. Under the more modern prudent investor approach, a fiduciary's performance is measured on the performance of the entire portfolio, rather than individual investments.

About Investment Policies Endowment monies can now be invested in any kind of assets (although financial statements will classify them by risk class and may assign lower values to riskier classes of assets). Endowment monies can also be pooled for investment purposes (to gain entry into portfolios with better investment returns, or to lower the cost of fund management). In general, under modern nonprofit investment law, investment decisions must be made in relation to the overall resources of the institution and its charitable purposes, with an eye toward the organization's entire portfolio, and as part of an investment strategy having risk and return objectives reasonably suited to the fund and to the institution. The organization's investment policy governs these matters. A well-drawn policy determines guidelines for asset allocations, establishes responsibility for various levels of investment decisions, determines eligible asset categories, and more. The leadership responsible for implementation of the policy (often an investment committee of the board, in consultation with finance staff and/or outside investment advisors) are responsible for monitoring and diversifying the endowment investment portfolio's performance in accordance with the policy and the fiduciary duties of care, skill, and caution.

A charitable institution is obligated to diversify assets unless special circumstances dictate otherwise. Assets that have recently been donated or otherwise acquired must be reviewed within a reasonable time after they come into the possession of the institution, in order to make sure they fit with the investment strategy and objectives of the organization.

The organization's financial professionals are entrusted with observing the asset categorizations just described, subject to the independent review of the auditors. Counsel can assist by reviewing the organization's assets in each of these categories together with finance staff, and by ensuring that the outside auditor's periodic reviews occur and that restrictions are observed.

Professional Investment Advising   The decision to move to professional investment advising is not one decision but several. Some organizations keep control over individual investment decisions while others rely on professional management to make such decisions, in part or in full. Organizations may set target ranges for asset classes, which the investment managers must adhere to. Others may specify investments only in index funds. Each of these decisions has implications for the level of activity, responsibility, and monitoring required of organization staff and officers. The organization should establish a process to select the advisor, and the process should provide for periodic review of the advisor's fitness and performance, perhaps every five years at most. Counsel can help ensure that the organization's processes for making these determinations and reviews are followed, and that those responsible for discharging these functions report their conclusions and recommendations to the governing body.

Once the determination is made to move to (or change) outside investment managers, counsel should then review the engagement letter retaining the investment manager, to make sure it is fair to the organization and complies with applicable law.

Legal Risks and Strategies Regarding Investment of Endowment Funds   Most states, particularly those whose nonprofit investment laws are modeled on UPMIFA, provide guidance to organizations that seek to modify donor restrictions on charitable funds. Sometimes a restriction imposed by a donor becomes impracticable, or wasteful, or may impair the management of a fund. For example, a fund may be restricted for use in a program that the organization no longer runs, or that may already be fully funded by other restricted gifts or sources. In such cases the organization will generally have to approach the donor for consent to release the restriction, if the donor is still alive and able to give such consent. If the donor is no longer alive or otherwise incapacitated, the charity can ask for court approval of a modification of the restriction. The trust law doctrines of *cy pres* (modifying a purpose restriction) and *deviation* (modifying a management restriction), taken together with UPMIFA where it applies, may authorize a modification that a court determines to be in accordance with the donor's probable intention. If the charity asks for court approval of a modification, the charity must generally notify the state's chief charities regulator, who may participate in the proceeding.

The broad-based adoption of UPMIFA in many states has provided beneficial flexibility to nonprofits looking at a significantly increased number and type of new investment products. It does not, however, excuse organizations from performing *due diligence* on various investment vehicles or managers before investing precious nonprofit dollars. The Bernard Madoff scandal of 2008 and other phony investment schemes that have hit many philanthropists—and many nonprofits—have wreaked budgetary and reputational harms on too many in the sector. Nonprofits lost twice: once because the value of their investment disappeared overnight, and again because donors who were heavily invested in those same scam investment vehicles lost their wealth and their ability to make good on their pledges. The negative publicity associated with large losses from scam investments may harm the organization yet again.

Investment losses in sham investments may even put the organization at risk for investigation by the state attorney general's office for potential breach of fiduciary duty. Moreover, the trustee in the Madoff case filed clawback lawsuits against many reputable nonprofits, including the America-Israel Cultural Foundation, a 70-year-old organization that gives scholarships to Israeli artists, and Hadassah, the women's Zionist charitable organization, to recover what the lawsuit claims are fictitious profits.[13]

By encouraging due diligence of new investments and requiring full disclosure of intertwined investment interests (for example, members of an organization's investment committee placing nonprofit funds in the same investment vehicle as the committee members themselves are invested in), counsel can act as an additional check on investment processes.

Pensions

A *pension* is a form of compensation paid to workers after they retire.

Federal law primarily governs pensions. The Internal Revenue Code and the Employee Retirement Income Security Act of 1974, or ERISA,[14] govern most types of pension plans for nonprofits. (Certain nonprofit plans may be exempt from ERISA's coverage.) The U.S. Department of Labor is the primary enforcer of ERISA, and the IRS is the primary enforcer of the Internal Revenue Code.

There are two types of pension plans: a defined benefit plan and a defined contribution plan. In a *defined benefit plan,* the employer sets aside, manages, and invests money in one aggregated account on behalf of its employees, to be paid out in a predetermined amount (benefit) upon each employee's retirement. The payout amount is normally based on the length of a worker's employment and the wages received. Typically, each employee does not have a separate account in these programs, as the money to support the pensions is generally administered through a trust established by the employer.

In a *defined contribution plan,* by contrast, the employee is not guaranteed to receive a given amount during retirement but only the amount in the account. Funds are deposited into an account established by and for each employee up to a certain maximum amount every year. In certain cases, the employer may contribute to the plan, based upon a predetermined formula (percentage of compensation); in other types of plans, employees are permitted to contribute a portion of their salary on a pre-tax basis. Such plans allow the employee to elect to defer receiving the monies until they retire. Once the amounts are withdrawn (generally at retirement, but maybe before that in certain cases), the withdrawals are taxed as ordinary income.

Employers are not required to establish a pension plan, but if they do have one, applicable laws specify when an employee must be allowed to become a participant, how long she has to work before she has a non-forfeitable interest in the pension (also known as *vesting period*), how long a participant can be away from her job before it might affect her benefit, and whether her spouse has a right to part of her pension after her death. An organization with a pension plan is also required to provide participants with certain information about the plan's features and funding. Pension law also specifies in great detail how pension funds are to be segregated, accounted for, and separately invested by the organization.

Anyone who exercises discretionary authority or control over a plan's management or assets, including anyone who provides investment advice to the plan, is considered a plan fiduciary, and is held accountable under law. Fiduciaries who do not follow these legal obligations may be held responsible for restoring losses to the plan.

⇨   **PRACTICE POINTER**

Counsel providing legal advice should avoid sitting as a member of the investment or pension committee so that her role as a legal advisor is kept clear of potential professional conflicts of interest.

Establishing and maintaining a plan, and complying with legal requirements, is definitely work for experts. Those charged with responsibility for the organization's legal, finance, and human resource functions should consult with qualified advisors to ensure the proper handling of these plans.

Insurance and Risk Management

Nonprofits, like other businesses, commonly carry insurance to help spread risk and protect the balance sheet against large losses.

The varieties of insurance commonly purchased by nonprofits vary according to the type of organization, the scope and scale of its activities, state law, and other factors. Nonprofits may face special insurance considerations that are different from other kinds of businesses.[15] Table 6.1 shows some common types of coverage, and some considerations for nonprofits.

Table 6.1   Some Types of Insurance Carried by Nonprofits

Type	What It Covers	Special Considerations
Property	Pays for replacement of building and contents in case of a loss such as a fire.	Revisit amount and adequacy of coverage periodically. Consider specific provisions for flood, earthquake, boiler/machinery, fire and other elements as appropriate.
Business Interruption (sometimes called business income)	Covers expenses in the event an organization's operations are interrupted due to covered events.	Consider what expenses would continue in the event of an interruption to a key revenue stream (e.g., paying key employees during downtime, provisioning temporary facilities).
Workers' Compensation	Replaces lost wages for employees who are injured on the job.	Compulsory in most states.
Commercial General Liability	Responds to lawsuits involving bodily injury and property damage allegedly due to organization's negligence, such as "trip-and-falls."	Covers personal injury claims of the general public, but not employees. Ask whether volunteers are covered.
Auto	Covers accidents caused by employees or volunteers driving organization-owned vehicles while conducting business for the nonprofit.	Consider adding coverage for non-owned auto protection if employees or volunteers frequently use vehicles not owned by the organization in conducting business for the nonprofit.
Directors' and Officers' Liability (D&O)	Covers breaches of duty by directors and officers, such as mismanagement of assets, employment discrimination, harassment, or wrongful termination.	The organization's bylaws may require indemnification of directors and officers, subject to any limitations imposed by state law.

(Continued)

Table 6.1   (continued)

Type	What It Covers	Special Considerations
Crime/Employee Dishonesty	Covers losses caused by dishonest acts of employees.	Watch for exclusions for employees with past criminal records; perform background checks in accordance with applicable law.
Professional Liability Insurance	Covers professional malpractice.	Carried by organizations with professionals on staff, such as legal aid societies, health care and human services providers.

As part of good risk management practices, counsel should clarify whether finance, legal or other overlapping personnel are primarily responsible for administering the organization's insurance program. In many nonprofits, particularly those without in-house legal counsel, the responsibility for insurance and risk management matters lies with the Finance department. In all cases, counsel should regularly discuss and coordinate risk and insurance matters with the head of Finance.

Here are some questions counsel should ask about the organization's insurance arrangements:

- What kind of insurance does the organization carry, and to what limits? How much are the deductibles, and what do premiums cost? Are defense costs included as part of the coverage?
- How regularly are these insurance arrangements revisited, by whom, and when was the last time they were reviewed to keep up with changing times?
- What representations and disclosures are made to the insurance carriers as a condition of receiving certain premium rates/discounts, and has counsel reviewed these representations and disclosures for continuing accuracy? Are they carried out in the organization's operations, and if so, who oversees continuing compliance?
- If a claim is made, whose responsibility is it to notify the insurance broker or carrier, respond to a declination of coverage, or address any reservation of rights?
- If the carrier assigns an adjuster and/or outside counsel to look into or defend the claim, who monitors their

progress and provides a primary point of contact within the organization?

- How may Legal best coordinate management of litigation with the organization's handling of insurance matters?
- What risks are uninsured or self-insured? Does the organization have a good handle on the potential size of these risks? How often are they reviewed by staff and discussed with the board and/or legal or audit committees?
- Who takes responsibility for and regularly reviews the costs and benefits of the organization's relationships with insurance advisors, consultants, brokers, carriers, and others?
- How else may Legal help analyze risks and participate in mitigation strategies?

Insurance, litigation, claims and risk management are key areas for counsel to partner with Finance and help protect the organization. (Chapter 11 discusses how to manage these matters.)

Income Taxes

As mentioned in Chapter 2, the tax exemption does not shield the organization from every kind of tax. Counsel should work with the organization's finance professionals to understand how applicable taxes and deductions are calculated.

One frequent source of confusion is the unrelated business income tax, or UBIT.[16] UBIT (pronounced YOU-bit) is a tax levied by the federal government on a nonprofit's unrelated business taxable income (UBTI). Organizations that derive income from an unrelated trade or business that they regularly carry on are subject to the tax.[17] The primary purpose of imposing a tax on exempt organizations for unrelated business activities is "to eliminate a source of unfair competition by placing the unrelated business activities of certain exempt organizations on the same tax basis as the nonexempt business endeavors with which they compete."[18]

Here are some helpful definitions:

- *Unrelated trade or business* is defined as "any trade or business, the conduct of which is not substantially related . . . to the exercise or performance by such organization of its charitable, educational, or other purpose or function constituting the basis for its exemption."[19]

- *Regularly carried on* means the activities "manifest a frequency and continuity, and are pursued in a manner, generally similar to comparable commercial activities by nonexempt organizations."[20]

If income meets these two criteria, it is probably taxable unless excluded or otherwise exempted. Just because the organization uses such income or funds for its nonprofit purposes does not cleanse the unrelated income of its taxable character.

Examples of *related* (i.e., nontaxable) business activities include:[21]

- Sale by a museum of reproductions, greeting cards, and books pertaining to the art in the museum.
- Lease by hospital of adjacent office building to a group of medical specialists to make specialized services available to hospital patients.
- Operation by medical school of a parking lot, cafeteria, and coffee shop for use by medical staff, students, employees and visitors.

Examples of *unrelated* (i.e., potentially taxable) business activities include:

- Operation by a university or religious organization of a TV station broadcasting primarily commercial programming.
- Lease of fair grounds by a county fair association to a horse auctioneer, where rent is based on net profits.
- Operation of a farm by a religious order.
- Lease of an outdoor amphitheater by an outdoor museum to a concert promoter.

Here are some *exemptions* from UBIT:

- Dividends, interest, rents from real property, gains from the sale of property other than inventory or "dealer property," and royalties.[22] (Organizations considering licensing and monetizing their copyrighted works in accordance with the discussion in Chapter 4 will appreciate the exclusion of royalties from UBIT).

- Any trade or business where "substantially all the work" is "performed for the organization without compensation."
- Activity carried out by the organization "primarily for the convenience of its members, students, patients, officers."
- Activity involving the sale of donated merchandise, that is, items "substantially all of which have been received by the organization as gifts or contributions."[23]
- Certain other kinds of passive investment income—except to the extent the property is debt financed.

The rules and exceptions governing unrelated business activities can be quite complex, and the organization should seek the advice of a knowledgeable accountant or attorney on UBIT questions.

Organizations operating an unrelated business must generally file form 990-T, a companion to the IRS informational return Form 990. Failure to identify and pay UBIT can result in the nonprofit being assessed back taxes, interest, and penalties.

Other Kinds of Taxes

Organizations such as private educational facilities, nonprofit hospitals, museums, soup kitchens, churches, and retirement homes, are generally exempt from state and local property taxation. Organizations that qualify as tax-exempt charitable entities under Section 501(c)(3) of the Internal Revenue Code for income tax purposes must apply separately for exempt status from property and/or sales tax in various states. This exemption request can be denied (or revoked) if the organization does not also operate as a public charity as defined under that state's law.

Tax-exempt organizations are not exempt from property taxes on portions of their property that are not used exclusively in furtherance of a proper or exempt purpose. Although property taxation of tax exempt organizations differs state by state and locality by locality, here is an example of one state's property tax scheme:[24]

- If any portion of a nonprofit's real property is not used exclusively to carry out one or more of its exempt purposes, but instead is leased or otherwise used for other purposes, such portion is subject to taxation and the remaining portion only shall be exempt.
- Even if another nonprofit rents the property for exempt purposes, the rental fee cannot exceed the amount of carrying, maintenance, and depreciation charges, or else the property will be subject to property tax.
- Exempt status may extend to the nonprofit's use for a non-exempt purpose, such as dining and residential facilities at a hospital or college, if those activities are incidental to the organization's overall exempt purpose.[25]

Although nonprofit organizations are often exempt from property taxation, as an economic matter these organizations nevertheless impose a cost on municipalities by consuming public services, such as police protection and roads. Over 117 municipalities in 18 states, including Baltimore, Boston, Philadelphia and Pittsburgh, have begun entering into agreements with nonprofits to make voluntary payments as a substitute for property taxes.[26] These voluntary payments are called payments in lieu of taxes, or PILOTs. Moreover, the property tax exemption for nonprofits is in jeopardy in a number of states and localities, due to budgetary pressures being faced by governments.

Counsel should ask the finance staff about the organization's mandatory and voluntary tax payments to assure compliance and assist with negotiation and documentation of new arrangements.

Financial Distress or Insolvency

If an organization's liabilities exceed its assets, it is technically *insolvent*. Nonprofit board responsibilities expand in times of economic stress. If a nonprofit approaches insolvency or bankruptcy, the board's responsibility expands to include all appropriate parties of interest—including creditors, lease holders, employee benefit plans, and retirement plans—not just the nonprofit itself. Board members cannot simply resign and let nature run its course. As long as the nonprofit organization continues to exist as a legal entity, the board has fiduciary duties. The board must ensure that the nonprofit reorganizes or winds down its affairs in an orderly fashion, provides the requisite notices and information to state and federal regulators, and then dissolves the nonprofit in accordance with state law. Typically, the state attorney general, a court, or other state entity has jurisdiction over the disposition of nonprofit organizational assets.

If the board members simply resign without following these steps, the state attorney general and/or the courts may step in. Former board members may incur legal expenses and liability, including for unpaid wages and payroll taxes and other acts or omissions of the organization that may have occurred while the organization lacked management. At this point the organization's liability insurance may not cover the directors and officers anymore!

Winding down a nonprofit's existence requires the same degree of attention and compliance with state law as establishing it in the first place.[27]

In Sum/Coming Up Next

This chapter has provided an overview of basic financial information—about nonprofits in general and about the client in particular—that counsel (and others) should acquire. It also sets forth some areas where counsel may be called upon to provide legal advice or assistance to staff in the financial area.

A glossary of financial terms is available on the companion web site to this book at www.wiley.com/go/goodcounsel. A Work Plan for surveying an organization's compliance with laws relating to nonprofit finances may be found after the Chapter 6 Focus Questions.

We now have an overview of the legal needs associated with an organization's corporate status, governance, program, fundraising, and financial functions. We now turn to the legal needs associated with the organization's human resources.

Focus Questions for Chapter 6: Laws that Matter to the Finance Department

1. Select a nonprofit of interest to you. Learn about its business model, obtain a copy of its strategic plan and associated financial or investment plan, and ascertain the governance steps surrounding its adoption and oversight. Learn about the main categories of its sources and uses of funds over the past several years and its performance against budget. Based on your review, do you conclude that its activities are sustainable in the long run? How would you measure its social return on investment?

2. What are the key financial materials that incoming counsel should review in order to support the organization's finance function?

3. What is the role of a nonprofit organization's outside auditors? To whom do they report? On what topics do they interact with counsel?

4. What are the key activities and milestones in the annual reporting cycle of a nonprofit organization?

5. What are internal accounting controls? What steps should an organization take if it encounters embezzlement or fraud?

6. Can nonprofits make a profit? What, if any, constraints are there on surplus revenue?

7. What is cash flow, and what is its relationship to a balanced budget?

8. What are some factors to consider in determining an appropriate loss reserve?

9. What is an endowment? What rules apply to the investment of endowment funds?

10. What are some of the authorizations and restrictions of UPMIFA?

11. What is a pension plan? What are some guidelines an employer must follow if it chooses to provide pension plans to its employees?

12. What is UBTI? Under what circumstances might a nonprofit be subject to UBIT?

13. What should board members of an organization do if the organization approaches insolvency?

Chapter 6 Work Plan

Laws that Matter to the Finance Department

This work plan can assist counsel or supervised law students in surveying an organization's compliance with laws impacting the finance function.

❑ Understand the organization's overall financial picture.
  - Study its business model and strategic plan.
  - Study its current operating budget and variances to date.
  - Study its financial statements.
  - Find out whether it operates on a fiscal or calendar year and determine when key events occur in the annual cycle.
  - Find out whether the organization accounts on a cash or accrual basis and determine what cash flow challenges it faces.
❑ Understand the organization's systems of preventive and detective internal controls and ascertain the role of legal counsel in supporting the control function.
  - Ask about any concerns, unusual book entries, accounts with balances that never seem to change over time, history of embezzlement or fraud perpetrated from within or outside the organization.
❑ Determine who provides legal information to the organization's external auditors.
❑ Obtain and review recent years' management letters from external auditors.
  - Note any significant deficiencies or material weaknesses.
  - Consider Legal's role to help address any such matters.
❑ Understand insurance arrangements and consider the adequacy of types and amounts of coverage.
  - Who interfaces with brokers, carriers, adjusters, and assigned counsel? Who handles reservations of rights and declinations of coverage? Who monitors litigation progress and potential settlements?
❑ Ascertain responsibility for handling of pension funds and compliance with law.
❑ Understand the organization's treatment of profits and reserves in light of applicable laws.
  - Discuss adequacy of reserves in light of pending or threatened legal matters and insurance coverage.
  - Reserves to cover unfunded pension and postretirement liabilities.
  - Reserves to cover planned workforce reductions.
  - Reserves to meet terms of contingent matching grants.

(continued)

❏ Review investment policies and procedures in light of applicable laws.

❏ Ascertain legal role in reviewing Form 990s and other filings and distribution to board.

❏ Understand the organization's sources of unrelated business taxable income.

  • Ascertain how UBTI arises, how it is reported, and how UBIT is paid.

  • Obtain and review its recent Form 990-T filings.

❏ Determine other ways in which Legal can support the Finance function.

  • Determine how the contracting process relates to Accounts Payable and Accounts Receivable areas.

  • Ascertain how minutes are kept for the finance, audit, and investment committees. Review recent meeting minutes for potential legal matters.

❏ If the organization is facing financial challenges, nearing insolvency, or considering dissolution, bankruptcy, or other restructuring, ascertain who is coordinating with board members, finance professionals, and, if required, the state attorney general's office to plan an orderly process for addressing circumstances.

Getting Personnel: Human Resources Law for Nonprofits

Nonprofit missions, programs, and fundraising plans don't execute themselves; they require the efforts of a dedicated and skilled staff. An organization's human resources professionals are responsible for the hiring, training, management, and departure of employees, all in a manner that serves the organization's best interests. Counsel has an active role to play in ensuring that these personnel matters are undertaken in compliance with law.

Many employment law issues are the same whether the employer is for-profit or nonprofit: what should (and should not) be in employment contracts and offer letters; what goes into employee handbooks and how best to convey policies to the workforce; how to ensure a fair workplace that is free of unlawful discrimination; what considerations apply in managing a unionized workforce; how to ensure compliance with immigration laws, and the like. This chapter provides an overview of these matters.

At the same time, some employment law issues present themselves differently in the nonprofit context: For example, how does an organization ensure that its volunteer and internship programs don't violate minimum wage laws? What special rules apply to setting compensation of nonprofit executives, in light of the rules against private inurement and excess benefit transactions? How does a board of directors effectively oversee the chief executive who founded the organization?

And there's more: Nonprofit workers are often a breed apart—they may be working for less pay, under more trying conditions, with broader responsibilities, than their counterparts at other kinds of businesses. What fundamental insights about a nonprofit workforce and organizational dynamics does counsel need to most effectively support the organization and its human resources team?

Establishing, training, maintaining, and rewarding a motivated and high-performance workforce—this is the mandate of any business organization's human resources function. The Human Resources department—sometimes called Personnel—is also responsible for creating job listings, overseeing the processes of hiring, training, promoting, and reorganizing the workforce, and separating employees from the organization at the end of their employment. Along the way, personnel managers keep job descriptions up to date, make sure workers are regularly and fairly evaluated and properly compensated, and maintain the organizational chart, ensuring that employees have clear lines of report to their superiors and from their subordinates. The senior human resources executive may be the staff liaison to a board-level personnel committee, if there is one.

Counsel may be asked to assist with employment law matters such as:

- Drafting and reviewing employment agreements.
- Preparing and updating employee handbooks.
- Explaining minimum wage and hours laws, and how they affect an organization with volunteers and interns.
- Assessing the classification of employees and independent contractors—an area of increasing scrutiny.
- Negotiating and drafting collective bargaining agreements, helping address labor union grievances and labor law/regulatory matters.
- Providing training and oversight of immigration law compliance, which is required even for organizations that do not have many (or any) non-U.S. citizens in their employ.
- Assisting with governance matters such as executive compensation and board independence regarding senior management.
- Keeping minutes of the board's personnel-related meetings and decisions.

We address each of these matters in turn.

Human Dynamics, Nonprofits, and the Law

While federal, state, and local employment laws apply in largely similar ways to for-profits and nonprofits, there are unique aspects of dealing with a nonprofit workforce that can make compliance trickier than in other contexts.

Many nonprofit organizations retain a mom-and-pop feel, particularly in the human resources area, long after they have outgrown this phase by other measures of their maturity: size of workforce, impact of program, age of organization, and amount of budget. The mom-and-pop sense shows up as a lack of standard procedures for listing job openings, hiring, orienting, training, evaluating, discharging, and otherwise professionally managing the organization's workforce.

At the same time, enforcement agencies at both the federal and state levels are setting their sights on the labor and employment law practices of nonprofits as a priority area for regulatory scrutiny. A growing organization and increasing regulatory complexity may make a sophisticated human resources function indispensible; but counsel recommending changes to HR procedures in a nonprofit should be mindful of the employees' emotional investment in the organization and in the ways of their work. In fact, many employees of growing organizations resent the perceived professionalization and homogenization that is implemented when the organization creates a human resources department, establishes written policies, and/or brings in an attorney to counsel in this area.

Nonprofit workers, from the top of the organization down through the ranks, tend to have a high degree of personal involvement with, commitment to, and even identification with, the organization and its cause. At the top, social entrepreneurs have invested their sweat equity in founding and developing the organization, while their counterparts in the for-profit business world may have built up valuable shareholder equity instead. Staff members at nonprofits may be working for less pay than their peers performing similar functions in commercial companies; many will say they take their salary in a higher currency. And the organization may have volunteers working alongside paid staff—in some instances even outnumbering them. For all of these good souls, mission means more than dollars.

Nonprofit employers also commonly have smaller staff than their for-profit counterparts, relative to the amount and nature of work required. This in turn contributes to staff members performing more diverse tasks, often at a higher level of responsibility than their peers elsewhere. Resilient and resourceful nonprofits make lots of lemonade for their workers out of economic lemons: greater opportunities for cross-disciplinary collaboration and learning, more rapid advancement of talented and responsible workers, more gratifying work, and even—sometimes—public recognition and prestige. The worthwhile mission of the organization and lean staffing can make it easier to attract and retain a deeply committed labor force, notwithstanding that the organization may offer lower wages and more demanding working conditions than local market averages.

But many of these same factors make it more difficult to enforce employment laws and workplace rules, especially those that were not written with the nonprofit sector in mind.

Nonprofit employees may expect fewer hassles from their boss about maintaining regular and punctual attendance, in light of their overall dedication to the work of the organization and typically lower pay. Job functions and even whole positions that no longer support the organization's current goals may continue to be filled by longtime employees, because of a vague sense of loyalty (by management), a strong sense of entitlement (by the employee), or inertia (by both). Employees may justify low-level pilfering, skimming, or even embezzlement because of lower wages or just because they can get away with it.

Harried executives concerned about balancing budgets or serving desperate societal needs may feel they simply don't have the time or resources for periodic employee evaluations or regular updates to job descriptions, let alone feedback, training, or rigorous oversight and controls. Board members may be preoccupied by other business, may not feel fully empowered or knowledgeable enough to exercise oversight over personnel matters, or may be too close to staff, or too insular among themselves to try.

And news of the latest trends in HR best practices may not have reached parts of the nonprofit workforce as quickly as those in the Fortune 500:

> **Example:** A wizened jazz artist who came up through the clubs decades ago now finds himself an adjunct professor in the

music department of a large university. Trying to make sense of the university's anti-sexual harassment training and policies, he says incredulously, "You mean to tell me, if a student comes into rehearsal looking fine, I can't tell her she's looking fine?"

Example: The leader of a conservatory's string instrument faculty opened her mail one morning to find the conservatory's new whistleblower policy. Scratching her head, she finally decided to send it back to the chairman of the music department with a note: "Misdirected mail, intended for the woodwind faculty?"

These are real examples.

Key Legal Elements of Employment Relationships

A number of legal matters arise at the outset of an employment relationship. Incoming counsel should check the organization's recruiting policies, background check procedures, job postings and advertisements to ensure that they comply with applicable federal and state law. If required notifications, such as Equal Opportunity Employer notifications, are missing, counsel should offer to help craft appropriate language. Some state laws also require other notices to be provided, such as New York's Wage Theft Protection Act.

Other paperwork generally collected from new hires includes benefits and pension enrollment, emergency contact forms, direct deposit forms, and, of course, tax forms.

About Employment Agreements

Employees commencing work for an organization should receive an *employment agreement* or an *offer letter*.

Generally, an employment agreement specifies a length of time for which the employee will work for the employer; the employee's title, salary, job duties, and reporting structure; bases for termination; and duties not to disclose confidential information. Organizations that produce intellectual property are wise to include a provision that work developed by the executive during his employment belongs to the organization.

Employment agreements generally are signed by both the employer and the employee and are binding in accordance with principles of contract law described in Chapter 4.

Figure 7.1 shows a simplified sample employment agreement with explanatory notes.

The employer and the employee should have separate counsel advising them about the agreement.

Offer Letters and At-Will Employment

Not every CEO has a contract, and most other nonprofit employees do not—at most they have an offer letter stating the key elements of the employment relationship, but not defining a specified period or duration of employment. In legal terms, most employment relationships without an employment contract are *at-will* relationships, meaning that they are terminable by either the employer (by firing) or the employee (by quitting) for any or no reason whatsoever. The at-will employment doctrine is generally considered beneficial to employers, as it provides a great deal of latitude to shape and size their workforce to meet their legitimate business needs without fear of a lawsuit for wrongful termination. This flexibility does come at a price, however: there is less surety of the employee's commitment to the post. For this reason, the organization may wish to consider a more binding relationship with employees deemed critical to the organization's success, such as the CEO.

Offer letters are a good way of memorializing the expectations of employer and employee in an at-will relationship. Organizations may provide new employees with letters describing the title, job functions, salary, and benefits (and indeed, are required to in certain states). However, counsel should review the form of such letters to ensure that they do not inadvertently undermine the at-will nature of the relationship, engendering in the employee a reasonable expectation of continued employment for a specific period of time or on a permanent basis. Such an implication may arise where, for example, an offer letter states that a project will last for three years or that grant funding has been secured for 12 months. Employers can avoid this mistake by stating that it is anticipated that the employee will work for the duration of the three-year project or the 12-month grant period, but that nothing in the offer letter is intended to alter the at-will nature of the employment relationship.

While much of employment law varies state by state, all states recognize the at-will employment doctrine.

SIMPLIFIED SAMPLE EMPLOYMENT AGREEMENT

EMPLOYMENT AGREEMENT ("Agreement") made this [date] between [organization name] ("Employer"), and _____, an individual ("Executive").

WHEREAS the Employer desires to employ Executive and Executive desires to be employed by the Employer, on terms set forth herein;

NOW, THEREFORE, in consideration of the mutual agreements set forth herein, the parties agree as follows:

1. **Term of Employment**. Executive's employment under this Agreement shall begin on [date] and shall end on [date] or such earlier date as Executive's employment terminates in accordance with Section 4 of this Agreement.

Anticipates employment for a period of years – contrast with at-will employment.

2. **Nature of Duties**.

(a) Executive shall during her employment be the President/Executive Director of [Organization], with overall responsibility for the management of the Organization, and will report directly to its Board of Directors.

Sets forth duties and reporting requirements. CEO reports to board.

(b) Executive will be expected to devote full working time and attention to the business of Employer.

Fiduciary duty of care

(c) Executive will not render services to any other business without the prior approval of the Board of Directors or, directly or indirectly, engage or participate in any business that is competitive in any manner with the business of Employer.

Fiduciary duty of loyalty.

(d) Executive will comply with and be bound by applicable laws and the Employer's personnel policies, operating policies, procedures and practices that are from time to time in effect during the term of Executive's employment.

Fiduciary duty of obedience. Reinforces that employer policies are applicable even to the CEO.

3. **Compensation and Related Matters**.

(a) **Salary**. Executive's beginning annual salary from the Commencement Date through_____[date] will be $_____. Salary will be payable in accordance with Employer's normal payroll practices with such payroll deductions and withholdings as required by law.In subsequent years of employment the Board of Directors, at its own discretion, will determine Executive's annual base salary based on the Board's review of Executive's performance for the preceding year as well as salaries of comparable executives in comparable positions in accordance with the Employer's executive compensation policies and applicable law.

Establishes periodic evaluations and comparison of compensation according to law. See Chapter 3.

Figure 7.1   Simplified Sample Employment Agreement (continued)

SIMPLIFIED SAMPLE EMPLOYMENT AGREEMENT (continued)

(b) **Standard Benefits**. During her employment, Executive shall be entitled to participate in the following benefits plans and programs, subject to the terms and conditions of those plans and programs (and subject to change by the Employer at any time): [medical insurance, dental insurance, life insurance, long-term disability insurance, retirement plans, etc.] Executive shall be entitled to paid vacation of [_____] days per year.

> Requires receipts for reimbursements and requires that expenses be reasonable; further to avoid private inurement or excessive compensation. See Chapters 2 and 3. The CEO's travel and expense reports should be signed by the Chair of the Board and reviewed annually.

(c) **Expenses**. Executive shall be entitled to receive prompt reimbursement for all reasonable and customary travel and business expenses she incurs in connection with her employment, but she must incur and account for those expenses in accordance with the policies and procedures established by the Employer as set forth in the Employee Handbook.

> The CEO's continued employment is in the hands of the board. Helps combat founders' syndrome.

4. **Termination**. If the Board of Directors of Employer elects to terminate Executive's employment without Cause (as defined below), Executive will receive the following benefits, provided Executive first signs a separation agreement [describe separation payment or other benefits].

For purposes of this Agreement, "<u>Cause</u>" shall include, but not be limited to: (1) Fraud or dishonesty; (2) Conviction of a felony; (3) Engaging in willful or reckless misconduct or gross negligence in connection with any property or activity of the Employer; (4) Material breach of this Agreement; or (5) Continued failure or refusal to perform her job duties (other than by reason of physical or mental illness, injury, or condition).

5. **Confidential Information**.

(a) **Non-Disclosure**. Executive promises never to use or disclose any confidential information of Employer.

> Establishes that the fruits of the CEO's labors belong to the organization. See work-made-for-hire discussion in Chapter 4.

(b) **Intellectual Property**. All work products developed by Executive pursuant to this Agreement shall be the property of Employer.

(c) **Survival**. This section shall survive the termination of this Agreement or Executive's employment for any reason.

Effective as of [starting date]:

EMPLOYER   EXECUTIVE

By:_____   By:_____

Date:_____   Date:_____

Figure 7.1

Exceptions to the At-Will Employment Doctrine

There are certain exceptions to the at-will rule, such as when the employee belongs to a union that has negotiated the circumstances under which union employees can be discharged.

Anti-discrimination laws are another exception to the general rule that the employer can fire an at-will employee for any reason or no reason. An employer may not base hiring, promotion, or termination decisions on race, gender, religion, national origin, or other factors that federal, state, or local laws recognize as protected. Other protected categories recognized by federal, state, or local laws include pregnancy, certain physical and mental disabilities, age, genetic information, military status or service, marital status, sexual orientation, and efforts to form or join a union. Employers that discriminate against employees on these bases may be subject to monetary consequences or even an order to reinstate a terminated employee with back pay. Anti-discrimination laws apply not only to termination and hiring decisions, but also to other employment decisions such as promotions, opportunities, assignments, and discipline. In addition, employers have an obligation to protect workers from harassment based on a protected category.

In addition to anti-discrimination laws, in certain places in the United States there is a *public policy exception* to at-will doctrine. According to the public policy exception, a decision to fire (or take other adverse employment action against) an employee must not be in *retaliation* for that employee's carrying out a public policy, such as informing regulatory authorities of unsanitary conditions at a humane shelter or overcrowding in a day-care center.

Moreover, terminations and layoffs of a group or category of employees by larger organizations may require additional steps to comply with the federal and state Worker Adjustment and Retraining Notification (WARN) acts,[1] the federal and state Age Discrimination in Employment laws, and other applicable laws, even if the employees are otherwise at-will employees.

Notwithstanding the at-will doctrine, employers must nevertheless compensate employees as agreed and treat the workforce fairly in accordance with applicable law. However, in the general case the organization has no obligation to keep an at-will employee on its payroll beyond the time it requires his or her services.

During an Employment Relationship

Common legal issues that arise in the Human Resources area involve performance appraisals, handbooks, and employment policies. We consider them in turn.

Performance Appraisals   Regular, annual performance appraisals of all employees are an important element in good personnel management. They are also a key area where counsel can proactively assist HR professionals. Employees whose performance is regularly reviewed and appraised generally perform better for the organization and grow faster into positions of greater responsibility. Negative performance appraisals also give the organization the opportunity to work constructively with an underperforming employee on specific areas for improvement. Moreover, if the organization has records of consistently negative appraisals of an employee, these appraisals will help support the organization's decision to terminate the employee, and defend it against allegations of wrongful termination or unwarranted claims for unemployment benefits.

Employee Handbooks   When an organization gets to be of the size or complexity where it is beneficial to have stated policies among its employees, it should work together with counsel to prepare and introduce an *employee handbook*. An employee handbook provides guidelines applicable to all employees, whether they work under an employment agreement or at-will, whether senior or subordinate. The employee handbook provides consistency that serves both legal and morale purposes. A handbook may also be used to support disciplinary action and avoid charges of unlawful discrimination.[2]

There is no hard-and-fast rule for when an organization needs a handbook, but some indicators include:

- There are more than a handful of employees.
- There are multiple people at each job category or level in several departments or functions.
- There is more than one reporting level between the lowest and highest-ranking employee.

- There is a history of complaints about disparate treatment.
- Any other time that management or the board feels the organization would benefit from a standard set of rules and statement of workplace expectations.

Depending on the needs, size, maturity, operations, and culture of an organization, its leadership may have a good sense of when it has reached the point where a handbook is advisable, or outside advisors, such as counsel, may recommend it. When that point has been reached, qualified counsel should help the organization prepare the employee handbook and keep it up to date.

What Goes into an Employee Handbook?   The employee handbook contains workplace rules of the road. Typical provisions include:

- Employer/employee rights, responsibilities, and expectations
- Pay policies and procedures
- Time and attendance policies
- Code of conduct or ethics, including personal financial interest disclosure provisions and a conflict of interest policy
- Equal employment opportunity statement
- Anti-harassment and antidiscrimination policies
- Accommodation of individuals with disabilities
- Drug and alcohol policy
- Background check policy
- Nonviolence policy
- Injury at work/safety
- Anti-fraternization/nepotism policy
- Wage and hour policies
- Vacation policy—accruals, uses, and forfeitures
- Meals, gifts, and entertainment
- Electronic communication policy
- Social media policy
- Confidentiality
- Company and customer equipment, property, and proprietary information
- Outside activities
- Disciplinary and employee conduct
- Performance appraisal process

- Employment separations, including notice
- Leave policies, including Family and Medical Leave Act policy (if more than 50 employees)
- Description of benefit plans and programs

Other provisions may be advisable if the organization operates internationally, if it has affiliates or members with shared or overlapping employees, if its employees work with particularly vulnerable populations such as children, seniors, sick or disabled persons, or if it has multiple locations. The matters covered in an employee handbook vary enormously depending on the organization's needs and culture, and likely will change over time.

How Is an Employee Handbook Introduced to the Workforce?   An employee handbook is typically provided to each employee at the time of hire. It is good practice to obtain a signed receipt from the employee. If an organization that already has employees provides a new or updated employee handbook, HR should explain the changes to all employees, perhaps in a group meeting, and each should sign a receipt for the new version. The HR team should review the employee handbook with employees from time to time, for example, at an annual staff gathering.

As an alternative to collecting signed paper receipts, organizations with an intranet computer system may make an electronic form of the employee handbook available on its system and provide a form of click-through acknowledgement by each employee once a year or upon the employee handbook being updated, whichever is more frequent. The click-through method is also a good way to advise employees of changes of other organization policies as well.

What Should Not Be in an Employee Handbook?   If properly written, an employee handbook will not create an expectation of or right to continued employment. For the reasons described in the at-will employment discussion earlier, the employer should be careful to include disclaimers so that the handbook does not imply to employees that they have an employment contract with the organization that gives them a right or reasonable expectation that they will be employed continuously, or permanently, or for a specified period of time, or absent the employer following certain specified conditions for termination. For example, the organization may consider it appropriate to provide two weeks' notice before termination or to grant severance pay for long-time employees being discharged; but unless the organization is prepared to be contractually bound to such practices and sets aside reserve funds for this purpose, it should refrain from stating them in an employee handbook.

As another example, organizations may choose to address employee performance or behavior problems through a system of *progressive discipline,* using increasingly severe steps of consequences if an employee fails to correct a problem after being given a reasonable opportunity to do so. Such a progression often begins with a warning and may end with a termination if intermediate steps (e.g., suspension, demotion) do not garner improvement. However, the organization may not wish to be strictly held to such measures in extenuating circumstances, maintaining its ability to terminate the employee in its discretion at any stage along the way. One common mistake is outlining a procedure in an employee handbook that *must* be followed before an employee is terminated, such as warnings or other intermediate or progressive disciplinary measures. If the employer fires an employee without following the stated procedure, the employee may have a claim for wrongful termination even if he is not under contract for employment of a certain duration.

⇨ PRACTICE POINTER

The employee handbook should use qualifiers such as "generally" or "typically" when outlining corrective and disciplinary action, reserving the employer's right not to follow each of these steps.

To avoid this problem, employers should include disclaimers in the employee handbook that it does not create a contract, express or implied; that it does not alter the at-will nature of the relationship between the employer and the employee; that it does not promise or guarantee employment for any definite period of time; that it is not all-inclusive and is only a set of guidelines; and that some of the guidelines may not be applicable to some employees (e.g., union employees may be covered by different rules in their collective bargaining agreements). The employer should also be sure to reserve the right to change the employee handbook as it sees fit.

Counsel should be sure to review with the human resources managers the systems and steps outlined in the handbook and ensure that the managers are equipped to follow through.

Avoiding Obsolescence of the Handbook   After the employee handbook is distributed, those responsible for the human resources function should periodically review the employee handbook with counsel for changes in law. They should also discuss revisions when the organization adds new classes or categories of workers, such as interns, volunteers, or non-U.S. nationals, or when it begins operations in new jurisdictions that may have different laws or cultural expectations regarding personnel.

The board or its personnel committee should have as part of its regular oversight duties a regular review of employee policies, including the handbook. Counsel can prompt and help lead this review.

Evenhanded Application of Workplace Policies   The policies of the organization should be equally applicable and enforceable to all employees, from junior and part-time employees to the president of the organization. The senior leadership sets the tone from the top for others to emulate. In cases where a senior leader of an organization does not follow the rules, counsel must remember that the organization—and not the leader—is the client, and help the board ascertain what action should be taken.

About Founder's Syndrome   Founders of an organization—who have invested a great deal of time and energy since inception to make it successful—may wish to retain a great deal of control over the functioning of organization even after it has grown. This problem is known in nonprofit circles as *founder's syndrome*. Although the founder—and the general public, and even at times the board—may regard the organization as the founder's organization, in fact he or she does not own it.

> **Example:** The founder of an organization registered its trademark in his own name and rearranged its financial and

other affairs without proper board notice and corporate action, leading to devastating results for the founder, the organization, and members of the board.

A leader with founder's syndrome has the erroneous sense that he or she owns the nonprofit and is fully in charge of its affairs, notwithstanding that no one owns a nonprofit and that the board and the public stakeholders have important roles. This misconception is ultimately inconsistent with the long-term health of the organization, its service of its mission, the morale of its employees, and the directors' faithful discharge of their fiduciary duties.

Counsel can help an organization and its board escape the grip of founder's syndrome by encouraging evenhanded application of policies and procedures, including:

- Adopting an employee handbook.
- Adopting a board handbook.
- Preparing and updating job descriptions, including for the CEO/founder.
- Ensuring that there are regular periodic evaluations of every employee, right up to the top.
- Ascertaining that employment contracts are in place for key employees, which are subject to review upon expiration or from time to time.
- Making sure the bylaws and other governing documents contain clear statements that the CEO takes direction from the board and can be replaced if he or she does not observe the policies set by the board or otherwise applicable throughout the organization.

A well-written board handbook should also help the board understand its proper role vis-à-vis the founder, with reference to organizational policies and the law.

Other Laws that Matter to Nonprofit Human Resources Professionals

Employment law is complex enough in the for-profit sector, the context envisioned by most lawmakers deciding what the laws are. The considerations become even more complicated in the nonprofit sector, which may not have been foremost in mind when the laws were written.

Here are some areas where the practice of employment law is particularly distinct in the nonprofit context: minimum wage and overtime hours laws, volunteers and interns, independent contractor classification, and the liability of the employer for the torts of volunteers.

Minimum Wage and Overtime Hours

The *Fair Labor Standards Act of 1938*, as amended, sets standards for minimum wage, overtime pay, and child labor.[3] The FLSA applies to nonprofit organizations as well as to for-profit employers. The FLSA requires employers to pay covered employees at least the federal minimum wage, plus overtime pay of one-and-one-half-times the regular rate of pay for each hour worked in excess of 40 in a work week. It restricts the hours that children under age 16 can work and forbids the employment of children under age 18 in certain jobs deemed too dangerous. The Act is administered by the Wage and Hour Division of the U.S. Department of Labor.

Exempt from the overtime requirements are employees who are paid on a salaried basis, earn at least $455 a week (as of 2011—this amount may change over time), and fall into one of the categories of exempt workers. Following are the most common categories of exemption:[4]

- *Executive Exemption*—Paid on a salary basis; primary duty is the management of the enterprise or a recognized department or subdivision of the enterprise; customarily and regularly directs the work of two or more other full time employees or their equivalent; and has the authority to hire or fire other employees.
- *Administrative Exemption*—Worker's primary duty is office or non-manual work related to the management or general business operations of the employer or the employer's customers, such as tax, accounting, insurance, purchasing, marketing, research, safety, human resources, public relations, government relations, computer network administration, or regulatory compliance, *and* the worker's primary duty includes the

exercise of discretion and independent judgment with respect to matters of significance.

- *Learned Professional Exemption*—Worker's primary duty is to perform work requiring advanced knowledge; that is, work that is predominantly intellectual in character and which includes work requiring the consistent exercise of discretion and judgment; the advanced knowledge must be in a field of science or learning; and the advanced knowledge must be customarily acquired by a prolonged course of specialized intellectual instruction.
- *Creative Professional Exemption*—Worker's primary duty is to perform work requiring invention, imagination, originality, or talent in a recognized field of artistic or creative endeavor, such as music, writing, acting, and the graphic arts.
- *Computer Professional Exemption*—Worker's primary duty is as a computer systems analyst, programmer, software engineer, or similarly skilled worker in the computer field.

Job duties often evolve depending on the changing needs of the organization, the capacities of the individuals performing the work, and conditions in the labor market. The organization's human resources leadership should perform an audit of job descriptions periodically to ensure that they remain accurate and that they properly reflect whether the worker is exempt or non-exempt. This review should be a collaborative effort between human resources professionals and counsel with knowledge of employment law.

Many states have laws regarding minimum wage, overtime, child labor, and exemptions that can differ markedly from federal law, and which in many cases provide additional protections to employees. Counsel should be very familiar with both federal and state wage and hours laws when advising human resources professionals.

About Volunteers

Volunteers are often the lifeblood of an organization. Certain individuals who work without compensation for charitable, civic or religious nonprofit organizations may be considered volunteers, and not employees, and therefore need not be paid in accordance with the FLSA.[5] With the guidance of counsel, nonprofit organizations can construct and continually review their volunteer programs to make sure that they do not unwittingly fall within the coverage of the FLSA.

An organization's relationship with its volunteers is exempt from the FLSA if:[6]

❏ The volunteer works solely for his own personal purpose or pleasure.
❏ The volunteer works without promise or expectation of compensation.
❏ The entity receiving the services is nonprofit.
❏ The volunteer receives, and expects to receive, no benefits from the entity receiving the services.
❏ The services are not performed under pressure or coercion.
❏ The services provided are not of the kind typically associated with paid employment.

There are also state minimum wage laws, which may contain overlapping or different requirements in determining whether an individual is a true volunteer. For example, New York's minimum wage law requires that:[7]

❏ The individual is performing tasks traditionally reserved for volunteers (that is, the volunteer is not being used to supplant or augment paid staff in performing staff activities).
❏ The individual is not being required to work certain hours or perform duties involuntarily.
❏ The individual receives no remuneration for his/her activities.

Some state laws require the organization to provide a written statement to its volunteers, signed by both the organization and the volunteer and maintained with the company records for 36 months, that the volunteers waive their right to receive the minimum wage.[8]

Interesting questions arise when an employee also volunteers to do certain work for the organization. If this occurs, ideally the work for which the employee is volunteering is different from the type of work for which he gets paid; no one else doing that type of work is being paid; and the employee is under no coercion or duress by the employer to volunteer his time.

Example 1: A church secretary is motivated of his own accord to volunteer as a server at the church picnic. All the other servers are volunteers as well.

Example 2: A member of a breast cancer research organization's janitorial staff decides to volunteer as a race-day timer at the annual footrace. All of the other timers are also volunteering. The janitor would experience no adverse result if she decided not to volunteer.

Not all volunteer situations are ideal from a legal standpoint, however, and counsel should review the organization's policies and practices from time to time for conformity with rapidly evolving law and enforcement patterns.

About Interns

Trainees, interns, externs, apprentices, graduate assistants, or similar categories of individuals may also be outside the coverage of federal and state wage and hour laws. The U.S. Department of Labor's Wage and Hour Division has developed six factors to evaluate whether a worker is an intern or an employee for purposes of the FLSA:[9]

1. The training, even though it includes actual operation of the facilities of the employer, is similar to what would be given in a vocational school or academic educational institution.
2. The training is for the benefit of the trainees.
3. The trainees do not displace regular employees, but work under their close observation.
4. The employer that provides the training derives no immediate advantage from the activities of the trainees, and on occasion the employer's operations may actually be impeded.
5. The trainees are not necessarily entitled to a job at the conclusion of the training period.
6. The employer and the trainees understand that the trainees are not entitled to wages for the time spent in training.

If all of the factors listed above are met, then an employment relationship does not exist under the FLSA, and the FLSA's minimum wage and overtime provisions do not apply to the worker.[10]

Much like the laws about volunteers, laws about interns vary from state to state. In New York, for example, three factors must be met in order for a student to meet the legal definition of an intern: the student receives school credit for his or her work; the student is supervised by an administrator, teacher, or professor (need not be day-to-day supervision); and the student's school must be accredited.

A recent crackdown on companies failing to abide by federal rules governing student internships in the for-profit sector has led to a decrease in the number of internship programs. The Wage and Hour division of the U.S. Department of Labor is also reviewing the need for additional guidance on internships in the public and non-profit sectors.[11]

Employees and Independent Contractors

Nonprofits tend to be leanly staffed—due in large measure to funding issues—and they often do more with less. Sometimes it is less costly to bring on needed helping hands as *independent contractors* (sometimes also called consultants or freelancers) rather than hiring them as employees. Employees' wages are reported on the federal Form W-2, and the employer is responsible for withholding income taxes, withholding and paying Social Security and Medicare taxes, and paying unemployment tax on wages paid to an employee. By contrast, contractors' earnings are reported on federal Form 1099, and the contractor, not the organization, is responsible for paying his or her own income taxes, Social Security and Medicare taxes, and unemployment tax.[12]

Hiring independent contractors helps the organization manage salary expenses, keeps headcount down, limits exposure to health and pension costs, reduces payroll taxes, and avoids certain overhead expenses. For these reasons it can be tempting for organizations to characterize the work relationship as a contractor relationship rather than an employment relationship, even if this characterization is inaccurate.

It is critical that organizations correctly determine whether the individuals providing services are employees or independent contractors. Nonprofits as well as for-profits must assiduously make and adhere to this distinction, notwithstanding the pressures of stretched budgets and daunting programmatic needs.

The complaint of a single individual—or an unemployment benefits filing by a former contractor who thought she was (or should have been) an employee—can trigger a Department of Labor audit of an entire organization's workforce. An employer can be held liable for employment taxes, plus interest and penalties, for any of its workers found to be incorrectly classified. Consequences may include liability for back withholding taxes, interest and penalties, and potential disqualification of employee benefit plans. For the worker, such consequences may include liability for self-employment taxes and denial of certain business-related deductions.[13]

Mischaracterizing a worker as an independent contractor can also result in minimum wage rules being applied retroactively to a relationship previously considered by the parties to have been an independent contractor relationship.

Officers and even volunteer board members can be held personally liable for failure to remit payroll taxes for misclassified employees.

Guidelines for Proper Worker Classification   In general, an employee is anyone who performs services for an organization if the organization can control what will be done and how it will be done; for example, by setting working hours, providing a work space, and supplying the tools and materials for the worker to do the job.

The IRS has provided some illustrative examples in the nonprofit context:

> **IRS Example 1**: Donna Lee works full-time as an appraiser for a tax-exempt museum. Donna works five days a week, and is on duty in the museum's office on assigned days and times. Her appraisals and proposals are subject to the museum curator's approval. Lists of leads of prospective sellers of art belong to the museum. Because of Donna's experience, she requires only minimal assistance in appraising art and preparing proposals, and in other phases of her work. In addition to paying Donna's wages, the museum pays the cost of health insurance and group-term life insurance for her.[14]

In analyzing this example, Donna works full-time, on a schedule designated by the museum, in facilities provided by the museum.

Her work is supervised by the museum, and she receives fringe benefits from the museum. The IRS concludes that Donna is an employee of the museum.

An independent contractor, on the other hand, is largely self-directed, that is, he or she is not provided with workspace or tools, and is not told by the company when, where, and how to work. A general rule is that the organization can control or direct the result of the work but not the means and methods of accomplishing that result.

> **IRS Example 2:** Vera Elm, an electrician, submitted a job estimate to a tax-exempt low-income housing organization for electrical work at $16.00 per hour for 400 hours. She is to receive $1,280 every two weeks for the next 10 weeks. This is not considered payment by the hour. Even if she works more or less than 400 hours to complete the work, Vera Elm will receive $6,400. She also is to perform additional electrical installations under contracts with other organizations, which she obtained through advertisements.[15]

In analyzing this example, Vera has control over when or at what pace she works. She is also able to accept other jobs without seeking the permission of the housing organization. Thus, the IRS concludes that Vera is an independent contractor to the low-income housing organization.

Various governmental agencies use different tests to determine whether someone is an employee. The U.S. Department of Labor's economic realities test inquires:

- Whether the worker provides services that are part of the employer's regular business (this factor weighs in favor of a finding that the worker is an employee).
- Whether management retains control over the work performed (this factor weighs in favor of a finding that the worker is an employee).
- Whether the worker has a permanent or extended relationship with the employer (this factor weighs in favor of a finding that the worker is an employee).

- Whether the worker has an investment in the work facilities and equipment (this factor weighs in favor of a finding that the worker is not an employee).
- Whether the worker can make a profit or incur a loss (this factor weighs in favor of a finding that the worker is not an employee).
- Whether the work requires unique skills or judgment (this factor weighs in favor of a finding that the worker is not an employee).

In evaluating whether a worker is an employee or an independent contractor under the FLSA, courts have applied this economic realities test on a case-by-case basis.[16]

While the Department of Labor economic realities test applies to enforcement of FLSA, the IRS applies other tests and factors when determining a worker's W-2 or 1099 tax status.[17] Therefore, a worker could theoretically be considered an independent contractor by the IRS for tax purposes but an employee by the Department of Labor in enforcing wage and hour laws. Qualified employment law counsel can help review the status of each worker in an organization for the purposes of all applicable laws.

Liability of the Organization for Employees, Independent Contractors   *Respondeat superior* is a Latin phrase meaning, "Let the master answer." It is an ancient but still viable legal doctrine that holds the employer liable for the *tortious* (negligent, harm-causing) actions of its employees while they are acting within the scope of their employment.[18] The doctrine applies to employees, and even to volunteers acting on behalf of the organization; but it does not hold an organization liable for the actions committed by independent contractors.[19] In addition, the doctrine applies only to tortious conduct that is generally a foreseeable consequence or risk of employment.[20]

In addition to the common law principle of *respondeat superior,* many employment statutes will hold an organization liable for the unlawful actions of its managers, supervisors, and sometimes staff employees. Through bylaws, many organizations take on additional duties to indemnify employees acting within the scope of employment.

Separation from Employment

An organization terminating an employee—particularly an employee threatening a lawsuit for wrongful termination such as alleged discrimination—should consult with qualified counsel. A knowledgeable attorney can help HR manage communications (and if necessary negotiations) with the departing employee, and obtain a written release and waiver of all potential claims. Separation agreements may also contain provisions regarding unpaid wages and vacation pay, confidentiality and nondisparagement, pension and benefits calculations, and continuation of health insurance under the federal COBRA law and state law.

Labor Law: Operating a Nonprofit in a Unionized Environment

The National Labor Relations Act of 1935 (NLRA) governs labor relations between employers and unions. The NLRA was enacted "to protect the rights of employees and employers, to encourage collective bargaining, and to curtail certain private sector labor and management practices, which can harm the general welfare of workers, businesses and the U.S. economy."[21] The Act, together with other federal and state laws, administrative agency regulations, and judicial decisions, are intended to provide an organized and coordinated set of rights and protections to workers, employers, and labor organizations.

Although the traditional focus of the NLRA and its authorities is the relationship between employers and unions, the law does have import for non-union employers. Most significantly, the law protects all employees' rights to act together, with or without a union, to influence terms and conditions of employment, including wages and benefits. These are known as protected concerted activities. Examples include:

- Two or more employees addressing their employer about improving their working conditions and pay.
- An employee speaking to his employer on behalf of himself and one or more co-workers about improving workplace conditions.
- Two or more employees discussing pay or other work-related issues with each other.
- Refusing to do any or all of these things.

Non-union employers may not realize that employees can file unfair labor practice charges with the National Labor Relations Board (NLRB) if their employer takes adverse action in response to employees engaging in protected concerted activities.

Federal labor law also requires the employer to bargain with the appointed representative of its employees; prohibits employers from discriminating against union members or interfering with employees' selection of a labor organization to represent their work unit; regulates the use of tactics such as strikes, lock-outs, picketing by each side in furtherance of their bargaining positions; and makes it illegal for employers to harass or retaliate against workers because of union membership.

Union members typically pay dues, for example 1 to 2 percent of pay, to help the union defray the costs associated with representing their interests. They may also participate in a union pension and health plan, to which the employer may be expected to contribute.

A collective bargaining agreement (CBA) is a contract that sets forth the terms and conditions that an employer and a trade union have reached regarding the wages and working conditions of employees who are members of that union. It is typically the result of collective bargaining, or negotiations, between representatives of the employer and union representatives. Once the union representatives and the employer have reached a deal, the union members employed at that workplace take a vote to decide whether to approve the deal. Once approved, the agreement is committed to writing and signed by both the employer and the union. The signed agreement governs the relationship between employer and the unionized employees for the period of years specified in the collective bargaining agreement. When that term expires, negotiations commence anew, unless the parties agree to simply extend the agreement for a longer duration.

Some of the terms typically contained in a CBA include:

- The requirement that the employer recognize the union as the sole bargaining agent for all employees.
- A statement of where the work is to be performed and the extent of the union's jurisdiction.
- What the work periods consist of (for example, 40-hour workweek, five days at eight hours per day followed by two consecutive days off).

- Descriptions of straight time pay and overtime pay.
- When meal breaks are and their duration.
- How much paid sick time a union member is entitled.
- The wage scales for different levels of senior, line, and new employees.
- What holidays are paid holidays.
- Number of training days and whether they will be paid or unpaid.
- Health, welfare and pension contributions by the employer.
- Vacation accrual rates.
- Provision for notice to employee and shop steward of any disciplinary issues (writeups).
- Prohibition against discharging an employee other than for good cause.
- Provisions regarding layoffs (e.g., notice periods).
- A no-strike clause during the term of the CBA.
- Agreement to arbitrate major questions.
- Grievance procedures, such as meetings between the employee, the shop steward/business representative of the union and the employee's immediate supervisor, and escalating to management/executive office.

In negotiating a collective bargaining agreement, past practices are often heavily influential in determining what conditions are expected to continue into the future (e.g., who does what work and what counts as overtime).

Benefits

An employer is required to pay social security taxes and make contributions on behalf of each employee toward unemployment and worker's compensation insurance.[22] In addition, some states, including New York and California, require that employers contribute to short-term disability insurance on behalf of employees residing in-state.[23] The law on healthcare requirements is complex. Effective beginning in 2014, a federal health care law establishes significant penalties to a company employing 50 or more full-time employees and not offering adequate health insurance, and where at least one of those employees purchases his or her own health insurance.[24] Additional benefits, such as dental insurance, life insurance, and retirement plans, remain optional.

A wide variety of legal and consulting firms can assist an organization with a review of benefits plans and recommendations for future action.

Immigration Law Compliance

Immigration laws apply to nonprofit and for-profit employers alike. Employers are required to determine the identity and employment eligibility of all newly hired employees, whether full-time, part-time, or temporary (but not independent contractors or the contractors' employees).

In order to comply with employment eligibility laws, employers are required to have all new hires, including U.S. citizens, complete *Form I-9* of the Department of Homeland Security U.S. Citizenship and Immigration Services (USCIS), also known as the Employment Eligibility Verification. All new hires must complete the I-9, on or before the first day of hire.[25] The employer must certify the employee's status on the I-9 within three business days of the first day of employment.

As part of the I-9 intake process, the employee must prove identity and employment eligibility by presenting certain documents, which can include a driver's license, Social Security card, and United States passport. The employer is held to a reasonableness standard in ascertaining whether documents are fraudulent. An employer should examine the documents for typos, strange fonts, errors in punctuation, irregularities in the photograph or the positioning of the photograph, and security features. If the prospective employee is under 18 or incapacitated, the employee's parent or guardian should fill out the I-9 form and provide the appropriate documentation. In requesting documentation of eligibility to work, an employer should be mindful to request only the documentation that is needed to complete the I-9. It is unlawful to require more or specified documentation from one type of employee or group of employees than from another.

⇨ PRACTICE POINTER

Requiring more work eligibility documentation from certain employees based on their appearance or ethnic group may subject the employer to discrimination claims.

The employer must keep the employee's form on file for the duration of his or her employment. In addition, the employer should maintain I-9 forms for terminated employees for the later of three years after the date of hire or one year after the date that the employment ends. The employer should store the I-9 forms separately from the personnel files in order to protect the privacy of the employees regarding other personnel matters in the event of an audit by US immigration authorities.

An employer has an ongoing obligation to monitor and re-verify the status of non-immigrant workers who present I-9 documentation that has an expiration date. The penalties for failing to do so include costly fines and criminal sanctions. Employers with sizable workforces or questions about past practices should engage periodic outside audits by a qualified immigration law professional.

The requirement to have employees fill out I-9 forms does not apply to unpaid interns or volunteers.

Certain employees who are not U.S. nationals or permanent residents must have a visa in order to work. Nonimmigrant visas are appropriate for those intending to work, study, or visit the U.S. for a temporary period, while immigrant visas are appropriate for those who intend to reside in the U.S. permanently. If an organization is asked to sponsor a non-national for either a temporary visa or as an immigrant, the organization should consult an independent attorney knowledgeable about immigration law and not rely on the attorney hired by the worker. An organization should also be cautious about entering into co-applications with other organizations for extended stays by foreign workers because each organization is responsible for the worker's compliance with his or her status during the entire visit yet will likely not be in a position to oversee the worker's activities for the entire visit.

In Sum/Coming Up Next

This chapter facilitates a review by counsel and HR professionals of the organization's employment contracts, offer letters and other on-boarding procedures; performance management protocols; employee handbooks and policies; compliance with minimum wage and hours laws; programs for interns and volunteers;

proper classification of independent contractors; labor unions; immigration law compliance; and more.

A glossary of human resources law terms is available on the companion web site to this book at www.wiley.com/go/goodcounsel. A Work Plan for assessing the state of employment law compliance follows the Focus Questions.

We're on a roll now: our organization has program leaders executing on mission with advantageous contracts and copyright arrangements; its fundraisers are successful and fully compliant; its finance department has the finances in perfect equipoise; and its human resources department has a dream team on the case. How does the organization get the word out? Start spreadin' the news, it's time for Legal to meet the Communications Department!

Focus Questions for Chapter 7: Getting Personnel

1. What are some similarities between human resources legal issues in nonprofit organizations and the for-profit setting? What are some differences between the two?
2. What matters does an employment agreement typically cover?
3. What is an at-will employee?
4. What are some matters generally included in an employee handbook? What should it *not* contain?
5. What is founder's syndrome, and how can it be addressed or avoided?
6. What are wage and hours laws, to whom do they apply, and what classes of employees are exempt from them?
7. What are some legal issues to consider in the use of volunteers? Interns?
8. What is the difference between an employee and an independent contractor? What are some legal implications of such classifications?
9. What is *respondeat superior*? To whom does the *respondeat superior* doctrine apply?
10. What is a collective bargaining agreement? What are some of the legal issues to be mindful of when interacting with employees who are members of a union?
11. What benefits must an employer provide its employees, and what benefits are optional?
12. What must an employer do to verify that a new hire is eligible to work in the U.S.?

Chapter 7 Work Plan

Human Resources Law for Nonprofits

This work plan provides an overview of legal issues that commonly arise for human resources professionals in nonprofit organizations.

❑ Review procedures for employee applications, hiring, promotion, discipline, and termination.
   • Review employment contracts and offer letters, including statements of job responsibilities, reporting relationships, compensation, confidentiality provisions for those with access to sensitive or proprietary information, intellectual property assignments, and term or at-will employment provisions.
❑ Review employee handbooks and methods for enforcing employee policies.
   • Leave policies.
   • Accommodations for employees with disabilities (temporary or permanent).
   • Policies implementing EEO, anti-discrimination, and anti-harassment laws.
❑ Review procedures for distributing employee handbooks, obtaining acknowledgements of receipt and assent.
❑ If the organization performs background checks, ascertain awareness of and compliance with laws for handling results.
❑ Review classification of workers as employees or independent contractors.
   • For tax purposes (W-2 or 1099) as well as for compliance with wage and hours laws.
❑ Review compliance with federal and applicable state and local minimum wage laws.
   • Determine whether employees have written job descriptions that accurately reflect what they do and whether they are exempt or non-exempt from wage and hours laws.
   • Ascertain whether internships and volunteer programs comply with legal requirements.
❑ Review termination and separation practices for compliance with law and sound risk management.
❑ Review any collective bargaining agreements and be familiar with the upcoming renewal dates, ongoing negotiations, current or recurring issues, and grievances.
❑ Review benefits programs and assess compliance with applicable laws.
   • Understand what benefits are provided to employees, including both required and optional benefits, COBRA requirements, and retirement benefit plans such as pension plans and 403(b) plans.
❑ Review compliance with immigration law, particularly I-9 Employment Eligibility Verification forms and work visas.

CHAPTER 8

Getting the Word Out, Legally: Counseling the Nonprofit Communications Team

Marketing, public relations, and communications executives play an important role in conveying the work of the organization to the public. Counsel can serve and support this important function by understanding the common legal needs of nonprofit communications professionals.

The chapter opens with information about trademark law—how to choose strong names with which to identify the organization's products and services, and how to protect the organization's good name from infringements and encroachments by others. Along the way it provides two illustrative case studies involving nonprofits and trademarks. The chapter then moves on to rights clearance, providing legal background that marketing professionals need to create materials that best publicize the organization's good works while respecting the intellectual property rights of others. After rights clearance, the chapter explains how communications and marketing campaigns comply with various consumer regulatory laws. It then continues with a discussion of the legal aspects of some of the most effective marketing techniques, including contests, games of chance, and digital media campaigns.

The chapter concludes with a discussion of other ways that counsel and the communications team can coordinate, especially in times of crisis.

Introduction to the Legal Aspects of Nonprofit Communications

Nonprofits, like other kinds of businesses, thrive when they create dynamic and innovative marketing and public relations campaigns to publicize their good works. Larger organizations may have separate departments for public relations and marketing, while smaller ones will bring these activities together under the general heading of communications. The communications function is responsible for the public identity of the organization, coordinating marketing and advertising efforts to create demand for the organization's offerings and support for its work. The head of the communications area sets media policies, creates strategy, determines budgets and spending priorities, and coordinates advertising buys. A worthy communications leader will continually evaluate results against stated goals and revise strategy in response to metrics. He or she will coordinate closely with the organization's chief executive, program leadership, fundraisers, and governmental relations team. Savvy communications leaders also interact frequently with the organization's counsel and/or corporate secretary, and coordinate external communications by the board and its chair.

Organizations have name brands under which they do business—possibly more than one if they are active in several lines of work. Using these brands, communications professionals help get the word out about the good works the organization does, and the need for support for that good work, by creating marketing pieces, press releases, a web site, brochures, social media presences, and other published material. From time to time, they may try to entice new members, subscribers, donors, and other members of the public to join common causes through signups for e-mail or text lists, giveaways, sweepstakes, contests, and games of chance. Each of these activities is subject to laws. When they are conducted interstate or online, yet other laws apply.

This chapter is about how communications professionals and counsel can collaborate to get the word out, legally.

What Nonprofit Marketing Directors Should Know about Trademark Law

A trademark is a brand: It identifies goods or services as originating with one person or entity, distinguishing those goods or services from the goods or services of others. A *trademark* is often the central focus of an organization's marketing or communications efforts. And yes, trademark law applies to nonprofit and for-profits equally. Trademarks are most commonly a word or a logo, although they can also be a number, design, color, sound, building design/shape, or even a smell, or a combination of any of these features.

Other names for trademarks are brand names (which are word marks) and logos (which are usually designs or symbols, although they can also include wording, which may be in a special script or typestyle). Trademarks identify the source or origin of goods or services, and are symbols of consistent quality of those goods or services and of the goodwill that has developed over the years of use of the mark.[1]

A *trade name* identifies an organization itself, while the *trademark* identifies its products, goods, and services. So, for example, General Motors (trade name) makes the Corvette and Cadillac autos (trademarks). Examples of trade names used by nonprofit organizations include the Jazz Foundation of America and Vanderbilt University.

Trade dress refers to the visual appearance of a product. Perhaps the most well known example of trade dress is the red labeling and white lettering on a Coca-Cola bottle.

Although trademarks are intangible assets, they are among the most valuable assets owned by many companies.

Trademark rights typically are acquired by usage. Therefore, a mark is protected under the common law beginning with the first time the organization uses it. The longer an organization has used a name or mark as its own distinctive moniker, or the more prominent or geographically varied the use, the stronger the common law trademark rights will be.

Registering a trademark with the federal and/or state government provides valuable additional protections, including nationwide priority of use of the mark, although as in the case of *copyrights*, registration is not necessary to establish ownership. The U.S. Patent and Trademark Office (USPTO) web site has information about the federal registration process.[2]

Whether registered or common law, and whether protected at the state, federal, or international level, trademark rights provide the owner with a mini-monopoly in the jurisdiction in which the mark is established—the exclusive right of the organization to use that name for those classes of goods or services with which it is most closely associated. Moreover, unlike copyrights, which expire after a period of years and the work passes into the public domain, trademarks can be owned and continually renewed in perpetuity. If all the rules are followed, the organization can continue to use its trademarks forever.

A *domain name* (or URL) is the address of a web site on the Internet. In business and nonprofit sectors, the domain name often encompasses the organization's trademark or trade name, followed by .com or .org. Traditionally nonprofits select the .org suffix to designate their non-commercial status (.com refers to commercial, .org to organizations, and .edu to educational institutions), although these designations are self-selected, not legally mandated or enforced.

Naming a Nonprofit

If an organization has not yet been named, or if it is launching a new line of goods or services that has yet to be named, it should consider the following:

- Is the proposed name protectable as a trademark?
- Is it available, that is, not already in use?
- Is it available as a domain name?

First, is it protectable as a trademark? While Apple can be a valid trademark for computers, it cannot be a valid trademark for apples, because it is the generic name of such goods. Also, Light for beer and White for bread cannot be brand names because they are generic adjectives. Apple cannot be a trademark for pears, either, because it is mis-descriptive of such goods or deceptive.

A Taxonomy of Names—From Weakest to Strongest Trademark Protection   The following hierarchy (from weakest to strongest) helps evaluate the protectability of words proposed as trademarks. Choosing a stronger mark will help truly distinguish the organization's goods or services from those of others.

Generic Names   A generic name of something can never become a trademark, because it defines a product, not its source, and must be free for all to use. An example of a generic name is the two-word moniker Homeless Shelter for an organization that operates a homeless shelter.

Merely Descriptive Names   A merely descriptive word or phrase that directly and immediately describes a product, or a quality or feature of the product, or an intended result of using the product, can become a trademark. But it is a weak type of mark and may be difficult to defend. Examples may include Feed The Children for an organization dedicated to providing food for children and families in need, or Public Broadcasting Service for an organization that provides programming to public television channels.

Suggestive Names   A suggestive word or phrase is a word or phrase that suggests an attribute or benefit of goods but requires one to use imagination, thought, or perception to reach a conclusion as to the nature of the goods. Suggestive words or phrases are protectable and registrable from the date of first use. Examples of suggestive marks are Habitat for Humanity for an organization that builds homes for those with low incomes; Goodwill Industries for an organization that trains people with disabilities; or Compassion International for an organization that fights child poverty.

Inherently Distinctive Marks   Inherently distinctive marks, such as fanciful, coined, or made-up words, or arbitrary associations of a word with an entirely different meaning, make for the strongest kind of trademark. Livestrong, as a mark of an organization that promotes cancer awareness, is an example of a coined mark; Cotton Candy, for an organization that promotes breast cancer awareness, is an example of an arbitrary mark.

⇨ PRACTICE POINTER

Selecting an inherently distinctive mark for an organization's goods or services helps project a memorable image in the public's mind and greatly increases the organization's ability to protect the mark against unauthorized use by others.

Next Steps: Assuring Availability   Once the organization has determined that the name is protectable, it must seek professional guidance to ensure that the name is also available. Qualified trademark counsel can help ascertain whether there are actual or anticipated uses of the mark, and identify whether there is a likelihood of confusion between the proposed mark and an existing mark or name. Factors for consideration include:

- Similarities in appearance, pronunciation, and/or connotation of the existing mark and the organization's proposed mark.

- Related or complementary nature of the respective goods or services offered under the mark.
- The channels of trade, target buyers, cost, complexity, and the environment in which the mark is used.

An organization may have selected the perfect mark for its purposes, but if the same or similar mark is already in use for the same or related goods or services by another entity, the organization will not be able to use or register it. Selecting and using a name that is already in use by another organization offering similar goods or services can be ruled an *infringement*, subjecting the organization to an injunction (court order) and an award of money damages. Another important consideration is the availability of a domain name that matches the proposed trademark, followed by .org. Other suffixes (.com) should also be checked to make sure there is not undesirable confusion. The availability of a domain name matching or mirroring the organization's desired name is an important part of the naming process. Organizations may even wish to obtain ownership of URLs similar to their name to avoid undesirable confusion by others seeking to exploit the similarity with the charity's official URL (called cyber-squatting or typo-squatting).

Trademark Warriors—A Case Study of Conflicting Names-in-Use and Domain Names An instructive example of trademark conflict in the nonprofit sector is the Wounded Warrior Project case. The Wounded Warrior Project (WWP) and Wounded Warriors Family Support (WWFS) are two different charities that assist injured veterans and their families. A military veteran founded WWP in 2002, as wounded veterans began returning to the United States from the Afghanistan war, to address gaps in services provided by the armed forces. With the donations collected, WWP delivered backpacks stocked with care and comfort items to nearby military hospitals. Over time WWP expanded its offerings, ultimately providing bedside training about veterans' and social security disability benefits, an adaptive sports program, college preparatory courses, and small group combat stress counseling. WWP grew to employ over 100 people, spending 75 to 82 percent of donations directly on wounded soldiers and their families. At present, WWP sends over 10 million mailers annually and appears on television and radio shows to publicize its activities and solicit donations in support. WWP operates two web sites, woundedwarrior.org and woundedwarriorproject.org, which were first registered in January 2003 and March 2004, respectively.

A member of the U.S. military serving in Germany founded the Wounded Warriors Hospital Fund, which later became the Wounded Warriors Family

WOUNDED WARRIOR PROJECT

Support (WWFS), in 2003, to purchase electronic equipment, sweat suits, and chewing tobacco for wounded soldiers in Germany. WWFS developed a web site to solicit donations, wounded warriorhospitalfund.org. In 2004, WWFS incorporated as Wounded Warriors, Inc. and started a new web site, woundedwarriors.org (with an "s" at the end of "warriors"). At the same time WWFS moved its operations to the United States. WWFS conducted little or no advertising, fundraising, or marketing. However, donations to WWFS increased dramatically upon the launch of the woundedwarriors.org web site. In 2006, WWFS bought condominiums in Florida and Texas with the donations. WWFS offers the condominiums to wounded veterans and their families for vacations. The condominiums' occupancy rate for soldiers and others staying for free was only approximately 30 percent, so WWFS rented the condominiums to others at a profit when wounded veterans, their families, or WWFS's employees were not staying in them.

At first, WWP tolerated WWFS because WWFS was operating in Germany under the www.woundedwarriorhospitalfund.org web site. However, WWFS renamed itself Wounded Warrior, Inc., moved its operations to the United States, and established a web site at www .woundedwarriors.org—in the process changing the web site's color scheme, font, and text phraseology to mimic WWP's web site. After these changes, WWFS began to receive—and cash—a large number of checks evidently intended for WWP. Some checks were made payable to Wounded Warriors Project; other checks were accompanied by correspondence indicating support for WWP or mentioning one of WWP's marketing or fundraising efforts. When WWFS established the www.woundedwarriors.com web site, donations to WWFS spiked from an average of $1,337 per month to $87,895 per month. WWP eventually obtained a court order shutting down the

WWFS web site and won a judgment holding WWFS accountable for the misdirected donations and reputational damage.[3]

The lessons to be learned from this example are many: Organizations should undertake frequent and consistent efforts to protect their name brands, their trade dress, their web site URLs, and other indicators of origin against nearby, competing efforts that may serve similar ends but in different ways or with different standards. If an organization identifies another, potentially competing use of its name but determines at the outset not to try to prevent the usage (as here, WWP initially tolerated the activities of WWFS because WWFS was originally based in Germany and had a sufficiently distinctive web address), the organization should nevertheless be on guard for progressive encroachments. Counsel can assist in reaching, documenting, and enforcing a written understanding with the other organization to circumscribe the other organization's activities under that name within acceptable limits, avoiding further encroachment. Interestingly, although WWP initially acted with restraint and reportedly undertook its lawsuit reluctantly, it received some criticism in the military and veterans' community for suing a fellow nonprofit with similar aims. Thus, nonprofit organizations and their counsel should be aware of the reputational and other impacts both of taking action and of refraining from action, and of the special sensitivities of trademark enforcement in the nonprofit context. Early and vigilant attention with the aid of qualified counsel can help deter or avoid such circumstances, or at least help address them before too much harm is done.

Should the Organization Register its Trademarks?

Trademark rights arise from use alone; no registration is required. However, a federal trademark registration can be of great value in protecting the mark, especially if it is intended for use throughout the country.[4] Registering provides:

- Evidence of ownership.
- Evidence of the validity of the trademark.
- Evidence of the registrant's exclusive right to use the mark for the goods/services recited in the registration.

- Protection against others' applications to register confusingly similar marks for competing or related goods.
- Nationwide protection of the mark.
- Easier licensing or sale of the trademark to others.

Federal registration protects trademarks according to the class of goods or services to which they are affixed. For example, trademarks registered in Class 9 are protected for electrical and scientific apparatus, while trademarks registered in Class 41 are protected for education and entertainment services. If the organization expands into new lines of goods or services, or it is licensing its mark to another entity that will apply the organization's trademark to a different class of goods or services, the organization should consider expanding its registration of its trademark into the classes associated with those new goods or services.

A mark must be used in interstate commerce before it can be federally registered, although the application can be filed initially with only an intention to use the mark, followed by actual usage within a set window of time in order to complete the registration process. Registration is a multi-step process that includes an initial determination of registrability by the USPTO, followed by publication in the Official Gazette for opposition.[5] If there is no valid opposition, the registration is issued.

State trademark registrations are also available for marks used within a state, but such registrations generally afford no greater rights than the user's underlying common law rights (that is, rights arising just from having used the mark).

Following the lessons learned in Chapter 4 regarding registration of copyrights (and unlike our exemplars at the Audubon String Quartet, in which one member of the quartet registered the trademark in his own name rather than in the name of the Quartet Corporation), organizations registering trademarks should be sure to register them in the name of the organization and not an individual.

Trademarks in Use: Licensing, Extending and Protecting Marks

The basic rule for trademarks is use it or lose it. The more the organization uses and promotes its mark, the stronger the mark becomes as an identifying symbol and a repository of goodwill for the organization and its goods or services. On the other hand, if use of a mark is discontinued for three consecutive years or more, the mark may ultimately be deemed abandoned by the U.S. Patent and Trademark Office.

Good trademark practices include the following steps.

Take Inventory of the Organization's Trademarks   Search the U.S. Patent and Trademark Office database (or commercial databases) under the company name, and run periodic web searches to see whether and how other entities may be using the organization's marks and similar marks.

Keep Track of Deadlines for Renewing Trademark Rights   For registered marks, diary ahead for all official maintenance deadlines. For example, an affidavit of use has to be filed between five and six years after registration; an application for renewal must be filed every 10 years after registration. A registration can be renewed every 10 years as long as the organization continues to use the mark. If minor changes to the appearance of a logo have been made, the registration can be amended to show its current form.

Regularly Police for Infringements   The organization should frequently check for third-party uses of its marks and act promptly to object to unauthorized uses, especially if such uses are likely to dilute, tarnish, or impair the organization's reputation and goodwill. Members and staff of the organization can assist counsel by serving as additional eyes and ears to detect infringements by neighboring businesses, similar nonprofits, and others. For marks with high value to the organization, professional trademark watching services can be engaged to monitor the filing and/or publication of applications to register similar marks, and to watch for incorporation of entities with similar names. Some state laws may provide additional protection for the names of nonprofit entities.[6] Keep records of all policing efforts and of all acknowledgments of the organization's trademark rights, as such evidence may be helpful in framing future objections and in proving to a court how diligently the organization has guarded its rights.

Enforce the Organization's Trademark Rights   The organization should send cease and desist letters to infringers (after confirming that it has priority of use), or reach a written understanding with the organization using a similar mark in order to define each party's rights. The organization should consult counsel and the organization may need to be follow up on threats of litigation where the damage from continued use of the infringing mark is direct and immediate. However, not all unauthorized uses of a trademark can be stopped, as the user may be making a "fair [descriptive] use" of your mark, or a use in comparative advertising, parody, news reporting, or a use in an artistic or other non-commercial context, or even in a commercial context that is so remote from your field of operations that no likelihood of confusion will result. In addition to consulting with counsel, the organization may also consult with public relations experts before firing off that letter of objection, as it may very well appear on the web the next day as part of the adversary's counter-attack, as seen in the Wounded Warrior case.

Extend Protection Efforts to the Web and Social Media Uses   If someone tries to register a similar name as a domain name, the organization may be able to recover the domain name in an electronic mini-litigation under the Uniform Domain Name Dispute Resolution Process. Also be sure to register the organization's trademarks on Facebook, Twitter, Flickr, Tumblr, and other social media sites commonly used in the organization's milieu, and police for infringements on these sites as part of periodic and regular sweeps. Most reputable sites provide a straightforward takedown method for use by intellectual property owners against infringements appearing on those sites.

Use the ®, ™, or ᔆᴹ Marks   The ® sign indicates a registered mark. The ™ or ᔆᴹ sign indicates rights in an unregistered trademark or service mark, respectively. Use of these designations is not mandatory—and the organization's creative designers may object to too much visual clutter if counsel goes overboard insisting on these designations—but use in at least one location per advertisement, publication, brochure, or web site will inform the public that trademark rights are being claimed. The organization might consider adding an unobtrusive legal line at the bottom of advertisements and other commercial uses of the organization's marks, stating the ownership of the marks.

Consider Creating a Branding and Style Guide   The Communications team, in consultation with counsel, may decide to issue a branding and style guide specifying typefaces, spacing, ®, ™ and ℠ placement, and other elements so that employees, affiliates, members, and licensees will use and promote a consistent visual image for the organization's brands.

Establishing and following through on these steps will help keep the organization's portfolio of trademarks safe from infringements, encroachments, and allegations of abandonment.

Licensing Trademarks   The organization may from time to time wish to *license* its trademarks to another entity for use. Common examples in the nonprofit sector include licensing to affiliates, joint fundraising collaborators, corporate sponsors (so that they may publicize their contributions to the organization), and commercial co-ventures or joint ventures. (Chapters 2 and 6 also discuss these arrangements from a corporate law, governance and tax point of view.) Such relationships are easier if the organization has its trademark portfolio in good order, with up-to-date registrations and full coverage in all pertinent classes. Organizations may also wish to obtain licenses to use the marks of others, under the circumstances described above or for other co-branding uses. In all cases, counsel can help prepare and review trademark licenses to make sure they protect the organization's interests.

Licensing should be carefully controlled, not indiscriminately undertaken. Trademark owners have a duty to control the quality of goods and services offered under their trademarks. Licensing to the wrong type of licensee can tarnish the organization's brand irreparably. Worse yet, uncontrolled licensing (also known as naked licensing) is considered inherently deceptive to the public, and it can lead to a finding that the organization has abandoned its trademark.

We turn to an example of how not to license a trademark.

Nonprofit Trademark Licensing Gone Bad: The Freecycle Case   The Freecycle case is an example of nonprofit trademark rights lost through naked licensing. In that case, the organization owning the Freecycle mark used it to identify the practice of giving unwanted items to strangers for further use, rather than disposing of them (the items, not the strangers). However, the organization allowed another local group to use its mark without a license, or contract, controlling the circumstances under which it could use the mark, and in fact simply let the second group use the mark in any manner it saw fit. When things went bad, the first organization then sought to prohibit the second group's use. An appellate court ruled that the trademark owner had not only failed to provide by contract for control over another party's permitted use of the mark, but it also failed to exercise actual control over the use, and also unreasonably relied on the user's own quality control measures. The trademark was deemed to have been abandoned.[7]

The Freecycle[8] case and the Wounded Warrior case demonstrate the importance of good trademark licensing and enforcement practices among nonprofit organizations, and the ways in which knowledgeable counsel may help. A great deal of additional information is available about trademark law in books, on web sites, and in articles.[9]

Special Trademark Considerations for Membership Organizations   Membership organizations are larger organizations that have chapters or member groups that use their name. Examples include the Boy Scouts of America and the YMCA. Membership organizations face particular trademark concerns. Membership organizations want to encourage their chapters or members to use their marks to signify membership, but at the same time the organization is less well-positioned to control the use. In such instances the organization should take the following steps to protect its trademarks and logos against claims of naked licensing:

- Add the word member or chapter to the mark, and register it as a *collective mark* with the U.S. Patent and Trademark Office. A collective mark is a word, phrase, symbol, or design owned by a collective group or organization and used by its members to indicate the source of the goods or services.
- Include trademark provisions in affiliation agreements between the national organization and the members or chapters, specifying permissible uses of the mark. Consider provisions in the organization's bylaws and policies that explicitly license the mark to members and chapters and bind them to specific controls or uses, such as a style manual and an obligation to cease using the mark if the chapter or member ends its affiliation with the organization.
- Conduct periodic checks to ensure that chapters or members are following the rules of use of the organization's marks or logos. If the rules, marks, or logos change, prepare and follow through on a plan to introduce and explain the new information to members and chapters, and obtain a promise to comply. Be prepared to take action against persistent noncompliance.

Counsel for organizations with members or affiliates should be sure to coordinate with the leadership of their chapters to ensure compliance with these steps.

International Protection for Trademarks   The good that nonprofits do is often not limited to national borders. Nonprofit activity sometimes occurs globally, and in such cases—or even where the organization's activities are located domestically but its web site or social media pages enjoy substantial traffic from international visitors—it may be a good idea to undertake international protection for its trademarks.

Unfortunately, there is not yet any global form of trademark protection. An international registration system, called the Madrid Protocol, does provide a cost-effective way to centrally file multiple national trademark applications. U.S. applicants currently can file applications in 85 nations through the Madrid Protocol.[10]

As we conclude the discussion of trademark law and nonprofits, note that a glossary of trademark terms is available on the companion web site to this book at www.wiley.com/go/goodcounsel. A
trademark law Work Plan follows the Focus Questions at the end of
this chapter.

Clearing Rights to Use the Protected Works of Others

In fundraising, marketing, and public relations materials, nonprofits may wish to use the works of others: photos, cartoons, books, articles, plays, music, or movies, for example. Organizations wishing
to use such materials must first clear the usage with the owner of
the material, ordinarily through a license agreement not unlike the
simplified sample license set forth in Chapter 4. Failure to obtain a
license to use protected materials belonging to others could expose
the organization to liability for copyright infringement. Negative
consequences can add up quickly.

The Communications team can help protect the organization
against expensive and embarrassing tangles by establishing rights
clearance protocols in collaboration with counsel, and by consulting counsel early in the process of creating new campaigns. Counsel
in turn can assist the organization's communications efforts by
undertaking swift and regular prepublication legal reviews of publicity materials and by providing training and assistance with rights
clearance procedures.

Rights Clearance by Type of Work

Following is a general description of how an organization may clear
rights for various types of copyrighted or otherwise protected works
commonly used by nonprofits: images, recorded music, books and
articles, plays, and films. Organizations with questions about how to
clear specific works should consult with qualified counsel.

Clearing Images In order to display and/or reproduce an image, an
organization must obtain permission from the copyright owner
of the image. Images include any pictorial representation, such as
photographs, paintings, drawings, and cartoons. Image archives are
mainly licensed for commercial purposes.[11] A nonprofit organization
seeking to reproduce an image from an image archive should explain

the planned educational or noncommercial use of the image in an effort to have the license fee lowered or eliminated. Underlying rights controlled by third parties either pictured in or involved in the creation of the images may also require clearance.

Corbis Images and Getty Images are two services that own and license a wide array of images. Both services offer some images that may be used free of charge. In addition, Corbis Images sponsors an Image Donation Program, which allows nonprofit organizations to use up to 20 photographs annually free of charge that normally require license fees.[12]

Clearing Music   If a nonprofit organization wishes to play music on its web site, promotional video, or as part of a live presentation or performance, it must obtain permission and negotiate a royalty payment to both the performer of the song and the composer/lyricist who wrote it. Permission is required and royalties are due even if the songs are used in a manner that does not generate revenue.

The organization may have to clear several different types of rights, depending upon its use of the music:

- The use of music in conjunction with visual elements requires a synchronization license and a master use license.
- Distribution of copies of a recorded work requires licenses known as a mechanical license and master use license.[13]
- The public performance of music requires a public performance license.[14]

The Library of Congress maintains an online searchable database of music and recordings, as well as books, visual materials, and other works dating back to 1978, with information about whether the work is registered, what entity registered it, and the year of registration.[15] Labels on recordings made after 1978 (mp3 file properties, compact disc booklet, or other format) have information necessary to locate the rights holder of the performance, usually the record company.

The legal issues involved in clearing music for use can be confusing and complicated. An organization should consult with counsel before large-scale or public use of music.

Clearing Books and Articles   If a nonprofit wishes to distribute copies of books or articles or selections of books or articles, for example at a conference or on its web site, it must first obtain permission from the work's copyright holder. If the organization has difficulty locating the copyright holder from the © notification on the publication, it may turn to the Copyright Clearance Center (CCC), an experimental electronic permission service that can assist in locating rightsholders and clearing rights. There is generally a 24- to 36-hour turnaround from the time that permission is requested to the time that the request is answered.[16] Permission to reproduce articles written by freelance writers can often be obtained through Ingenta, which handles rights for the Publication Rights Clearinghouse, a collective licensing agency representing over 13,000 publications with over 5 million articles.[17] Finally, to reproduce news articles, it is best to consult the news organization's web site, which generally contains information about the use of articles and archived materials.

A word of caution: It is common for nonprofits to want to celebrate their positive press coverage by sending out copies with their fundraising appeals or by reprinting the article in their newsletter. If permission hasn't been obtained in advance, however, this violation of copyright can have expensive repercussions. Newspapers do police such uses, and they typically charge for permitting copies of their articles to be used. The cost may vary based on type of use and number of copies. A particularly compelling nonprofit advocate may be able to persuade the publication to provide a *gratis* (free) license for a particular period of time or usage, but this is rare. The nonprofit can avoid having to obtain permission and pay a fee by just quoting a short excerpt from the article, with attribution. See the discussion of *fair use* further on.

Clearing Plays or Theatrical Works   In order to perform a play or copy a dance routine, an organization must obtain permission from the copyright owner. Play publishing houses such as Music Theatre International, Rodgers & Hammerstein Theatre Library, Anchorage Press (plays for young people), Samuel French, Baker's Plays, Dramatists Play Services, or Dramatic Publishing can ascertain whether plays are available for production and make arrangements for scripts and payment of royalties. Their web sites may also provide a community for users; for example, educators with limited budgets may be able to contact other educators to borrow/trade props, costumes, and sets.

Clearing Films and Videos   In order to screen a film or video at an organization's event, or include a sizable clip in the organization's fundraising or promotional materials, the organization must obtain permission. Motion Picture Licensing Corporation, Movie Licensing USA, and Swank Motion Pictures, Inc. grant most public performance rights in movies.

Internet Archive has a selection of educational public domain films available for download. Films are stored in MPEG format. However, organizations wishing to use such films may also need to investigate whether any rights need to be additionally cleared—actors, producers, writers, performers, guilds, or composers. Agent representation for living people can be found at the WhoRepresents web site.[18]

Once the organization has ascertained who owns or controls the rights in a work it wishes to use, it should follow certain procedures for obtaining permission.

Steps for Clearing Protected Works

Some organizations that use large quantities of media, such as public television stations, may have an entire department or team devoted to rights clearances. Others learn as they go. Important steps to take when seeking a license from a rights holder include:

Step 1: Correctly identify the entity that is administering the rights the organization wishes to use. In some cases (particularly with music) the person or company administering license requests may be different from the copyright owner. This may require some research, either by an Internet search or on one of the clearinghouses or archives listed above.

Step 2: Request permission to use the work from the appropriate party. Clearly and accurately explain the proposed use, extent, and duration.

Step 3: Understand and be prepared to comply with any restrictions on use. In seeking permission to use copyrighted work, it is always best to seek rights in perpetuity, in all locations, and in all forms of media. If securing such broad rights is not agreeable to the copyright owner/administrator or is cost-prohibitive, determine what limitations the organization can live with and still carry out the program or project for which the use is needed.

Step 4: Document the agreement reached with the copyright holder. Upon obtaining permission to use copyrighted work, document the agreement in a written license agreement. Key provisions of the agreement include rights granted, duration of license, geographic restriction (if any), limitations on sublicensing, a fee (if any), and may also require crediting (see simplified sample license in Chapter 4). If the copyright holder sends a license agreement for the organization to sign, be sure to review it carefully with counsel to accurately reflect the terms discussed, and ensure that the organization complies with these terms. In particular, if the license is granted for a *limited purpose or time*, be sure that someone within the organization is responsible for ending the use when the license runs out.

If the Copyright Owner Orally Grants Permission   The organization should send a confirmation letter describing the terms agreed upon and requesting the copyright owner's countersignature. If the owner fails to countersign and return the letter, send a follow-up confirmation letter in which the previous conversation is referenced and the prior correspondence is attached. If the copyright owner still does not sign and return the letter, then prepare a written memo to file, documenting the conversation: how the copyright holder was reached, with whom the conversation was held, on what date, what terms were discussed and agreed, and subsequent efforts by the organization to follow up and obtain written confirmation of the conversation. Attach to the memo a copy of any e-mails or other correspondence with the copyright holder. This course of action in the absence of a written agreement carries some risk, however; the organization may still be exposed to liability for infringement if the rightsholder later reappears and denies that it gave permission.

If You Cannot Reach or Identify the Copyright Holder   This is the so-called *orphan works* problem. Many works are still under copyright but the owner cannot be located or reached, for a variety of reasons: The owner is unaware of its ownership, for example, or has died or gone out of business without leaving information establishing to whom ownership of the copyright has passed. Organizations needing or wishing to use such works do so at their own risk.

Here are some steps that can be taken to minimize (but not eliminate) that risk:

1. Undertake a diligent effort to locate the owner, and document all steps and efforts undertaken. A search may be considered reasonably diligent if it is conducted in good faith, with resources and technology reasonably available to the user.
2. Provide attribution to the extent possible, based on information obtained during the course of the search.
3. If the owner emerges after the use has commenced, promptly engage in discussions toward a licensed use of the work, and cease such use in the event terms cannot be reached.
4. Be prepared for an owner to emerge and claim copyright infringement. It may be entitled to injunctive relief (a court order prohibiting the use) as well as money damages and possibly attorney's fees.

If the organization follows these steps and nevertheless receives a claim of copyright infringement from a purported owner, it should ask counsel to assist in investigating the veracity of the claimant's assertions and try to negotiate a resolution. If the copyright owner is adamantly opposed, cease using the infringing material.

Larger nonprofits that make substantial, visible use of the copyrighted works, such as television or radio programs or webcasts,

---

⇨ PRACTICE POINTER

Sometimes an earnest explanation of the organization's good-faith and diligent efforts to clear the rights, together with an explanation of the worthy nonprofit uses to which the work is being put, will pave the way toward resolution.

---

may consider obtaining *Media Errors and Omissions Insurance.* Media E&O insurance defends and indemnifies the organization against claims of infringement; however, it can be expensive.

Rights Clearance Alternatives   Users of rights-protected works have been pushing owners toward a more open-source model: encouraging broader, or even unlimited, access without having to go through a potentially costly and time-consuming clearance process. Some owners have been responsive while others have maintained a more traditional approach.

For those willing to share, an internationally recognized non-profit organization called Creative Commons has developed an alternative approach to allow free, limited, noncommercial copying and distribution of works uploaded to it, either because the works have entered the public domain or because their owners are willing to permit free licensing on certain terms. Creative Commons' free tools permit the granting of licenses to users while still reserving various rights to owners. For example, the owner of an image may decide to permit a free license through Creative Commons, pro-vided that it is used for noncommercial purposes, is attributed to the author, and is not modified.[19] Wikimedia Commons is another very useful tool in locating open source images.[20]

The Fair Use Defense   Generally speaking, the use of a copyrighted work without permission from the owner is an infringement. However, the federal Copyright Act allows copyrighted materials to be used "for purposes such as criticism, comment, news reporting, teach-ing (including multiple copies for classroom use), scholarship, or research."[21] This allowance is known as fair use.

There is no clear-cut test for determining whether a use is fair use, but courts have identified four factors to help with the analysis.

The four factors used to determine whether the use of a work without a license is fair use are:

1. The purpose and character of the use.
2. The nature of the copyrighted work.
3. The amount and substantiality of the portion used.
4. The effect of the use on the potential market for the copy-righted work.

☐▷ PRACTICE POINTER

While a proposed nonprofit use of copyrighted works without permission may very well be a permissible fair use, it is always advisable to consult with an attorney con-versant in this area for advice.

First Factor: Purpose and Character of the Use   The first factor asks, what is the purpose and character of the use? A noncommercial purpose, such as nonprofit or educational use, is more likely than a commercial purpose to be regarded as fair use.[22] In this regard, nonprofit organizations are at an advantage over for-profit organizations making the same use of the same material. However, noncommercial purpose alone does not automatically qualify unlicensed use as fair use; all four factors must be weighed.

In addition, courts will look more favorably upon uses that are transformative in character, that is, uses that give the work some new expression, meaning, or message not present in the original work. For example, a nonprofit might change the lyrics of a song to reflect the organization's goals. This novel use of the song could be regarded as transformative, although again, transformative use alone would not be sufficient to justify unlicensed use without other factors also being met.

Second Factor: Nature of the Copyrighted Work   The second factor asks, what is the nature of the copyrighted work? A finding of fair use is more likely when the nature of the work is further from the core of copyright protection, such as a listing of information, which involves a minimal level of creativity, as opposed to a musical composition, which is very creative and at the core of copyright protection. For example, an organization devoted to the legal needs of domestic violence victims may wish to copy a list of local matrimonial lawyers from a copyrighted publication; such use of a listing might tend to be supported by this second factor of fair use analysis.

Third Factor: Amount and Substantiality of the Work Taken   The third factor evaluates the amount and substantiality of the portion used. With respect to this factor, the likelihood of a finding of fair use increases when less of the work relative to the whole is used. Although some organizations use a 30-second rule or a 10 percent rule, neither of these rules of thumb is a reliable definition of substantiality for purposes of fair use analysis. The amount of the work taken is less important than whether the heart of the work is taken; this can occur even where a relatively small amount of the work is used. For example, a magazine published verbatim quotes from

President Ford's forthcoming memoir about his years in the White House without his or his publisher's permission. The article quoted only about 300 to 400 words, which in absolute terms was an insubstantial portion of the memoir. However, the excerpts included factual material drawn exclusively from the chapters about President Ford's pardon of former President Nixon. These excerpts were held by the Court to be the heart of the memoirs and thus the use was an infringement and not fair use.[23]

In another case, the use by a television news program of one minute and 15 seconds from a 72-minute Charlie Chaplin film in a report about Chaplin's death was found to have taken the heart of the film and thus was not fair use.[24]

Fourth Factor: Effect on Market   The fourth factor, arguably the most important, evaluates the effect of the use upon the potential market for the copyrighted work. If the use of a copyrighted work without a license cannibalizes revenues from the licensed sale of the work, then the use will not be considered fair use. If on the other hand the potential market for a copyrighted work is not harmed by the proposed unlicensed use, then a finding of fair use is more likely. Examples of uses that do not cut into the sales of a copyrighted work include short segments from a film or novel, if the overall context of the use would not provide a substitute means for the public to have access to the heart of the protected work. In one case a nonprofit organization's use of one minute and 25 seconds of a five-minute song, which was part of a movie that was 136 minutes long, was held to be fair use in light of the amount used, and also in light of the fact that it was used for nonprofit purposes.[25]

As this example illustrates, the rules for fair use analysis are applied somewhat more liberally in the nonprofit context. The law provides that if the challenged use is noncommercial in nature, the burden is on the copyright holder to prove that the noncommercial use will harm the sales of the work. By contrast, the alleged infringer has the burden if the challenged use is commercial in nature.[26]

Nonprofit status is not a free pass, however. Courts have repeatedly ruled that distribution of substantial portions of copyrighted publications, even for educational purposes, requires permission of and compensation to the copyright owner, and does not constitute fair use.[27]

Nonprofits seeking to use copyrighted works without permission under the fair use doctrine are advised first to consult with counsel who is knowledgeable about copyright matters.

What happens if an organization gets it wrong—fails to clear the rights, violates the terms of a license, or thinks it has a fair use defense but is mistaken? The rightsholder may sue the organization for copyright infringement, the unauthorized use of the copyrighted work of another.

Copyright Infringement Remedies and Enforcement   If an organization is sued for copyright infringement and loses, the court will then consider what the organization owes to the rights holder:

- *Actual damages* are available if the copyright owner can measure and prove a dollar value of how much it was damaged by the infringement. The owner may also force the infringer to pay over any profits that the infringer may have acquired from unauthorized use of the work. The owner is entitled to obtain information needed to prove the infringer's gross revenue from the unauthorized use of the work.
- The owner can instead elect to recover *statutory damages.* Statutory damages are in amounts written into the law, or statute. At the time of this writing, statutory damages are between $750 and $30,000 for each work, based on the court's discretion. If the infringement was willful, knowing and intentional, the court may increase the amount of the award up to $150,000 per infringed work. If, however, the infringer was unaware and had no reason to believe that its acts constituted an infringement of copyright, the court may reduce the award to $200 per work.
- Courts may also allow the owner to get the full costs of its efforts to enforce its rights, including reasonable *attorney's fees.*
- *Injunctive relief,* which is a court order to stop the infringing activity, is also available to a copyright owner in limited circumstances. To obtain an injunction, the copyright owner must show:
    1. That it has suffered irreparable injury, or is likely to suffer irreparable injury if the activity continues.

2. That monetary damages are inadequate to compensate for that injury.

3. That, considering the balance of hardships between owner and the infringer, an injunction is warranted.

4. That the public interest would not be disserved by an injunction.[28]

Registering the copyright in the works with the U.S. Copyright Office is a prerequisite to any enforcement action.

The severity of consequences for infringement serves as a valuable reminder of several lessons in this chapter as well as Chapter 4: the importance of properly clearing and obtaining licenses from others whose copyrighted works one seeks to use, and the importance to the organization of protecting and policing its rights in the works it owns.

Other Rights to Be Cleared

In addition to copyrights, there are other kinds of rights that must be cleared before an organization may use, reproduce, or distribute materials belonging to others.

Guild or Union Rights   Materials created by members of certain creative guilds or unions, such as stagehands, choruses, corps de ballet, scenic designers, and costume designers may require a payment to be made to the union in order to clear the rights in such materials for use. Organizations wishing to use such materials should investigate and, if necessary, negotiate for these rights.

Rights of Publicity   The *right of publicity*, recognized under some states' laws, is the right to control commercial uses of a person's identity. This right allows celebrities and private citizens alike to control how their likeness (including their picture, name, signature, or other identifying aspect of their person) is used in commercial materials. If an organization wishes to feature a person's photo in a brochure, or use the name of a celebrity to endorse a cause, the organization must first obtain permission from that person.

Use of a person's identifying features without permission may subject the organization to a lawsuit for violation of publicity rights under state law. There is also a federal cause of action for use of a person's name or likeness to falsely imply her endorsement of a product or service.[29] In some places, even deceased persons continue to have rights of publicity for a certain period! In such states, permission to use the deceased's name or picture must be sought from the deceased's estate.

Knowledgeable counsel should assist the organization in developing form releases or consents to be obtained from attendees of an event at which photographs or video will be taken if those photos are to be used in organizational publicity materials and if the individuals depicted are recognizable.

A simplified sample release form might include text such as shown in Figure 8.1.

If it is impracticable to obtain signed releases from all participants in an event that the organization wishes to publicize, the

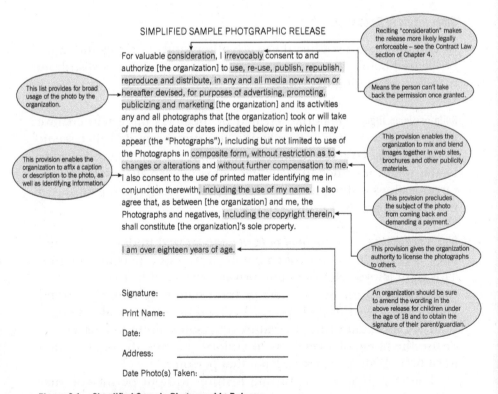

Figure 8.1   Simplified Sample Photographic Release

organization may consider using photos in which no individual is recognizable (blurred crowd shots, shots from behind). In that case, the organization should also post signs prominently at all points of sale (web site, box office, scripts for phone operators, back of ticket stock) and at the entrance to the event (especially if it is a free event), notifying participants that the event will be recorded or photographed:

> By entering into this event, I irrevocably consent, on behalf of myself and accompanying children in my care or custody, to be photographed or videotaped by an authorized media professional.

This approach is helpful but not failsafe, especially as some state laws, including New York, require that an individual's consent to certain commercial uses of his or her image be in writing.

As we conclude the discussion of rights clearance and nonprofits, note that a glossary of rights clearance terms is available on the companion web site to this book at www.wiley.com/go/goodcounsel. A rights clearance Work Plan follows the Focus Questions at the end of this chapter.

Consumer Regulatory Laws

A wide variety of federal, state, and even international laws govern business entities' interactions with the general public. At the outset of each new fundraising or publicity campaign, counsel can help coordinate among the organization's program executives, its fundraisers, and its communications function to ensure compliance with consumer regulatory laws: What is it telling the public and its donors about its activities, and does it match its practices to its promises? These efforts help protect and preserve the organization's good name with the public it is intended to serve.

Truth-in-Advertising Laws

Truth-in-advertising laws vary from state to state. But in general, whenever a nonprofit advertises to the public, such as offering tickets to an event, providing services for a fee, or seeking charitable donations, it must be truthful and accurate about the nature of the services being offered and the ultimate uses of the funds being raised. Although the law is somewhat unsettled in this area, organizations should be aware that their words may be scrutinized as commercial speech in just the same way as the words of a for-profit organization. If a communications campaign is found to be inaccurate, the organization may be held liable for false advertising and deceptive practices.[30]

Contests, Sweepstakes, and Other Promotions

Contests, sweepstakes, and other promotional activities attract new supporters and subscribers to the organization. Games of chance, including raffles and sweepstakes, are regulated by all states as well as by the federal government. (Chapter 5 also touches upon laws and regulations affecting raffles, bingo, and other games of chance that are part of a fundraising campaign.)

States commonly require that before publicizing such an activity, the organization either already possesses the prizes or has written agreements with the sponsor regarding the delivery of the prizes. In some states, the organization offering the contest or sweepstakes must also register with the secretary of state, pay a fee, and/or maintain an escrow account or post a bond in an amount equivalent to the value of the prizes.

Rules Pertaining to Contests and Games of Chance   Generally speaking, entry materials should clearly state the eligibility requirements, such as age and residence, what the prizes are, how to win the prizes, and how to claim the prizes. Neither a purchase nor a contribution may be required to enter or improve chances of winning. Simple surveys can be a condition of entering, but the organization must not require that participants fill out complicated surveys or provide a great deal of information. The organization should expressly retain the sole right to determine the winner and resolve any disputes.

Contest activities that are advertised across state lines, such as on the Internet or in interstate mail, are also subject to federal law. In addition to a general requirement that mail not be deceptive, federal law requires that no purchase can be required to enter; the mailing must not contain a facsimile check; the contest should not falsely state or imply that it is sponsored or endorsed by the government; and the mailing must give the recipients a way to remove themselves from the mailing list. The mailing should also disclose the sponsor (and contact information for the sponsor), and include the quantity and retail value of each prize, estimated odds of winning each prize, and a schedule of payments of a prize if it is not one item or a lump sum. If the contest ballot is mailed, the required disclosures must be in the mailing, in the rules, and on the order or entry form. After the contest's conclusion, the sponsoring organization must notify winners and post or make available winner lists.

The U.S. Postal Service has the right to seize non-compliant mailings and impose fines. Fines for failure to comply with federal law begin at $25,000 and increase depending on the number of pieces of mail sent. A violator may also be subject to criminal liability. Nonprofits are not exempt from these rules, and in fact may be subject to greater scrutiny because of subsidized nonprofit postal rates.[31]

Skill Contests   Organizations conducting *skill contests* must disclose additional information. A skill contest is defined as a game, puzzle, competition, or other contest in which a prize is awarded or offered, the outcome depends predominantly on the skill of the contestant, and a purchase, payment, or donation is generally required to enter. In addition to the information that must be disclosed for games of chance, sponsors of skills contests must include the number of rounds or levels of the contest and the cost, if any, to enter each round or level; that subsequent rounds will be more difficult; the maximum cost to enter all rounds; the number or percentage of entrants who may correctly solve, or the percent of entrants correctly solving the past three skill contests conducted by the sponsor; identity or description of judges if not judged by the sponsor organization; method of judging; and date by which winners will be determined and date or process by which prizes will be awarded.[32]

Organizations seeking to engage the public in games of chance or skill—whether in-state, across state lines, or via the web or social media—should have counsel review the promotion in light of applicable laws.

How Not to Run a Game of Chance Figure 8.2 offers a negative example, aggregating and exaggerating many of the failings of noncompliant games of chance. Don't make these mistakes![33]

Counsel and marketing staff should familiarize themselves with how to structure a compliant marketing campaign based on a game of chance, and follow these rules meticulously.

Getting the Word Out, Digitally

Publicity campaigns that include creation of an organizational web site or use of social media platforms, text, e-mail or mailing lists, and groups and messages via Facebook, Twitter, and other social media, involve all of the above considerations—clearances of copyrights and other rights, protection of trademarks, consumer

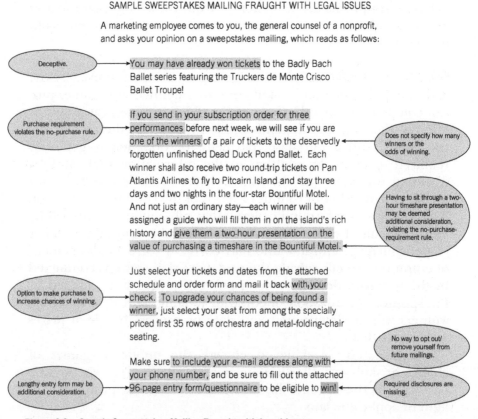

Figure 8.2   Sample Sweepstakes Mailing Fraught with Legal Issues

regulatory matters—and also present digital media-specific legal issues as well.

Web Site Terms of Use

When an organization establishes or relaunches a web site, counsel should review the terms of public use of the site, including the following:

- The terms should begin upon the user's first access of the web site and end when such access is terminated by either party.
- The terms should indicate that any content downloaded from the organization's web site by the user is for noncommercial, educational, or personal use only.
- The terms should shield the organization from liability resulting from access to third-party web sites via links on the organization's web site.
- The organization should establish (and include in the terms and conditions) an e-mail address such as counsel@your organization.org or a postal mail address.
- The terms should include a privacy policy, which is explained in greater detail below.

An organization that maintains a web site permitting the downloading or uploading of content or information (including user information) should be mindful of additional risks and liabilities. In the case of downloading content, such as video or documents, the terms and conditions should absolve the organization of liability resulting from harm caused as a result of the download. Where users upload content to the organization's web site, the organization should limit its liability for content that may infringe upon the rights of others. The terms of use should require users to agree not to upload anything slanderous, obscene, offensive, libelous, defamatory, or unlawful. Content posted by users should not be fraudulent, infringing, violative of any law, contain any viruses, shall not constitute any form of advertising, shall not constitute spamming, and not incite physical harm against another.

Before a user can initiate the download or upload, the organization should display its terms of use (for example in an inset window) and require assent, such as checking off a box. The essential

element is that users must be able to see that there are terms and
conditions, read them, and indicate their agreement. A button
allowing the user to finalize the action, such as a submit button or
an upload button, should be located *below* the terms of use and the
acknowledgement of assent.

The organization should retain the right (but not the obligation) to monitor, edit, or remove any activity or content. It should
also include terms limiting its liability for harm caused to other
users as a result of user-submitted content. Additionally, the organization should establish a method by which individuals who own
content submitted by users of the organization's web site without
authorization can notify the organization (a *take-down notice*). The
organization should respond promptly to take-down notices.[34]

Web Site Privacy Policy

Privacy policies set forth the manner in which both personal and
nonpersonal information is gathered. A common way of collecting
information about users of a web site is in the form of *cookies*. Cookies
are text files placed by a web site on a user's hard drive that enable
a web site to recognize repeat visitors. This information can be used
to automatically remember log-in information to facilitate purchases
and participation in promotions, and to compile usage statistics. Data
collected from cookies can also prove valuable to third parties, and
can be given or sold to other organizations (both for-profit and not-
for-profit). For example, if an organization is dedicated to eradicat-
ing malaria, and a visitor to its web site has repeatedly followed links
relating to malaria in sub-Saharan Africa, the organization can sell
targeted advertisements to a company or NGO, to be served on that
visitor, offering insecticide-treated mosquito nets in the region.

A web site's privacy policy should be sure to specify what
information, if any, it retains the right to disclose to third parties.
Further, the organization should not collect personally identifiable
information relating to minors. The organization should indicate
that it retains the right to disclose personal information if required
by law enforcement. Finally, some foreign countries are stricter
regarding what information may be collected, and an organization
should indicate in its terms and conditions that it does not know-
ingly collect information from international users.

Other Privacy Considerations   An organization should be mindful of privacy considerations based upon the type of organization. For example, special privacy laws such as HIPPA (Health Information Patient Privacy Act) apply to patients in hospitals and other health care settings. Counsel to such organizations should review patient disclosures pertaining to the handling of such data and should advise on the implementation of internal controls and procedures for safeguarding such information. Similarly, educational institutions should be mindful of student privacy laws such as FERPA (Family Educational Rights and Privacy Act).

All organizations sending bulk e-mail to customer, subscriber, client, or donor lists must ensure that their practices comply with the CAN-SPAM Act and similar applicable federal, international, and other privacy laws.[35]

Social Media Laws   The use of social media sites—Facebook, Twitter, Flickr, Tumblr, and others—by nonprofits is widespread and growing. Organizations should bear in mind that laws that are applicable in other contexts, such as practicing good trademark habits, policing its own intellectual property and respecting the rights of others, safeguarding customer data and respecting consumer privacy, and complying with required disclosures such as for games of chance, are equally applicable in the social media context.

As we conclude the discussion of consumer regulatory law and nonprofits, note that a glossary of consumer regulatory terms is available on the companion web site to this book at www.wiley.com/go/goodcounsel. A consumer regulatory law Work Plan follows the Focus Questions at the end of this chapter.

Other Places Where Legal Meets Communications

In addition to trademark review, third-party rights clearance, consumer regulatory compliance, and other legal matters described here, counsel may assist communications professionals by generally being aware of the organization's ongoing or forthcoming PR strategies.

Media Relations

Counsel should preview press releases if they involve matters of a sensitive legal nature. Counsel may also assist in developing standby statements in the event a delicate situation with legal implications is expected to arise or come to light. Counsel should also review the boilerplate that appears at the end of the organization's press releases for its continuing consistency with the organization's mission and nonprofit status.

Crisis Communications

If the organization is or may soon be the subject of unflattering media attention, counsel should be part of the crisis management team that may include members of senior management, board members, outside public relations experts, outside litigation counsel, government relations experts, and others. Often the professionals from these various disciplines will have to consider competing interests, such as balancing the need for transparency—to restore and promote public trust—with legal protection. Such trying circumstances require extraordinary discipline, political skills, and judgment. Members of the team should listen carefully to one another and to trusted outside advisors whose perspectives they require, to make sure the organization's best interests are served.

> **Example:** In two separate incidents, one involving the community organizing group ACORN and the other involving National Public Radio, recordings of nonprofit organizations' staffers were secretly made, edited and released to the public. The recordings purportedly showed those staffers making statements against the policies or interests of the organization.

Under such trying circumstances, the organization should plan a coordinated strategy of internal review, external communications with the media, funders, and government agencies, and legal defense. In the event such circumstances result in litigation, counsel, the public relations professionals and other members of the crisis management team should continue to coordinate their response.

Whether the organization's communications function is divided among marketing, public relations, and web professionals or whether a smaller team is responsible for all of these efforts, counsel should maintain close touch with those responsible for representing the organization to the outside world.

In Sum/Coming Up Next

Communications professionals can serve the organization's interests and minimize risk by learning the fundamentals of trademark law, rights clearances, and the fair use defense to infringement. They should also have a good grasp of applicable consumer regulatory laws, such as truth-in-advertising laws and laws governing contests, sweepstakes, and other promotions. In taking the organization's communications digital, communications staff should be conversant with basic requirements of web site and social media terms of use and privacy considerations. Communications professionals and attorneys who work closely together—on media releases, on crisis management and communications, and on general public relations strategy—serve the organization well.

With introductions now complete for the legal needs of the organization's Program, Fundraising, Finance, Human Resources, and Communications departments, we turn now to the legal needs of the Operations department.

Focus Questions for Chapter 8: Getting the Word Out, Legally

1. What is a trademark? How are trademarks acquired?
2. What are some of the lessons of the Wounded Warriors and Freecycle cases?
3. How may an organization clear the rights to use a copyrighted work that belongs to someone else?
4. How may an organization evaluate whether a use of a work is fair use?
5. In addition to trademarks and copyrights, what are some other kinds of rights that must be cleared? What are the risks if an organization fails to obtain necessary rights clearances?
6. What key terms should an organization include in the terms and conditions for access to its web site? What additional terms should be included for a web site which allows users to upload or download content to or from it?
7. What terms should an organization include in its privacy policy?
8. When conducting contests of chance and skill, what are some of the key legal requirements? Rewrite the Ballet de Monte Crisco hypothetical example in this chapter to make it comply with law.
9. Other than by helping with trademark, copyright, and consumer protection matters, in what other ways can counsel assist and support the work of an organization's communications professionals?

Chapter 8 Work Plan

Getting the Word Out, Legally: Laws that Matter to the Communications Team

These three work plans can assist counsel or supervised law students in surveying an organization's compliance with laws of concern to the Communications department: marketing, public relations, and web site/social media professionals.

Work Plan 1: Protecting and Enforcing the Organization's Trademarks

❏ Take inventory of the organization's trademarks.
  - Note all protectable marks in use by the organization.
  - Search the U.S. Patent and Trademark Office database (or commercial databases) under the company name.
  - Determine which marks may not have full protection in every class or every jurisdiction needed.
❏ Understand who is responsible for keeping track of deadlines for renewing trademark rights, expanding coverage to new classifications and jurisdictions if the organization's activities warrant.
❏ Ascertain steps taken by the organization to regularly police for infringements of the organization's marks, both in traditional and digital media.
  - Inquire whether there are any pending disputes over the organization's marks.
  - Note what actions are generally taken by the organization to object to unauthorized uses or to respond to objections received by others.
❏ Collect brochures, publications, web pages, and other places where the organization uses its marks to determine whether the organization appropriately applies the ®, ™, or ˢᴹ marks
  - Weigh in on the branding and style guide so that it affords appropriate legal protections while promoting a consistent visual image for the organization's brands.
  - Strike a balance between protective use of marks and visual clutter.

Work Plan 2: Clearing Rights for the Use of Intellectual Property Belonging to Others

❏ Ascertain whether the organization is using, or wishes to use, the rights-protected works of others.
  - Trademarks belonging to others.
  - Copyrighted works of others.
  - Rights of publicity—note special sensitivities regarding children, clients, patients, and disabled.
  - Guild or union rights, patents, trade secrets.

❏ Understand the organization's protocols for clearing rights and ensure that they include:
  • Correctly identifying the owner/administrator of those rights.
  • Requesting permission to use the work from the appropriate party.
  • Upon reaching agreement with the copyright holder, documenting that agreement in a written license agreement.
  • Understanding and complying with any restrictions on use.

Work Plan 3: Ascertaining Compliance with Consumer Protection Laws Relating to Communications and Marketing

❏ Review web site terms of use and privacy policy for compliance with applicable laws.
  • The terms should begin upon the user's first access of the web site and end when such access is terminated by either party.
  • The terms should indicate that any content downloaded from the organization's web site by the user is for noncommercial, educational, or personal use only.
  • The terms should shield the organization from liability resulting from access to third-party web sites via links on the organization's web site.
  • The organization should establish (and include in the terms and conditions) an e-mail address such as counsel@yourorganization.org or a postal mail address.
  • The privacy policy should accurately disclose the various uses of personally identifiable data collected and provide opportunities to opt out or correct information.
❏ Determine whether mass-marketing e-mails and postal mailings provide required disclosures and the opportunity to opt out.
  • Periodically check to ensure that opt-out notices are complied with, in both electronic and other forms.
❏ If the organization runs sweepstakes, contests, games of chance or skill, ascertain procedures for complying with applicable laws.
  • Advance possession of prizes, no purchase necessary, posting of bonds as may be required, disclosure of rules containing required provisions.
  • For skill contests, additional rules apply.
  • Other disclosures may be required to comply with federal law (if mailed or otherwise in interstate commerce) and state law.
❏ If the organization engages in social media, ensure that good practices with respect to all matters listed in this chapter (trademark protection, rights clearance, consumer regulatory compliance, and general coordination with PR strategy) extend to the social media context as well.

CHAPTER

9

Legal Meets Operations, Facilities Management, and Security

This chapter examines the legal needs of the organization's Operations area. These matters are complex and varied. The chapter begins by focusing on four key areas where Legal and Operations collaborate: real estate arrangements; contractor, supplier and procurement relationships; regulatory, law enforcement and security matters; and the planning, execution, and funding/financing of major capital projects. The chapter continues with a detailed exploration of nonprofit leasing, subleasing and space-sharing. Along the way, the chapter identifies several areas where corporate governance and risk management matters figure prominently in the Operations area.

T he Operations department of a nonprofit, sometimes also called facilities management or general services, manages the physical facilities of the organization. Depending on the nature of the organization, the physical location might be a wildlife refuge, a theater, a training institute or school, an office, a place of worship, a community center, a hospital, a residence, or another location. The organization may have one location or type of location, or it may have many.

In addition to the program-related spaces where the mission-related work of the nonprofit is accomplished, the organization may also operate ancillary facilities, such as its administrative offices, parking garages, restaurant or cafeteria facilities, mechanical rooms or plants, and storage areas.

The leader of the operations function may have the title of chief operating officer, director of operations or a similar title. In coordination with Finance, Human Resources, Government Relations, Legal, and other personnel, and generally reporting to the chief executive officer, the responsibilities of the head of operations may include the following, and then some:

- Managing the physical plant.
- Coordinating and scheduling regular and special uses of the facilities.
- Working with buildings and systems engineers.
- Managing a calendar of routine maintenance and repairs.
- Staffing and training facilities workers, janitorial, and security staff.
- Procuring supplies, contractors, and vendors.
- Obtaining permits and complying with their terms.
- Complying with building codes and life safety requirements, facilitating inspections, and responding to building violations.
- Overseeing security detail.
- Contracting for maintenance of vertical transportation (i.e., escalators and elevators).
- Coordinating ancillary services, such as food service and parking garages.
- Managing construction projects.
- Renting or purchasing new locations.
- Planning ahead for capital needs (anticipated renovations or improvements).
- Renting out and possibly sub-leasing portions of the location.

Although many of these individual tasks seem mundane, the operation of facilities may be at the very heart of the organization's activities. Thus, the ultimate goal of the operations staff is to help the organization realize its mission by providing for the safety and comfort of residents, patients, visitors, patrons, members, exhibitors, students, performers, clients, workers, and members of the general public who may visit the facility. Some organizations have an operations committee of the board to oversee this important work. In that case, the chief operating officer likely is the staff liaison to this committee.

Laws That Matter to Operations

The organization's counsel should have a firm grasp of the organization's operations, how the facilities fit in with the business plan, and how they help meet the mission. Counsel to the organization should be prepared to work closely with the Operations area, to help keep the organization running smoothly and progressing toward its goals. The attorney should be prepared to answer legal questions about present and planned real estate arrangements, procurement contracts, governmental compliance, and major capital projects.

Figure 9.1 depicts some key areas of collaboration between the Operations and Legal teams.

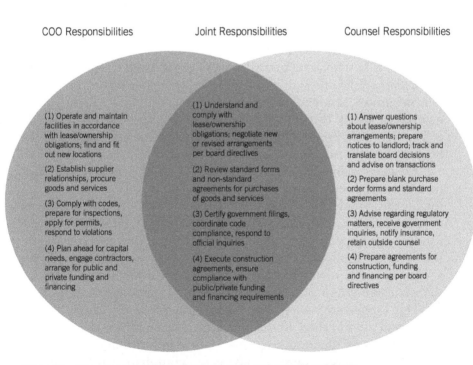

COO Responsibilities   Joint Responsibilities   Counsel Responsibilities

(1) Operate and maintain facilities in accordance with lease/ownership obligations; find and fit out new locations

(2) Establish supplier relationships, procure goods and services

(3) Comply with codes, prepare for inspections, apply for permits, respond to violations

(4) Plan ahead for capital needs, engage contractors, arrange for public and private funding and financing

(1) Understand and comply with lease/ownership obligations; negotiate new or revised arrangements per board directives

(2) Review standard forms and non-standard agreements for purchases of goods and services

(3) Certify government filings, coordinate code compliance, respond to official inquiries

(4) Execute construction agreements, ensure compliance with public/private funding and financing requirements

(1) Answer questions about lease/ownership arrangements; prepare notices to landlord; track and translate board decisions and advise on transactions

(2) Prepare blank purchase order forms and standard agreements

(3) Advise regarding regulatory matters, receive government inquiries, notify insurance, retain outside counsel

(4) Prepare agreements for construction, funding and financing per board directives

Figure 9.1   Some Areas of Collaboration between Operations and Legal Teams

Let's explore each of these matters in turn.

Real Estate Arrangements

The attorney and the operations leadership should review together what facilities are owned, leased, operated, or otherwise used by the organization. They should determine together that records of facilities are complete and properly organized by facility. If these documents are not well organized, Operations and Legal should cooperate to establish and maintain a workable system for maintaining originals, working copies, and back-up sets of leases, permits, insurance certificates, warranties, and key contracts. They should also include among their key documents a copy of the property owner's certificate of occupancy, certificates of completion for any subsequent build-outs, public assembly permits, records of Fire Marshal visits/citations, records of Department of Health visits/citations, site plans and surveys, floor plans, as-built drawings, and any environmental surveys that have been done on the property.

Real Estate and Corporate Governance   The primary purpose of the organization's real estate arrangements is to help it fulfill its mission.

If the organization is growing, serving new clients, or adding new programs, the leadership must consider whether to add, build, or expand space. If it is contracting or consolidating, the decisions will instead involve selling, subdividing, subleasing, assigning, or terminating (or nonrenewing) leases.

Trustees, management, and counsel must understand the long-term commitments embodied in its existing and proposed real estate arrangements—costs, functionality, balance sheet impacts of purchasing or leasing and associated capital investment, and fundraising impacts of acquiring and building out new space. For this reason, some states require a board vote—sometimes even by a supermajority of members—before a nonprofit incorporated in that state can sell or otherwise divest itself of real estate it owns.

The Operations team will execute on these decisions, under the supervision of the CEO, and it is up to counsel to advise on the legal aspects of the resulting new real estate arrangements. Legal may also be called upon to advise on compliance with, and/or modification of, existing real estate relationships.

Other Legal Aspects of Operation, Maintenance, Repair, Replacement, and Insurance of Facilities

Operations should brief counsel as to who is responsible for basic operational matters, such as cleaning, maintenance, routine repairs, and security of the organization's physical facilities. Be sure to cover matters such as who is responsible for interior maintenance including equipment, utility systems, and heating, ventilation, and air conditioning (HVAC); and who is responsible for each building's exterior, including roof clearing, façade cleaning, parking lot maintenance, snow removal, exterior lighting, landscaping, and signage. Counsel should then review contracts pertaining to these matters, such as contracts for installation and upkeep of important systems, equipment, and utilities, to make sure they conform to legal requirements.

Next, Operations management and counsel should understand who is responsible for capital repairs, capital maintenance, improvements, replacement of obsolete equipment and systems, and major repairs after a casualty loss, and any real estate taxes or other user fees. Again, counsel should review the contracts relating to these matters to make sure the organization is properly addressing its responsibilities.

Counsel should understand property and casualty insurance arrangements—amounts, types, and durations—and periodically review with operations and finance/risk management teams the suitability and adequacy of such coverage. He or she should also review with the head of Operations the basic terms of warranties for key equipment and know where the warranties are stored.

Counsel should know who operates ancillary facilities, such as retail, food service, garage management, and concessions. Sometimes employees carry out these functions, and sometimes the department contracts out these functions. Counsel should have a good command of any contractual arrangements with outside companies if any of these functions are outsourced, including insurance arrangements and any profit-sharing provisions.

If the organization rents its space, it should be sure to identify key landlord personnel, and be sure to designate a point person within the organization who is responsible for contact with the landlord in case of emergency. Counsel should also review the lease to make sure that addresses for legal notices (such as renewals, breaches, termination) are current for all parties.

If any of the functions described above are carried out by union-ized personnel, such as building services employees, cleaners, security, or other service workers' unions, counsel should study the collective bargaining agreements between those unions and the organization.

Purchases of Goods and Services

Operations and Legal should cooperate in preparing, understand-ing and administering agreements for the purchase of goods and services from vendors, suppliers, consultants, and contractors. To this end, counsel and Operations staff should together review agreements with key vendors as well as reviewing form agree-ments for more routine purchases of goods and services, such as blank purchase orders, service agreements, and contractor agree-ments. (Chapter 4 contains a discussion of contract law basics.) If needed, counsel can prepare new or revised standard forms for ordering supplies (purchase orders) and contracting for services (service contracts).

The Operations team should establish or revisit protocols for apprising Legal of upcoming major purchases. Legal should be pre-pared to step in to assist with requests by vendors, suppliers, and other contracting parties to diverge from the organization's form agreements. Together the Operations and Legal teams should establish and maintain procedures for filing contracts.

Insurance arrangements with contractors who are entering the organization's premises to do work should command the attorney's particular attention: does the contractor carry adequate insur-ance, is the organization named as an additional insured, and has the contractor provided a certificate of insurance that conforms to contractual requirements and kept it in force? The attorney should also be sure to review provisions for indemnification and any limita-tions on contractor liability.

Government Interactions

Legal and Operations together should review building permits, certificates of occupancy and completion, and any variances. Legal can also be instrumental in helping the Operations team apply for and secure permits, comply with applicable local and state building codes,[1] and comply with federal laws, such as the Americans with Disabilities Act (ADA)[2] and the Occupational Safety and Health Act (OSHA).[3]

Operations managers commonly handle mountains of local, state and federal paperwork. When the forms require that statements of a corporate officer be certified, notarized, sworn under penalty of perjury, or stamped with the corporate seal, the organization's counsel should review and assist. Because many of these documents have deadlines and penalties, counsel should avoid creating a bottleneck.

Handling routine violations, such as notices from the fire department or noise complaints from applicable local authorities, requires coordination between Operations and Legal. Together they should establish protocols, including devising a database of such notices, establishing clear lines of authority, and monitoring to ensure that all matters are properly and timely addressed. Improper handling of even routine violations can ripen the matter into a criminal case, potentially endangering users and certainly causing the organization to waste unnecessary staff time and pay significant fines. Counsel should work with operations to review all documents responding to violations, draft cover letters addressing any outstanding issues, attend hearings when necessary, and negotiate or avoid fines. Operations should make Legal aware of all such governmental communications. They should cooperate in responding and record the outcome of such proceedings.

Counsel needs to keep up with professional reading about changes to relevant laws, governmental forms and instructions, and industry-accepted form agreements.

Responding to Investigations and Lawsuits Most governmental interventions are minor or routine, but from time to time the organization may face a significant governmental action, such as an investigation or a lawsuit. Such matters may include serious or ongoing involvement with the Department of Buildings, environmental protection authorities, occupational safety and health agencies, Department of Labor, federal, state, or local prosecutor's office, and others.

If the organization is served with a lawsuit or receives a governmental inquiry, subpoena, or notice of investigation, the communication should be immediately referred to the Legal department. Counsel should ascertain whether any insurance carriers should be placed on notice; if coverage applies, the carrier may appoint defense counsel. If none is available, the organization's regular counsel should consider whether the matter is so serious or specialized as to warrant retaining outside counsel. Either way— whether appointed by the carrier or retained by the organization directly—outside counsel's work on the matter should be coordinated by the organization's regular counsel, to insure rapid investigation, to help gather and safeguard pertinent documents and information, to facilitate communications between the Operations team and the outside counsel and, ultimately, to help determine the appropriate response to the investigating agency. Counsel may also be responsible for reporting on major matters to members of the organization's leadership, such as finance, risk management, the CEO, and pertinent members of the board, such as the chairs of committees overseeing legal, audit, and operational matters.

⇨ PRACTICE POINTER

Government inquiries, lawsuits, subpoenas, and other important communications are not always sent to or served directly on the Legal department. Sometimes they arrive at the doors or on the desks of security officers, buildings, or maintenance personnel. Legal should work with Operations leadership to make sure matters are promptly referred to the organization's attorneys.

Legal and Operations may also wish to brief Public Relations personnel so that they may prepare a stand-by statement or, in serious circumstances, consider hiring a crisis management team to help manage public messaging.

Security and Interface with Law Enforcement

Legal should understand the organization's security needs, and help the operational leadership to coordinate security arrangements with law enforcement agencies.

The purpose of security is to provide for the safety and well-being of people who use the facility. Security personnel establish and maintain a safe environment and serve as first responders.

Some tools for accomplishing this purpose involve direct interaction with the general public at the nonprofit's facilities, including:

- Conducting foot patrols.
- Answering alarms.
- Investigating disturbances.
- Responding to illness or injury, and providing assistance to emergency medical personnel.
- Conducting interior vehicle checks (for a parking facility).
- Conducting bag checks (for indoor facilities).
- Operating detecting devices to screen individuals and prevent prohibited articles from entering restricted areas.
- Maintaining safety, comfort and order in public gatherings at the facility.
- Providing assistance to police, fire, and other public authorities.
- Assisting in emergency evacuations.
- Answering general inquiries from the public.

A key task of private security forces is to deter, detect, detain, or evict disorderly, threatening, or violent persons from the premises, using force only when necessary. Security team members charged with this task may be armed or unarmed. In consultation with local authorities, counsel should be prepared to advise on the legal implications of having armed or unarmed security forces.

Security forces also observe and identify safety risks and undesirable conditions on the premises. In this respect, the security function may overlap with the facilities function. Security forces should alert maintenance personnel of the presence of tripping hazards, loose wires, protruding objects, and unsafe accumulations of water, snow and ice. These steps in turn will reduce accidents and personal injury claims.

In addition to their ongoing interaction with the general public, security personnel play a critical role behind the scenes, sometimes in a manner that intersects directly with law enforcement and the organization's legal function. Security personnel may interact with police and other municipal authorities, prepare written or electronic reports about incidents, and, where applicable, provide sworn testimony or other reliable and truthful information to judges, insurance adjusters, and opposing counsel in legal proceedings. Counsel can help prepare security personnel to provide testimony or other sworn statements and may occasionally be called upon to represent the organization in prosecutions, claims, and lawsuits. It is recommended that counsel be present when security personnel are interviewed by insurance adjusters and/or police to ensure appropriate and adequate cooperation.

⇨ PRACTICE POINTER

Security personnel are occasionally approached directly by counsel representing the plaintiff in a lawsuit against the organization, for example in a personal injury case. Security officers should be advised not to speak with anyone outside the organization, instead referring the matter to the Legal department.

Inquiries that come directly to security personnel from government officials such as OSHA, USCIS (federal immigration officials), or other federal, state, or city officials should be referred to the organization's counsel. Media inquiries should go to the organization's public relations point person, who may decide to confer with Legal as well. Individual members of the public who approach security personnel with questions of a legal nature regarding an accident, incident, pending investigation, or other sensitive issues should be referred to Legal.

In light of the wide range of responsibilities that fall to security personnel and the degree of judgment and discretion that is required, the organization should take a particular interest in how this function is staffed. Counsel can help the Operations department and human resources professionals craft a proper job description that will pass legal muster and that will ensure security personnel have the requisite physical abilities, communication skills, and problem-solving abilities.

Counsel should also verify that security personnel have met state-mandated background and training requirements, where applicable. In some states, a security guard must have a security guard license.[4]

Where security personnel are unionized, counsel will help Operations management navigate other legal and practical considerations. (See the collective bargaining agreements section of Chapter 7.)

Construction Planning, Execution, and Funding/Financing

In accordance with board decisions and the CEO's directives, Operations will set about planning, executing, and lining up funding for construction projects. Operations and Legal together should discuss and review contracts for the planning, architectural design, and construction of facilities to be acquired or renovated. Their review should also include the terms of purchase of major equipment and associated warranties.

Where these activities are funded with public dollars, the legal team should be prepared to help negotiate and close on funding agreements and to help ensure compliance with ongoing reporting and reimbursement procedures. The organization's Government Affairs (lobbying) and Finance teams may also be involved. Private funders or lenders may impose other requirements that should be reviewed by Legal.

We turn next to a more detailed discussion about nonprofit leasing.

About Leases

A major lease is often the most significant contractual obligation of a nonprofit. If the governing board is considering authorizing the organization to enter into a major new lease, experienced leasing counsel should be engaged early in the planning stage to review the organization's goals, program, and budget and to assist in structuring the business and lease negotiations.

A well-negotiated and well-drawn lease contains the resolution to almost any what-if situation that could arise between the landlord and the tenant during the term of the lease. A fair lease creates a stable long-term relationship between the landlord and the tenant; a one-sided or problematic lease can cause no end of problems.

Since nonprofit organizations are more often the tenant, rather than the landlord, this portion of the chapter is written with the tenant's perspective in mind.

Types of Leases

The two main kinds of leases are *net leases* and *gross leases*. In a net lease, the tenant is solely responsible for paying all costs related to maintenance in a building, in addition to its monthly base rent.

The most common form of net lease is the *triple net lease*, by which the tenant agrees to pay all operating costs of the building, including property taxes, property insurance, and maintenance costs. While triple net leases are more typical of stand-alone buildings, they are sometimes found in multi-tenant facilities. As discussed in previous chapters, nonprofits are not necessarily exempt from property taxes; it depends on whether the owner is tax-exempt *and* the property is being used for exempt purposes. In a *gross lease*, the tenant pays a gross amount to the landlord so that the landlord can pay for all the costs that the tenant is responsible for, such as utilities and insurance. In many gross leases, operating expenses are considered to be included in the rent for the first year of the lease but, in later years, tenants pay increases in operating expenses as they rise above that baseline.

In most leases, the tenant pays for electricity and other utility usage as well as any services in the building that the tenant uses specifically, that other tenants do not share. Sometimes the tenant pays the actual cost of utilities plus an administrative charge. In other instances, the tenant pays a fixed or escalating amount with the possibility of adjustments if the landlord's actual costs are substantially higher.

It is important for budgeting purposes to understand any extra costs, often referred to in the lease as additional rent, *operating expenses*, or *pass-through expenses*. If the tenant has bargaining power, it should attempt to negotiate a cap on the operating expenses to prevent unwelcome, unaffordable surprises, for example, dramatic increases in building labor expenses or fuel prices. Note, also, that many operating expense clauses include a pass-through of the tenant's share of capital improvements (whether through a sharing of depreciation, subject to certain limits, or keyed to reductions in expense resulting from such improvements). If a nonprofit tenant can't get out of paying for capital improvements, it can try to pay only the pro-rated amount based on the expected life of the improvements and the remaining term of the lease—for example, a tenant in half of a building with only one month left on its lease shouldn't be forced to pay for half of the job of repaving the parking lot and walkways.

⇨ PRACTICE POINTER

Operating expense clauses are often buried in the fine print of a lease. They can be a trap for the unwary and require careful review and understanding.

A lease may also have a rent escalation keyed to price indices, labor rates, or other variables—these, again, should be carefully reviewed with both Operations and Finance personnel.

Major Lease Issues

Following is a discussion of key matters that may arise in the context of a nonprofit organization's lease.

Term   The *term* is the duration of the lease. The lease term usually commences on the date that the landlord completes its preparatory work and provides the premises to the tenant so that the tenant may perform any of its own *fit-out* (or build out) of the premises.

Renewal Term   Some landlords will grant renewal options to the tenant for one or a number of shorter terms, to be exercised at the tenant's option usually during the last year of the term. These renewal options are valuable to the tenant to avoid the disruption and expense of a move. Boards (or their Operations Committee) that fail to obtain renewal options at the inception of a lease, or fail adequately to plan for the upcoming expiration of a lease without renewal options, are risking a significant interruption of operations that could seriously harm the organization and those it serves.

Utilities   The tenant's costs for electricity may be *submetered* and paid as a separate charge to the landlord each month as additional rent; or included as part of monthly base rent; or payable directly by the tenant to the local utility. The tenant will almost always be responsible for its own telephone, computer, and data services. Typically the landlord provides HVAC, cold water (and sometimes hot water), and may provide security and cleaning services to the premises. The lease should set forth the days/hours and dates of the year that HVAC is provided without additional charge, and should set forth any overtime HVAC charges and how they are calculated for any after-hours use. Again, the idea is to avoid budgetary surprises.

Alterations   As a general rule, all work performed by the tenant in the premises, either prior to its occupancy of the premises or alterations performed during the lease term, is subject to approval of the landlord. The tenant and its contractors should take care to understand insurance requirements, and counsel should help assure compliance.

Use Clause   The *use clause* describes the activities for which the tenant may use the leased premises. Ideally this use clause will be as broad as possible to ensure that the tenant will be able to perform the type of work and services offered by the organization now and in the future during the term of the lease (including any renewal terms). A very broad clause might say that the premises may be used for "any legal use," but office leases are often written to allow only "executive and general office uses." In addition to envisioning its own future activities, the organization that negotiates the broadest possible use clause protects itself in the event it needs to assign or sublet during the lease term.

Nonprofits providing programs or services of any kind should take care that both the anticipated activities and the number of persons expected to visit the premises are permissible under the lease.

Assignments and Subleases   An *assignment* is when the tenant transfers its entire interest in its lease to a third party. A *sublet* is when the tenant transfers only a portion of the premises to a third party or for a shorter period of time than the entire lease. In order to assign or sublet the premises, most leases require the consent of the landlord. Tenants may be able to negotiate that such consent will not be unreasonably withheld, conditioned or delayed. The tenant should negotiate as best as they can for flexibility in the case of a future merger or reorganization. If the organization's governing board is forward-looking, it may ask counsel to negotiate the right to assign or sublease to affiliated or supporting organizations, specified nonprofit entities with which the nonprofit collaborates regularly, and successor nonprofits. Nonprofit landlords may require that assignees or sublessees also be nonprofits, so as not to jeopardize the facility's property tax exemption.

Permits   Certain uses of the premises (for example, health care facilities, child care centers, auditoriums, theaters, dormitories, or cafeterias) require special permits. It is the tenant's responsibility to determine if permits are required. The tenant's architect can advise about obtaining the requisite permits.

Termination Options   Tenants rarely have early termination rights. If an organization has a five-year lease but shuts down with three years left on the lease, the organization may be held responsible for the entire amount of remaining rental payments. This circumstance is called *tail-end liability*. The landlord may be responsible for mitigating its damages by making reasonable efforts to re-let the space.

⇨   PRACTICE POINTER

If the board of an organization is considering dissolving or ceasing operations at a leased location, counsel should advise whether the lease contains a tail-end liability provision, and if so, should work with finance staff to plan appropriately for this financial obligation. The organization can help manage this risk by negotiating for an early termination option if the board believes the organization may cease to exist at some point during the term.

Living with a Lease

Once the leasing process is complete, counsel can assist those with operational and financial responsibility by preparing a *lease abstract*, or summary, and by explaining key provisions, dates, and deadlines. Key lease terms to be covered in an abstract for use by a facilities manager might include:

- Duration.
- Key financial terms.
- Operating expense provisions.
- Permitted uses.
- Tenant's right to make improvements.
- Intellectual property or signage requirements.
- Affirmative obligations on the part of the tenant.
- Assignment and subletting.
- Renewal and termination provisions.

Counsel may also be called upon from time to time to write a notice letter to the landlord, for example to lodge a formal complaint (e.g., that there is not enough heat or there is a vermin infestation), or to officially inform the landlord of the organization's plans (e.g., to renew, extend, sublet, or terminate the lease).

⇨ PRACTICE POINTER

It is important for tenants to document unsafe or improper conditions in writing and notify the landlord in accordance with the notice requirements set forth in the lease.

The lease abstract is a handy tool but should not be a substitute for legal advice. Operations or other staff with questions about the lease should get in touch with counsel.

Beginning or Renewing a Lease

To be prudent and avoid any interruption to its business, a nonprofit should start the leasing process well in advance of expiration of its current lease term to give itself time to find suitable space, agree to favorable lease terms in a *term sheet*, negotiate a full lease, and perform any build-out or alteration of the premises if required.

The tenant usually retains a broker to locate suitable space based on the tenant's current occupancy needs and its growth plans.

Nonprofits should have an attorney review any brokerage agreement in advance of its execution to make sure that the broker is working for the tenant on market terms or better.

The leasing process can take as little as a few months or a year or more, depending upon the availability of suitable space in the marketplace, the tenant's space requirements, and other factors that the nonprofits should discuss in advance with the broker before he or she begins the search. The organization should retain an architect early in the leasing process to evaluate the potential premises for the nonprofit's space needs. Counsel should be prepared to review the contract with the architect.

A Note on Subleasing

Some organizations may find it convenient to *sublease* someone else's premises, that is, to occupy some or all of the space previously let out to a tenant for some or all of the remaining term. Because subleases are *subordinate to* (subject to the terms of) leases, the organization should be aware that it has two sets of rights and obligations, one with the sub-landlord (also known as the *prime tenant*) and the other with the *prime landlord*. Subleases typically *incorporate by reference* (import the terms of and make applicable) the terms of the *prime lease*, and they should never be regarded as standalone documents.

⇨ PRACTICE POINTER

Be sure to get copies of both the prime lease and the proposed sublease when negotiating a subletting arrangement.

A sub-tenant should request back-up copies of all official notices sent by the landlord to the prime tenant/sub-landlord, to minimize the sub-tenant's likelihood of being surprised when a problem under the prime lease becomes the sub-tenant's problem. Also, a sub-tenant should review the credit-worthiness of the sub-landlord and the sublease provisions related to a default by the sub-landlord. Typically, if the sub-landlord defaults on the prime lease, the sublease will be put at risk as well. If the sub-landlord fails, the landlord will sometimes then try to set up a direct deal with the sub-tenant, but if there is another more attractive company interested in the building, the sub-tenant can be evicted, creating unbudgeted costs.

Sharing Space with Other Nonprofits

Some forward-looking communities nationwide have begun creating shared office space for smaller-sized nonprofit organizations looking for flexibility, efficiency, and collaboration. Typically, such arrangements include both workstations (cubicles) and a limited number of private offices, with access to shared office equipment, telephone/data/Internet service, and conference rooms.

Oftentimes these shared spaces are grouped thematically, incubating start-up social entrepreneurship programs, arts endeavors, or complementary health-related programs.

Nonprofit space sharing arrangements pose interesting legal questions—for example, regarding equitable division of maintenance costs, office support services, insurance (including deductibles), and access to common spaces and other resources. As with any space rental, prospective tenants should review the lease carefully with counsel before signing.

Risk Management and the Chief Operating Officer

In addition to the risk management matters identified elsewhere in this chapter, here are conversation starters that may help reveal some others:

- How confident is Operations leadership in the organization's crisis management plan? In what areas is the organization most vulnerable, and what are we doing to address those vulnerabilities? Has the board or audit committee fully considered all major risks? Are reasonable insurance arrangements in place?
- When money is tight, how do you balance short-term needs with long-term planning? Do you sometimes defer maintenance in order to balance a budget; if so, how do you measure/ account for the inherent risks—to the organization, to its clients, to its workers, to the general public?

In Sum/Coming Up Next

A nonprofit's real estate arrangements are a direct result of decisions made by the governing board, and the manner in which it operates its facilities reflects profoundly upon its execution of its mission. Counsel can help advance the nonprofit organization's objectives by translating board decisions and CEO directives into legally binding actions that set the stage for operations.

If the organization's board is planning ahead for an upcoming expansion or renovation, counsel can assist with the legal aspects of the necessary real estate transactions, construction contracting, public and private funding agreements, and financings.

Counsel can also help the operations team establish beneficial terms for hiring and paying contractors, ordering supplies, and procuring other goods and services.

Counsel facilitates the operations department's interactions with governmental agencies, whether assisting with paperwork for permits and approvals, handling investigations, or addressing violations. Counsel can also assist with the security function and its interaction with law enforcement authorities.

Day to day, counsel can assist the operations manager in understanding and complying with the often complex matters contained in lease documents.

Counsel, in collaboration with both operations and finance professionals, can help identify and minimize risks inherent in the organization's operations.

A glossary of operations, facilities management, security, and leasing terms is available on the companion web site to this book at www.wiley.com/go/goodcounsel. A Work Plan for assessing the legal needs of the Operations department appears after this chapter's Focus Questions.

The next chapter, Chapter 10, discusses political activities and governmental lobbying in the nonprofit context. It sets forth guardrails for the organization's involvement in political matters.

Focus Questions for Chapter 9: Legal Meets Operations, Facilities Management, and Security

1. How does the operations function relate to the mission of the organization?
2. What are some of the responsibilities of the head of operations? What are some of the operational matters that counsel may encounter? On what topics may operations and legal teams be expected to collaborate?
3. How can counsel help operations staff operate and maintain facilities in accordance with lease/ownership obligations?
4. What role(s) may counsel play in setting terms for supplier relationships and procurement of goods and services?
5. Outline the steps that the organization's legal counsel and head of operations should take in the event of a governmental inquiry, investigation, or regulatory action.
6. How may counsel assist operations in addressing code violations?
7. How can counsel help support the security function of a nonprofit organization?
8. What legal matters can the organization anticipate when the operations team is planning to address major capital needs, such as construction, renovation, or structural repairs?
9. What are some of the key terms specified in a typical lease?
10. Which professional advisors should a prospective tenant retain prior to entering into a lease term sheet? How can counsel help?
11. What are some leasing matters that a nonprofit board should consider when deciding whether to dissolve or cease operations at a particular location?

Chapter 9 Work Plan

Legal Meets Operations, Facilities Management, and Security

This work plan can assist counsel or supervised law students assess the legal context for an organization's Operations department.

❑ Review all real estate arrangements and understand how they serve the organization's mission.
  • Understand procedures for board review and approval of key real estate arrangements.
❑ Chart out what facilities are owned/leased/operated/used by the organization.
  • Summarize key terms; prepare an abstract of leases and other key real estate agreements.
  • Ascertain responsibility for equipment, maintenance, systems, utilities, capital repairs, improvements, casualty losses and relevant contractual relationships for each location.
  • Know basic terms of warranties for key equipment and know where warranties are kept.
  • Review building permits, certificates of occupancy, and insurance certificates.
  • Understand key points of interaction with government and ascertain procedures for handling permits, approvals, and violations.
❑ Determine what construction, expansion, or refurbishment plans are underway or contemplated.
  • Ascertain what special legal arrangements are appropriate and necessary, and determine who will handle them.
❑ Review forms of purchase orders and service agreements.
❑ Understand arrangements for security and interface with law enforcement.
❑ Review property and public liability insurance arrangements.
  • Make sure facilities risk management protocols comply with applicable law, lease/contractual requirements, and other expectations.

CHAPTER 10

Political Activities and Governmental Lobbying

This chapter discusses the limits on nonprofit organizations' political activities. Directors, senior executives, government relations staff, and counsel must remain acutely aware that Section 501(c)(3) organizations are strictly prohibited from intervening or participating in political campaigns. This chapter provides some examples of impermissible and permissible political activities. It next describes permissible lobbying and advocacy, and summarizes certain recordkeeping, registration, and disclosure requirements. It ends with a list of permitted pursuits involving government or politics.

Reminder: For purposes of this book, the words nonprofit or non-profit organization refer to public charities under Section 501(c)(3) of the Internal Revenue Code. This definition is particularly important in the context of this chapter. Different restrictions and rules apply to other types of nonprofit organizations that may be tax exempt under other provisions of the Internal Revenue Code Section 501(c).

Thou Shalt Not Politick

Section 501(c)(3) organizations are banned from participating or intervening in political campaigns on behalf of (or in opposition to) any candidate for public office. A *candidate* is someone who offers himself or is proposed by others, as a contestant for public office, at the national, state, or local levels. Forbidden campaign intervention includes any and all actions by the organization that favor or oppose a candidate for public office, including endorsing a candidate, contributing funds to a political campaign, publicly stating a position on an issue about which the candidates are in clear opposition to one another (implied endorsement or opposition), distributing statements authored by others, or allowing a candidate to use an organization's assets or facilities without giving equal opportunity to all candidates.

Federal tax law imposes stiff penalties on any organization and its managers that violate this prohibition, including intermediate sanctions or even revocation of status.[1]

Table 10.1 depicts the most common types of prohibited political campaign activities by 501(c)(3) organizations, as detected by the IRS in campaign years 2004, 2006, and 2008, according to the IRS's Exempt Organizations Workplan for Fiscal Year 2011.

In this period, the Exempt Organizations unit of the IRS revoked the tax-exempt status of seven noncompliant organizations.

State charities laws are also exceedingly exacting: state charities enforcers have been known to require Section 501(c)(3) organizations to refund as little as $10 unwittingly contributed to a political action campaign.

Table 10.1   Prohibited Political Campaign Activities, 2004 to 2008

Allegation	2004	2006	2008
1. Exempt organization (EO) distributed printed documents supporting candidates.	24	14	24
2. Church official made a statement during normal services endorsing candidates.	19	14	47
3. Candidate spoke at an official EO function.	11	16	2
4. Organization distributed improper voter guides or candidate ratings.	14	8	3
5. Organization posted a sign on its property endorsing a candidate.	12	13	11
6. Organization endorsed candidates on its web site or through links on its web site.	15	11	16
7. Organization official verbally endorsed a candidate.	8	5	2
8. Organization made a political contribution to a candidate.	7	11	12
9. Organization allowed a non-candidate to endorse a candidate during a speech at the organization function.	4	2	1
10. Other	0	16	15
TOTAL	114	110	133

An Example of Impermissible Intervention in a Political Campaign

In the days leading up to Bill Clinton's nomination for president by the Democratic National Committee in 1992, Branch Ministries, Inc., a Section 501(c)(3) religious organization, took out one-page ads in two national newspapers accusing then-Governor Clinton of "promoting policies that are in rebellion to God's laws." The ads also solicited tax-deductible donations to Branch Ministries.

The IRS investigated and ultimately revoked the organization's tax-exempt status. The revocation was upheld on appeal.[2]

Branch Ministries is a potent example of why Section 501(c)(3) organizations must avoid participating in political campaigns by, for example, endorsing or opposing candidates.

Coloring Inside the Lines: Permissible Political Activities

Not all politics is politicking. Section 501(c)(3) organizations may undertake the following types of nonpartisan political activities:

Voter Education and Voter Registration Drives   Voter education and registration activities are fair game for Section 501(c)(3) organizations, as long as there are no biased references to particular candidates or political parties.

Timing is everything when it comes to the permissibility of voter education activities by a Section 501(c)(3) organization. The publication of a newsletter that contains the voting records of Congressional incumbents on selected issues important to the organization likely would constitute participation or intervention in a political campaign if distributed to voters during an election campaign.[3] In contrast, if the newsletter was distributed outside the election season, or covered a broad range of issues, the newsletter would be permissible.

Speeches by Candidates: Equal Time   An organization may invite a political candidate to speak at an event, so long as opposing candidates for the same office are given equal opportunity to speak. The event as a whole must not advocate for a certain position.

Speeches by Candidates in a Personal Capacity   Political candidates may also speak at an organization's event if their appearance is in a non-candidate capacity. The organization should take strong, affirmative steps to ensure that the line is not blurred between the individual's appearance before the nonprofit and his campaign for office.

For example, in 2006, then-Senator Barack Obama was invited by the United Church of Christ to address its national meeting the following year. Although he was invited in his personal capacity to speak about the intersection of his personal faith and his public life, by the time the speech occurred in 2007 he had announced his campaign for president. Ten thousand people attended the convention. The church organization took special efforts to verbally communicate to those in attendance that Senator Obama was there as a member of the church and not as a candidate for office, and that the audience should not attempt to engage in any political activities. The church's counsel apprised the candidate of the ground rules for his speech. Outside the civic center where the speech was held, on public property not under the control of the synod, campaign volunteers set up tables on behalf of the candidate. Under these circumstances the IRS concluded that this appearance did not violate the political activity prohibition on the church.[4]

Facility Rental, List Sharing   A nonprofit organization with space for public gatherings, such as a senior drop-in center's community room or an opera theater, may rent space to a candidate seeking to make a speech, so long as the organization charges the campaign its customary fees and makes the space available to other, opposing candidates on an equal opportunity basis. Further, the activity must be regularly offered by the organization and not specifically for the candidate. The organization should make clear to the campaign renting space that it must not state or imply that the candidate's appearance at the venue constitutes an endorsement by the theater.

Similar rules apply to the sale or rental of an organization's mailing lists, or other goods or services it may offer to the general public. The equal-opportunity, regular-offering, and no-endorsement rules apply.

Political Activities by Nonprofit Leaders in Their Personal Capacity   Leaders of Section 501(c)(3) organizations acting in that capacity must not make partisan comments, raise funds, or expend organizational resources on a political campaign. However, nonprofit leaders are not expected to check their First Amendment free speech rights at the door when they become involved with a Section 501(c)(3) organization: they may endorse candidates or make donations in their personal capacity, on their own personal stationery, personal e-mail account, social media page, listserv, or blog they maintain in their individual capacity. Similarly, an online campaign contribution from their personal computer and e-mail account at home during non-working hours is fine.

The situation gets murkier when they donate personal funds from their work e-mail account and/or during working hours. Nonprofit executives and board members, particularly those who are publicly identified with their charity, should exercise caution in these circumstances, and consult with counsel if they are unsure of the bounds.

Lobbying: Advocacy with Limits

Section 501(c)(3) organizations are permitted to *lobby*, or to advocate, to a limited extent, in support of or in opposition to, proposed legislation.

An organization lobbies when it "contacts, or urges the public to contact, members or employees of a legislative body for the purpose of proposing, supporting, or opposing legislation, or if [it] advocates the adoption or rejection of legislation."[5] The IRS defines legislation as including "action by Congress, any state legislature, any local council, or similar governing body, with respect to acts, bills or similar items . . . or by the public in referendum, ballot initiative, constitutional amendment, or similar procedure" and excluding "actions by executive, judicial, or administrative bodies."[6]

Taking a Stand on Public Policy Issues

Section 501(c)(3) organizations may take positions on *public policy* issues. For example, if a pending piece of legislation proposes to restrict a nonprofit cultural or educational institution's ability to deaccession, or sell, property from its collections, it is perfectly natural—and permissible—that an affected nonprofit would wish to take a position in favor of or against the bill.

However, such organizations should steer clear of issue advocacy that functions as campaign intervention. In particular, if a candidate is closely identified with a particular issue, the organization should proceed with caution before making repeated or regular statements about that issue. For instance, an animal welfare organization may take out a newspaper advertisement endorsing a bill prohibiting the use of animal testing and urging the public to contact their senator to support that bill. It may do so, even if that advertisement is published shortly before an election in which that senator is a candidate—if the ad does not mention the election or the senator's candidacy, animal welfare issues have not been raised as distinguishing the senator from any opponents, and the timing of the ad and identification of the senator are directly related to the specific legislation and appears immediately before the legislature is scheduled to vote.

The IRS and many state charities regulators provide resources for non-profits to determine if their actions are permissible under applicable laws.[7] Section 501(c)(3) organizations should also check federal, state, and local election laws that may apply to their lobbying activities.[8]

Limits on the Amount of Permissible Lobbying

Not only the type of lobbying but the amount of lobbying is limited by federal law. Generally, a non-profit organization may not qualify for Section 501(c)(3) tax-exempt status if a substantial part of its activities consist of attempting to influence legislation through lobbying. Organizations that lobby in excess of permitted limits may have to pay excise taxes and may even lose their tax-exempt status.

Although the definition of substantial is unclear, there is a straightforward way to avoid uncertainty: consider filing IRS Form 5768 (Election/Revocation of Election by an Eligible Section 501(c)(3) Organization to Make Expenditures to Influence Legislation). Most informed Section 501(c)(3) organizations that lobby choose to make the election (unless they spend more than $1 million a year on lobbying, in which case they are disqualified from making the election). Filing the form (also known as filing the 501(h) election) allows nonprofits to elect to be measured by a more straightforward expenditure test rather than the vague substantiality test that applies to those who don't file the form.

Once the organization makes the election, it must not spend more than the allowable amount on lobbying efforts:

(i) 20 percent of the first $500,000 of its expenditures on exempt purposes, plus
(ii) 15 percent of the second $500,000 of such expenditures, plus
(iii) 10 percent of the third $500,000 of such expenditures, plus
(iv) 5 percent of the remainder of such expenditures, with a cap of $1 million in annual lobbying expenses. [9]

Lobbying expenditures include both the costs of direct lobbying by the organization and the costs of grassroots lobbying (urging, directly or through its members, that the public contact legislators about an issue). In addition to the spending limits stated above, an organization may not spend more than 25 percent of its permitted lobbying total on grassroots lobbying.

If an organization exceeds the amount allowed under the expenditure test, it must pay an excise tax of 25 percent of the excess. If it engages in excessive lobbying over a four-year period, it may lose its tax-exempt status altogether.

Note that merely contacting a legislator about an issue is not considered a lobbying expenditure unless the organization expresses a view for or against pending or proposed legislation.

The Section 501(h) election is not for private foundations, churches, and integrated auxiliaries of churches. Nonprofits that receive federal funds are not permitted to use those funds to lobby.

Organizations taking part in any activities attempting to influence legislation should seek the advice of qualified counsel so that they do not unwittingly cross the line into taxable amounts of lobbying activity or threaten their tax exemption. [10]

Risks and Alternatives

Organizations that cross the line risk sizable excise taxes or even revocation of exemption. For example, Christian Echoes National Ministry lost its exempt status because its weekly newspaper ads and media broadcasts were seen as attempts to influence legislation by promoting desirable government policies consistent with the organization's objectives—even though no specific legislation was ever mentioned. [11]

Some 501(c)(3) organizations that feel hamstrung by the strict prohibition against political campaign activities have converted to 501(c)(4) status, the tax code classification for civic leagues, social welfare organizations, and local associations of employees. While Section 501(c)(3) organizations are absolutely prohibited from participating or intervening in political campaigns on behalf of any candidates for public office, Section 501(c)(4) organizations are allowed to conduct such activities, as long as they are not the primary activity. (Contributions to 501(c)(4) organizations are generally not tax-deductible, and a Section 501(c)(4) organization may incur a tax if it makes political expenditures.) Other Section 501(c)(3)s have spun off a separate 501(c)(4) entity or set up a Section 501(c)(4) subsidiary corporation.[12] As long as the Section 501(c)(4) organization is separately incorporated, operates independently of the Section 501(c)(3) organization, and keeps records adequate to show that tax-deductible contributions are not used to pay for nonexempt purposes, the political activities of the Section 501(c)(4) organization are generally not attributed to the parent. However, an organization that has lost its exempt status due to excessive lobbying is not then permitted to convert to a Section 501(c)(4) organization.[13]

In sum, while Section 501(c)(3) organizations may never endorse or oppose a particular candidate, they may engage in *advocacy* to a limited extent. They risk fines and possibly loss of exemption if their political activities become a significant part of their staff time and operating budget.

The next section describes the record-keeping and disclosure obligations associated with political advocacy.

Recordkeeping, Registration, and Financial Disclosure

If a Section 501(c)(3) organization engages in lobbying, it must fill out IRS Form 990 Schedule C. The organization must keep careful track of its expenditures on these activities throughout the year. Once filed, the Form 990 is publicly available information and used by organizations such as Charity Navigator and Guidestar to rate nonprofits and provide the public (including potential donors) with information regarding an organization's lobbying expenditures.

Federal law requires lobbyists, whether for-profit or nonprofit, to register and file financial disclosure reports every six months if the person has made at least two legislative contacts and has spent at least 20 percent of his or her time on lobbying activity in that period, and if the employing organization spent at least $24,500 on lobbying during that same period.

State and local laws may also require registration and periodic financial disclosures of lobbying activities. While state laws generally do not limit how much lobbying a charity can do, they may well require disclosure of an organization's advocacy expenditures, even if the organization does not use outside paid lobbyists. Counsel for nonprofits that lobby should be familiar with applicable registration and disclosure requirements.

What Isn't Lobbying?

Not every activity that bears on politics or government counts as lobbying. In general, the following activities do not constitute lobbying for those organizations that have made the Section 501(h) election:

- Nonpartisan analysis.
- Discussions of broad social problems.
- Technical advice to a governmental body in response to a written request.
- Self-defense lobbying to preserve the organization's exempt status.
- Communications between an organization and its members.
- Communications with a governmental employee for reasons other than to influence legislation.

Because there is a great deal of uncertainty in this area, and the penalties can be severe for 501(c)(3) organizations that get it wrong, organizations with questions should consult with qualified counsel.

In Sum/Coming Up Next

Section 501(c)(3) organizations must not endorse or oppose political candidates. They may advocate for or against particular policy issues, but the extent of these activities is limited. Lobbying activities must be disclosed and may be taxable if they go beyond a certain limited extent.

A glossary of lobbying law terms is available on the companion web site to this book at www.wiley.com/go/goodcounsel. A Work Plan for assessing the legal needs of the government relations team appears after this chapter's Focus Questions.

This chapter concludes Part II of this book, the department-by-department tour of the legal issues facing nonprofits. Part III begins with Chapter 11 and is primarily aimed toward attorneys, providing tools and insights to manage and administer the sizable portfolio of legal matters identified throughout the text and Work Plans of Chapters 1 to 10.

Focus Questions for Chapter 10: Political Activities and Governmental Lobbying

1. What kinds of political activity must a Section 501(c)(3) organization avoid altogether?
2. What might happen if a Section 501(c)(3) organization endorses or opposes a political candidate? Cite a case example.
3. What are some politically related activities that nonprofits are permitted to undertake?
4. What steps can a nonprofit executive take to ensure that his personal political activities are not ascribed to the organization?
5. What is lobbying?
6. May Section 501(c)(3) organizations lobby? How do lobbying rules differ from rules about intervening in political campaigns?
7. How much lobbying may a Section 501(c)(3) organization do? What happens if lobbying activities are more than an insubstantial part of the organization's activities?
8. What disclosures must a lobbying 501(c)(3) make?
9. Activity: Check your state's registration requirements for nonprofit lobbying activities and provide a link to the government web site where registration and disclosure forms are available.

Chapter 10 Work Plan

Political Activities and Governmental Lobbying

This work plan is designed to assist counsel or supervised law students assess a Section 501(c)(3) organization's compliance with the prohibition on political activities and limitations on advocacy activity.

❏ Review policies and practices for compliance with the absolute ban on intervening in political campaigns.
❏ Review lobbying activity to ensure it complies with applicable laws.
  • Public policy issues.
  • Limited, insubstantial part of the organization's activities.
❏ Check bylaws for conforming provisions permitting lobbying activity.
❏ Determine compliance with recordkeeping and registration requirements.
❏ Ascertain compliance with federal, state, and local reporting requirements and Form 990 disclosures.
❏ Find out whether the organization has any significant history of regulatory action (missed filings, excise taxes, significant audit findings) that may bring additional scrutiny or heightened penalties in the event of a further violation.
❏ Find out whether the organization has made a 501(h) election.
  • If not, explore whether such election would be beneficial.
  • If so, ascertain compliance with limits.
  • Make sure grassroots lobbying does not exceed the 25 percent cap.
❏ Assess whether planned or desired political activities suggest a change in corporate form, a spinoff, or establishment of a subsidiary Section 501(c)(4) entity.

PART III

FOR GOOD COUNSEL ONLY

CHAPTER

11

Taking Charge of the Legal Function

These chapters are primarily directed toward incoming counsel at a nonprofit. In-house counsel in any company or organization is a critical member of the management team. Good in-house counseling demands top-flight legal advice as well as good business judgment and the ability to establish a rapport with the CEO, the board of directors, department heads, and staff. At the same time, in-house counsel must be a good manager of the organization's legal function.

This chapter helps an organization to bring a new counsel on board, and helps the new counsel organize her work. It also provides a context for trustees, executives, and counsel to crystallize their joint understanding of counsel's role, setting her up to succeed. Along the way, it points out several respects in which the in-house counsel's role at a nonprofit differs from the job of her counterpart at a for-profit business.

The list of potential legal issues outlined in the previous chapters can be daunting: Where to start? After discovering the legal needs outlined in the department-by-department tour just completed, counsel should join forces with members of the organization's executive team, perhaps under the leadership and oversight of one or more trustee groups, and work together through the Work Plans offered to get a detailed look at the organization's areas of legal needs. (The Work Plans are consolidated on the companion web site to this book at www.wiley.com/go/goodcounsel for easy reference.) Counsel should add other topics to the Work Plans to cover state-by-state issues as well as specialized areas of the nonprofit's activities, for example, federal Food & Drug Administration laws for a blood bank, applicable international laws for an international relief agency, or local, state, and federal education law issues for a private academy.

Catalogue and Prioritize Legal Needs

The project of assessing the organization's legal status and needs through the Work Plans can take weeks or months. Incoming in-house counsel should establish a close working relationship with the head of each function to carry out this work. A law student or intern, as part of a semester-long assignment or clinical program, can be of great assistance to in-house counsel. The student will gain important professional experience along the way that will set her up to succeed in a variety of practice settings after graduation.

Once the initial assessment is done, counsel and leadership will need to prioritize the issues and establish a schedule and a budget. Whether working within the organization or outside, counsel should be sure to have the buy-in of key members of the executive team and board before embarking on this journey.

This review is just the beginning, though. While counsel is busy cataloging and prioritizing, the organization is evolving and the regulatory environment is shifting all around it. New initiatives may get underway; changes in laws or regulations may require prompt implementation; a process server may be at the door with a new summons and complaint. Counsel may get stopped in the hallway and asked for spot advice—and not every quick question has a quick answer. In the meantime, she may be preparing minutes for the last board or committee meeting and resolutions for the next ones. She is supervising the work of outside counsel (e.g., defense counsel appointed by an insurance company on the organization's behalf), responding to requests by auditors for information, training the organization's non-lawyers in legal basics, assisting with legal aspects of new hires and departures, reviewing a new media campaign that's going live tomorrow, and helping the facilities manager answer the fire department's questions about the spate of false alarms. Then there is the occasional large-bore crisis. Good counsel keeps track of it all and is ready for more.

In this moving-target environment, counsel needs great organizational skills and excellent connections within the organization and with the outside world. Here are some ways that counsel stays on top of their workload and maintains a high profile.

Maintain a Docket of Legal Matters

Organizing and tracking legal matters helps counsel to monitor the workload and progress of the legal function, and makes Legal accountable to the CEO and the board. Counsel can start by creating (or taking over responsibility for) a *docket*, or listing, of all current and planned legal activities. The docket should list the matter, the internal client or department, and if there is more than one attorney doing legal work for the organization, which attorney is assigned. Docket control also furnishes a record from which the counsel can recap—for himself, for the CEO, and for the board—all work completed in the course of a year. This review also prompts a busy CEO and board to pause and reflect on the legal needs of the organization and whether any require additional resources to be properly addressed.

Docket listings can take any of a number of forms, but Table 11.1 shows a simplified sample docket sheet.

Additional enhancements to the docket sheet could include columns indicating priority of task, risk or threat level, and expected duration/amount of effort required to resolve.

Updating the docket sheet continuously, at least once a week at the beginning or end of a workweek, helps the attorney maintain focus and provides important accountability to the organization. Counsel should periodically review performance of her department and outside attorneys, and at least annually report out the results of the department's work to the chief executive and the board (or its legal committee, if there is one). This exercise helps ensure that counsel is on track, prevents overlaps or gaps in coverage, provides an overview of risks, and helps establish an accurate budget for the following year.

Manage and Administer Contracts

Supervising the flow of contracts is a key function of an organization's counsel. At the outset, counsel should establish a system for keeping track of new contracts—arising from which department

Table 11.1   Simplified Sample Legal Docket Sheet

Matter Name/ Description	Internal Contacts(s)	Outside Contact(s)	Status	Deadline/Notes
Analyze effect of new state statute regarding investment of endowment funds, assist with compliance.	CFO; Comptroller; Fundraising department head; Legal, Audit, and Investment Committee Chairs	Exempt organizations counsel, outside auditors	In progress	90-day deadline per statute: 12/31/xx. Assist with donor search. Draft notification letter for fundraising department review. Draft revision of Audit Committee Charter and Investment Committee policies to reference new oversight provisions.
Complete application for expanded trademark protection to cover new program initiative.	Program staff, Marketing staff	Trademark counsel	In progress	Deadline to file has been extended to 6/30/xx. Continue gathering specimens.
Ongoing review and purge of legal files that are past their document retention times or no longer the subject of a litigation hold.	Records department; Information Technology Department; Legal, Audit Committee	Records management consultant	Continuous/ quarterly	Consider reducing amount/cost of warehousing physical documents. Discuss cloud computing storage solution with IT.
Prepare and mail agenda, minutes, and resolutions for upcoming board meeting.	CEO, Board Chair	—	Completed	Board meeting 3/31.

or function, reviewed by whom, signed by whom, implemented by whom, and tracked for compliance, payment or invoicing, renewal, and termination by whom.

Technology can assist this daunting task, and there are several worthy and inexpensive systems available for contract database management. Helpful functions include searching and indexing capabilities, a linkage with the organization's archives, and accessibility through the organization's information technology function to the organization's finance professionals, who facilitate prompt payments or billings consistent with the organization's systems of internal control.

A contracts database also serves as a repository of standard, preapproved contracts and forms, making contract administration more efficient for counsel and the users. When introducing standard forms, counsel should educate the clients about the meaning of the key provisions of contracts they are responsible for implementing. (See Chapter 4 for help explaining basic contract law to nonlawyers.) The organization's staff should develop good habits of consulting with counsel before negotiating or agreeing to any changes to substantive provisions that may be requested by the other party to the contract. For counsel's part, she should regularly review the contracts in the database with the end users to ensure timely and helpful responses to requests for changes to forms, and consider modifying a form if the law changes, business circumstances dictate, or counterparties repeatedly object to the same provision.

A contracts database can help counsel and users keep track of deadlines, renewal dates, expirations, and milestones embedded in agreements. Renewals, extensions and amendments also get uploaded to the database, and should be reviewed and approved by legal counsel in the same way as the underlying agreement. Counsel should also review notices, opportunities to cure, and terminations of contracts, whether for cause or for convenience.

Manage Litigation and Regulatory Activity

Broadly defined, *litigation* matters are court cases, claims, disputes, and regulatory activity (government inquiries, investigations and prosecutions). Counsel must quickly gain an understanding of what litigation matters are currently pending, what matters have been recently concluded, and what matters may be threatened or imminent. The litigation list should distinguish garden-variety matters such as a claim for a refund from a disgruntled client, or a minor personal injury by a member of the public, from a bet-the-company case, such as a challenge to its tax exemption or a major scandal in progress.

In creating or reviewing this listing of litigation matters, counsel should be sure to delineate and discuss with finance professionals, the auditors, the CEO and the board the degree of risk (uninsured exposure), upcoming deadlines, and expected outcomes if known.

Unless the business of the organization is bringing impact litigation (e.g., lawsuits brought by civil rights, environmental, or other nonprofits for the purpose of effectuating social change), in most litigation matters the organization is the *defendant,* or the party defending itself against an action or complaint by someone else. The litigation list should record which outside attorneys are in charge of handling all defensive litigations. Counsel should ensure that all matters—pending and threatened—have been reported to all conceivably applicable insurance carriers and assigned to outside counsel appointed by the carrier. The organization's in-house attorney should coordinate the defense of all matters, respond to any denials of coverage or reservations of rights by carriers, and be prepared to review draft pleadings, supply documents and information, identify witnesses as needed by carrier-appointed counsel, and, in some cases, sign sworn pleadings or statements on behalf of the organization.

The organization may also be the *plaintiff* in a lawsuit, meaning that it is the party with the grievance against another. These matters are rarely handled by insurance-appointed counsel, but instead require the organization to select and retain counsel directly. It is rare that in-house counsel will prosecute these matters on her own, because of the time, expertise, and attention required and also because counsel's role in the matter may disqualify her under professional ethics rules from also representing the organization in the dispute.

Counsel should sensitize clients within the organization about the attorney-client privilege and the attorney work product rules. Although these doctrines have been cut back lately by the courts, it is worth conveying to non-lawyers within the organization that communications between legal counsel (whether in-house or outside counsel) and employees acting on behalf of the organization are confidential and may be privileged. The attorney-client privilege is meant to encourage open and honest communications. The work product doctrine protects materials that are prepared by counsel or at her direction in anticipation of litigation. When an employee in his role on behalf of the organization receives legal advice, the information may be privileged; not the facts but the legal advice provided based on the facts and the specific communications with the attorney about those facts. This privilege can be waived, for example by forwarding the communications or discussing legal advice with individuals outside of the organization. This privilege can also be inadvertently waived by discussing them with individuals within the organization who are not involved in the matter at hand. In-house counsel should keep abreast of developments in this fast-moving area, and in general maintain sensitive awareness of how to increase the chances that communications with clients will be cloaked in privilege.

If the organization is party to a lawsuit (or has reason to believe a claim is likely to be made in the future), counsel should be sure to activate the organization's *litigation hold* procedures for gathering and securing all potentially relevant documents, whether stored on paper, electronically on hard drives, network servers, flash drives or other storage media, in the "cloud," on voicemail, SMS message, or in any other form. Counsel should have ironclad procedures for stopping the cyclic destruction or deletion of documents that may be relevant to the case. The penalties for noncompliance are high. Counsel may also be called upon by outside litigation counsel to help prepare and produce evidence pertinent to the case, identify and prepare witnesses to give sworn statements at trial or in pre-trial proceedings, assess whether the matter is ripe for an out-of-court settlement, and participate in mediation efforts.

For minor matters that have not yet risen to the level of a legal claim, counsel may work with insurers and the organization's finance professionals to decide whether to engage in an early and private settlement to avoid litigation, such as modest restitution in exchange for a release and waiver of claims.

Responsible counsel will also lead the organization through a post-mortem review of past litigation matters of importance, to avoid repeat litigations, to take steps necessary to correct deficiencies in procedures, or to advise where retraining is in order. These activities are an important part of the organization's risk management strategy.

Special Considerations in Managing a Nonprofit's Litigation Docket   The forego-
ing section on litigation management applies similarly to for-profit
and nonprofit organizations. However, litigation in a nonprofit
context can also give rise to certain unique issues.

In some states, the doctrine of *charitable immunity* provides
nonprofit organizations with a level of protection from tort liability. Charitable immunity protects nonprofits in some states from
liability (legal responsibility, obligation to pay damages) for inju-
ries or harms caused to other people.[1] Also, the federal Volunteer
Protection Act provides qualified immunity to volunteers working
with Section 501(c)(3) organizations.[2] As a general matter, though,
nonprofit corporations and the people associated with them should
exercise reasonable care not to injure, harm, or damage the person
or property of others.

Charities officials in most states have the power to bring special
regulatory proceedings against nonprofits, for example, to prevent a
nonprofit from disposing of all or substantially all of its assets without approval from their state attorney general; to stop a nonprofit
board from undermining donor restrictions on uses of a gift without
donor permission; or to intervene in pervasive, ongoing activity that
is outside the organization's charitable purpose. In cases of egregious
misconduct by the leadership of the organization, charities officials
may bring legal action to remove a rogue director or officer, restrain
actions of the corporation, or even annul or dissolve the corporation. While the state Attorney General has the discretion to bring an
action against a nonprofit to protect the public interest, the decision
is reviewable by the courts.[3] (Charities and the people within them
are also subject to ordinary law enforcement activities, such as a district attorney's prosecution under state fraud or theft laws.)

It takes a counsel of unusual competence and fortitude to
guide an organization through such events. Fortunately, such proceedings are exceedingly rare, especially if the organization has
been assiduously attending to the matters described in this book.

Nonprofits are also particularly sensitive to negative public relations that may accompany litigation, not only because of adverse
reputational consequences that face other kinds of businesses, but
also because of potential harm to donations and public funding.
For this reason, counsel should be sure to notify and involve the
organization's PR team early on about potential litigation matters

that may be of interest to the media and work together with public relations professionals to coordinate the response.

The Softer Skills of Good Counsel

Beyond understanding and managing the legal matters that arise, effective nonprofit counsel knows that a key part of her work is synching the legal department's goals with organizational and programmatic goals. Counsel's effective relationships organization-wide can be an important element of the organization's success, promoting the legal department as an integral part of institutional policy-making initiatives as well as new business operations.

Build Relationships and Establish Great Communication

Actively managing the legal function means that matters don't slip through the cracks, that queries are answered promptly and efficiently, and that the attorney is as resourceful and nimble as the needs of her clients require. Counsel should maintain an approachable demeanor—door open, prompt return of phone calls and e-mails, plain English answers to questions.

One of the most frequent complaints from management about counsel is timeliness of legal advice. If counsel is not immediately available to address the question, she (or her assistant) should at least take down the information and set a time for follow-up and a time frame for completion. A good rule of thumb is that the sun should never set on an unanswered telephone message or e-mail from a client.

Find a Responsible Way to Make the Answer Be Yes

Effective in-house counsel develop and maintain a reputation for facilitating clients' legitimate objectives—finding a responsible way to make the answer be yes, instead of being the Department of No or Department of Delay. Too frequently, clients view in-house counsel as a stumbling block that interferes with a proposed project or activity. Lawyers have a reputation for finding legal defects without simultaneously offering creative suggestions to cure them. Truth to tell, lawyers occasionally elevate form over substance, to the detriment of institutional progress. This routine inevitably leads to excluding counsel from project development or ignoring counsel's advice, often to the peril of the project or even the organization. Counsel's goal should be to become a regular part of the team who is invited to brainstorm as early as possible in the development of a major project. To be sure to receive that invitation, counsel needs to figure out how to make herself welcome at the table. Here are some ideas:

Be a Legal Educator

Some client education may be needed, as nonprofit executives may not realize that their work or activities have legal implications. Make sure that employees enjoy a basic level of legal literacy— about nonprofit corporate law and the tax exemption, contracts, intellectual property, and all the rest. Counsel in larger organizations would do well to convey these important lessons not only to the senior staff but also to middle management and below. Every individual in the organization should know how to bring a legal matter to counsel, and when. Early is always better than late, and late is better than never.

Clients appreciate when counsel shares information about breaking legal developments and circulates memos translating new laws, judicial decisions, and articles about hot legal topics into plain English. Counsel can also offer mini-sessions for clients to help explain legal developments of particular pertinence.

Be Inclusive

If the legal department identifies the need to issue a new legal policy, counsel should include the internal clients on the planning, execution, and implementation so that they, too, have a sense of ownership and a feeling of inclusion. At the same time, counsel should welcome learning opportunities offered by leaders of other disciplines within the organization. Counsel should set the bar high by supporting organizational diversity initiatives, mentoring programs, and other policies.

Be Trustworthy and Respectful

Trust and mutual respect are quintessential elements of a working relationship. The organization's staff may be suspicious of counsel at the outset, whether because the legal issues are unfamiliar, the profession does not enjoy the most sterling reputation, or the employees may be confused about whom the lawyer represents. A strong working relationship with the organization's staff comes about through consistency, thoroughness, timeliness, cooperation, dedication to mission, and team spirit.

Sometimes the Best Legal Review is Invisible—A Personal Example

Sometimes the best compliment a lawyer can get is that she left no visible fingerprints on a great new initiative. The cultural critic for the *Washington Post,* Pulitzer-nominated journalist Philip Kennicott, paid this compliment, perhaps unwittingly, to Lincoln Center's legal team. Kennicott gave a rapturous review of Lincoln Center's billion-dollar redevelopment effort shortly after its completion, calling the complex "livelier, smarter, hipper and more inviting." After describing the dynamic new glass façade of Alice Tully Hall and The Juilliard School building, the new streetscape, the new lighting and fountain, and other praiseworthy features, he turned his discerning eye toward the new roof lawn atop the new restaurant:

> On top of the restaurant, a grass roof offers passersby a gently inclined hillock on which to sit, stretch out, daydream and cruise. It is a surreal space, a grassy patch of park thrusting out of the rigid geometry of the plaza. It offers views of the city that seem as if they were invented on Photoshop, and it creates a play zone in the middle of a plaza that often feels windswept and barren. It is an eccentric vision, an invitation to spontaneity and informality and the gentle chaos of urban life.[4]

Then came the clincher:

> Somehow *the lawyers never got at this idea,* never sank it with fears of imaginary dangers. It feels fresh and accidental, adolescent and fun. (Emphasis added.)

What higher praise could there be for the legal team than that this most remarkable feature of the renovation appeared as though "lawyers never got at the idea"? Naturally, both the green roof and every other aspect of the redevelopment were fully reviewed by

Building the Framework for Lincoln Center's Illumination Lawn

lawyers—from every conceivable rakish angle. The concept proposal of the inclined roof lawn—technically a hyperbolic parabo-
loid—was first posed by our visionary architects to our captivated
board. It was then rigorously reviewed by engineers for proof of
concept, by construction managers for constructability, and yes, by
lawyers, insurance specialists, and the biomechanics safety experts
consulted by the legal department. We reviewed it, independently
and together, in design, in prototype and again "in the grass." At
the grand opening, it was counsel who made the first ceremonial
roll down the hill to prove it was safe. Yes, Mr. Kennicott, lawyers
got at the idea—lawyers who know how to make way for the excellent execution of daring new ideas.

Inadvertently or not, this critic's comment sets a new high bar
for counsel: Advise your visionary trustees and entrepreneurial
executives as thoroughly, knowledgeably, and deftly as possible—so
that it appears to an admiring outsider that they bypassed counsel
altogether!

In Sum/Coming Up Next

This summary of the role of in-house counsel may lead the organization's staff and trustee leadership to wonder: Is it time to bring

on a new in-house counsel? In describing the activities and traits of a good in-house counsel, this chapter outlines a job description as well—a job description that should then be tailored to each organization's specific needs. The general traits include being generally knowledgeable about the matters contained in this book, its work plans, and the resources located in the endnotes and appendices. Counsel must have excellent organizational skills to assemble and maintain a docket of legal matters, review contracts, oversee litigation, and educate and counsel clients about the legal aspects of their important mission-related work. Good time-management habits are a must, as is the ability to juggle many issues of disparate subjects and sizes. Having a passion for the purpose of the organization is a *sine qua non*. So are diplomatic and communication skills, at the board level, interacting with the CEO, with individuals at every level of the organization, and the outside world—regulators, government agencies, auditors, and more.

This summary may lead attorneys who are tantalized by the prospect of devoting their professional energies to a worthy nonprofit to wonder: How do I find such a job? This is the subject of Chapter 12, which offers some suggestions for job-seeking to aspiring nonprofit lawyers who are undaunted—or even energized—by this description.

12

Finding Your Dream Job as In-House Counsel at a Nonprofit

This chapter outlines career pathways for attorneys wishing to enter the nonprofit sector. In-house counsel jobs at nonprofits are hard to find. Paid in-house jobs are even harder! The sector has not (yet) fully embraced the value of having regular legal counsel—although readers of this book may be convinced that the time has come for the nonprofits they care about to add a budget line for an in-house lawyer.

For newly established nonprofits, the initial hires are, of course, the CEO, chief program officer and staff. Perhaps a professional fundraiser is next, then a finance person, and eventually operations, marketing, public relations, and human resources professionals and staff to follow.

But a lawyer may be the hundredth hire, if that. Indeed, many major nonprofits do not have in-house counsel. For instance, if you want to get to Carnegie Hall, practice, practice, practice—but don't practice law.

Where to Begin Searching for an In-House Job at a Nonprofit

For those new to the sector, the challenges of finding an in-house legal job may seem insurmountable. When an in-house legal job does open up, whether because a lawyer left one of these coveted positions or the organization has determined to create a position, the organization or its search firm may receive a hundred, if not more, applications for the slot.

Recruiters, also known as search firms or headhunters, often round up the usual suspects, seeking out people already success-ful in nonprofit executive positions who are looking to move on to other organizations. Moreover, open positions may not be publicly listed, as only the largest organizations can afford placement fees.

Attorneys working with placement counselors should certainly mention their interest in or willingness to consider a nonprofit post. However, nonprofits often do not think to list a legal open-ing with legal recruitment firms, and may not even accept resumes from outplacement counselors because of associated fees for a suc-cessful placement.

Because of all of these challenges, lawyers looking to break into the nonprofit world have to be creative and resourceful—a good test of things to come! There are jobs in nonprofit organizations for lawyers—it may just take a little extra time, tenacity, creativity, imagination, and powers of persuasion.

How to Position Yourself to Win an In-House Job in a Nonprofit

For those undeterred by the challenges and absolutely dedicated to the idea of finding—or creating—an in-house paid legal position within a nonprofit, here are some things to do.

Build Up the Resume

It is rare for an entry-level attorney to become an in-house attor-ney, in any sector. Being in-house counsel has been likened to playing with live ammunition—you'd better learn what you are doing by firing some practice rounds first. Ideally an attorney will probably have at least two or three years of experience before going in-house. Important skills to develop early on include draft-ing and negotiating, corporate law basics, and exposure to some other areas, such as employment law, intellectual property, and/ or real estate.

Building your legal resume doesn't mean you have to prac-tice in a specific area, however. Because of the generalist nature of many in-house legal positions in nonprofit organizations, a broad array of experiences can be useful in building up and refining an attorney's skills. Helpful and transferrable legal experience can be acquired in varied settings—law firms, government offices, the district attorney's office, corporate positions, and elsewhere. Carefully read job descriptions and string together pertinent experiences from prior positions, whether legal or non-legal, volunteer or paid, that answer the call. Even if an attorney has only served in private practice, there are plenty of practice management skills that can be knitted together to write a truthful, attractive story about the candidate's skills as a potential executive.

Sometimes there is an obvious internal candidate waiting in the wings for these rare in-house counsel positions. By the time the position gets posted or known more broadly, the organization may already be down to a (very) short list, making the interview process a frustrating exercise for the applicants who don't realize they have little or no chance at the job. Some have likened this process to Kabuki theater, where the interviewers and interviewees are going through elaborate motions but the outcome is pre-ordained.

But there are cases of serendipity, where real and non-obvious candidates have a chance to land a gratifying and exciting position. For example, the general counsel of the nonprofit National Public Radio (NPR) started out as a tax lawyer in private practice; she then worked on international franchise deals as in-house counsel for Southland (now 7-Eleven, Inc.). After that she parlayed her experience into an in-house position at a children's entertainment group best known for producing Barney & Friends, and its subsequent owner, HIT Entertainment. To this day she touts the benefits of on-the-job training![1]

On-the-job training is a time-honored tradition—in both the for-profit and the nonprofit sectors. An applicant transitioning from a law firm or an in-house counsel position at a for-profit company should not be deterred by a lack of experience as an in-house nonprofit lawyer; to the contrary, they can feel confident that they will not be the first to learn the job while already in place, and they should not feel shy about asking and answering questions accordingly.

It helps to have some context for on-the-job learning, however, and here are some additional steps job seekers can take to improve their chances and steepen the learning curve.

Do the Public Good

Some attorneys have found great success locating an in-house position by starting out as a volunteer. Serving the type of organization you would eventually like to be employed by will help you build the skills you will need and understand the types of issues that will arise in that organization. Volunteering will make you a more obvious candidate for the job because of the understanding you will have of the unique issues that may arise. You can incorporate extracurricular and volunteer activities into your resume using a skills section. This is an excellent way to show organizations the skills you've developed and the level of your interest in their type of work.

Some lawyers will even approach the executive director of a nonprofit they admire with an offer to take on a project without a fee. Working on an important or recurring legal matter for a nonprofit can be a great selling point for an eventual job search. Be sure to follow the formalities of obtaining a signed engagement letter that spells out the scope and terms of the pro bono work. Needless to say, treat the matter with the same attention and skill as if it were a billable matter.

Another productive way to develop relevant experience is by serving on boards. As described in Chapter 3, being on a board involves overseeing the management and operations of a nonprofit. The same fiduciary duties of care, loyalty and obedience apply to board members as to senior managers. (Do note the warnings in Chapter 1 about lawyers acting as board members, however: It's all-too-easy to slip into the role of pro bono general counsel but minus the requisite malpractice insurance or conflicts-check, with the dual position of trustee and legal counselor creating role strain, professional ethics challenges, or worse.) Done right, board service is great training for running an organization—or for becoming an in-house lawyer and member of the senior management team. But choose wisely: Be passionate about the mission of the organization, do homework to fully understand the condition of the organization, and be prepared to take on solemn fiduciary duties—board service is no mere vanity gig. Check the organization's recent informational filings, such as the IRS Form 990, and inquire whether director's and officer's liability insurance is in place, and whether the organization's bylaws provide indemnification to board members to the fullest extent allowed by law.

A resource that helps match boards with prospective board members is Boardnet USA.[2] Boardnet compiles a list of organizations seeking directors according to category, such as arts and culture, education, environment and animals, health, human services, international/foreign affairs, public and societal benefit, religion, and many subcategories as well.

Build or Activate Your Network

If you want to work in a certain field, look through your address file and figure out if you know someone or someone who knows someone in your area of interest. Friends or business contacts may serve on boards of organizations of interest; board lists are generally public knowledge under the About Us section of most nonprofits' web sites. Social networking web sites such as LinkedIn.com and alumni networks can also be helpful in this endeavor.

Join Bar Associations

Bar associations and their committees provide an excellent way to meet and work with other lawyers who share professional interests. Try to get involved in a substantive project such as a written report, a continuing legal education program or a themed event, to show what you can do. Working side-by-side with people already in the industry provides a great opportunity to demonstrate character, skills and energy.

Ask for Informational Interviews

While doing Internet research and building up your contacts you will identify individuals who you might want to target for conversations and information gathering. There's no harm in cold-calling them to see if they are willing to meet for an informational interview or brainstorming session. This is an accepted and proactive step in getting your interest and your name into the field. Ask each of the people with whom you conduct an informational interview about who else you should see. They will often give you the name and contact information of other people in the field. They may also know about upcoming conferences and meetings that you might be able to attend. Although many nonprofit in-house legal positions that become available are not posted or listed with search firms, if the people in your field of interest are aware that you're looking and that you've been proactive about introducing yourself, they may think of you when they have a position available or hear that a colleague has an open position.

One word of warning, though: Do not go into a meeting on the guise of an informational interview or brainstorming session and then ask for a job! This is considered bad form.

Show an Interest

Figure out what specific part of the sector interests you the most—the nonprofit world is large and varied. Nonprofit organizations will be more inclined to be interested in a candidate who shares their passion about the organization's mission. A candidate can show interest in a variety of ways—examples include traveling to a troubled area to do relief work, subscribing to a theatre company, contributing to or raising money for the cause, volunteering, or starting a blog. If you always turn first to the sports section of your favorite periodical, you would mention that in an obvious place in your cover letter applying for a job with Special Olympics. Any activities that demonstrate an interest in the mission of the organization will certainly help land a coveted paid position, and cover letters as well as the skills section of the resume need to be tailored to connect the applicant to that specific institution and its mission.

In all of these endeavors, sell your personal attributes: intelligence, analytical abilities, tenacity, people skills, organization, dedication to the mission, enthusiasm, and leadership abilities. Allow the deciders to see your work ethic and commitment. All of these personal attributes are just as important as the skills you list on your resume. In sum: It's largely about confidence!

Where to Locate Job Listings

In addition to legal profession headhunters who carry in-house listings in all sectors, there are a few good resources that specifically serve or include nonprofit positions.

- Executive search firms with developed practices in the nonprofit area, such as Phillips Oppenheim or Spencer Stuart.

- Legal profession listings, such as in-house bar associations (e.g., Association of Corporate Counsel, www.acc.com/jobline) or affinity groups (such as Corporate Counsel Women of Color, www.ccwomenofcolor.org).
- Idealist is a web site that connects people and organizations searching for roles and resources in nonprofit social, legal, and environmental issues (www.idealist.org).
- The Chronicle of Philanthropy is a news and job-information source for charity leaders, fundraisers, grant makers, and others involved in philanthropic enterprises (www.philanthropy .com).
- The Chronicle of Higher Education is a weekly news and job-information source for college and university faculty members, administrators, and students (www.chronicle.com).
- Nonprofit Times and NPT Jobs is a national business publication focusing on nonprofit management, with a weekly list of job openings (www.thenonprofittimes.com).
- Arts Journal is a daily arts news and job information source from more than 100 newspapers, magazines and e-publications, including job listings in the arts and cultural sector (www.artsjournal.com).
- Newspaper and web site searches. Many newspapers and job web sites offer the option of setting up RSS feeds for narrowed searches. The RSS feeds will allow you to check all your job-search resources in one stop.

Counsel listings are few and far between, but occasionally they do arise. In the meantime you can learn a great deal about the sector while you search. Careful and persistent readers of these web sites will find industry-insider information about specific nonprofits in transition, nonprofits facing regulatory or legal challenges, and general issues of importance to the sector. Job seekers can pick up clues about which organizations may be hiring at some point in the future—or which could be susceptible to a pitch to create a new legal position now.

Even if none of the jobs listed in these resources seems exactly right—timing-wise, geographically, or otherwise—it is a worthwhile exercise to draft a cover note and write a sample resume as if applying for the job. Show your drafts to a friend or willing acquaintance in the sector for critique and advice. Practice job interviewing with friends in the sector or with career counselors through your law school alumni association.

Law students who eventually wish to work as in-house counsel in the nonprofit sector may also wish to keep an eye on these job listings in the years before they are ready to apply, so that they can start preparing suitable resumes when the time comes.

Create a Legal Job Where There Is None

A more challenging—but not unheard of—way to get an in-house job is to create one. Many organizations use volunteer outside counsel; occasionally these positions turn into paying work and ultimately to a salaried in-house position.

With all of the issues described in the preceding chapters, the checklists and diagnostic tools will inevitably uncover a number of matters that need to be addressed. The organization may or may not be able to locate volunteer (pro bono) or discounted-rate (low-bono) counsel willing and able to address all the matters that have surfaced. Even if there are one or more good-hearted attorneys addressing the array of legal needs faced by the organization on an affordable basis, the organization may conclude that it would benefit from having an in-house counsel to coordinate the work.

In addition to coordinating complex legal needs, in-house counsel working as part of a management team can instill trust, collegiality, intimacy, and familiarity with legal matters on the part of non-legal staff. Legal issues tend to surface much earlier when counsel resides in-house than when a non-legal executive within the organization has to spot legal issues and affirmatively reach out to outside counsel. Having a lawyer in-house will make these issues easier to identify and easier to solve and it will often be less costly, in terms of both money and time, over the long run.

Outside counsel can help an organization appreciate the value of hiring an in-house counsel, and volunteer counsel may be best situated to persuade the chief executive and the board of directors to create the salary line to bring the legal function in-house.

Take a Non-Legal Job (Which May Turn into a Legal Job)

In addition to applying for existing positions or creating one, another strategy for lawyers intent on serving the sector is to consider applying for non-legal positions that use similar skills at a more abstract level. Ask yourself what skills you have built that are translatable or transportable. If you get involved with work in a non-legal role you'll realize how much your legal background can help you. Also ask yourself what skills you would like to learn. If you want to build your legal skills in a certain area, stepping out of the traditional legal role or into a non-legal role can help you build these skills.

Fundraising   Fundraising is one of the most valuable skills a person can bring to a nonprofit organization. Fundamentally, fundraising is about being a zealous advocate for the organization, involving excellent persuasive writing skills and oral expression. Sound familiar? These are some of the same skills that go toward being a great lawyer. Being fearless is also an attribute common to both professional fundraisers and lawyers: better to overreach and ask for forgiveness than to fail for lack of trying. A lawyer who has become an extremely successful executive director of a Chamber of Commerce organization, via the fundraising track, characterizes his work as "bragging and begging."[3] Sounds a little like client advocacy or rainmaking in private practice!

Many elements of fundraising call directly upon legal knowledge, such as planned giving or trusts and estates law. Grant writing is essentially persuasive writing, which relates to writing briefs and memoranda. Fundraising pitches are essentially oral advocacy—representing a client at its best. Prospect research is not unlike legal research, but with a different database—linking donors to causes like the ones they have already shown an interest in supporting. As is evident from Chapter 5, the connections between fundraising and law are legion.

Government Affairs/Lobbying   Government affairs positions are a great fit for lawyers with political experience, policy research and analytical skills, good relationships, keen instincts and powers of persuasion. Although government affairs executives are not always lawyers, a lawyer may distinguish himself among applicants with an understanding of how governmental funding works and how legislation is drafted, marked up, debated and voted. Because the lobbying area is so heavily regulated, lawyers also can help organizations navigate the fraught and sometimes confusing territory between prohibited campaign intervention and permissible lobbying, and help coordinate complex governmental filings.

Corporate Secretary/Board Liaison   Some organizations, particularly those with large boards, have a corporate secretary position that's distinct from the general counsel role. The secretary coordinates communication between the board and management and takes primary responsibility for keeping corporate records, taking minutes, and disseminating information. He may also advise on bylaw matters and draft amendments or resolutions.

Although corporate secretaries are not always lawyers, lawyer applicants may receive special attention because of the significant legal elements in this role.

Operations/Administration   Becoming involved with operations or administration requires organizational skills, which many lawyers with busy dockets have in abundance. A great operations/administration manager looks at the organization's needs and structure in an analytical way, envisioning efficient processes and effective checks and balances, not unlike running a legal practice or office.

Human Resources   Human Resources is a department shot through with legal issues, as seen in Chapter 7. Hiring, firing, compliance with wage and hour laws, recruiting and retaining top talent, maintaining high morale, crafting and fairly enforcing employee policies, overseeing nondiscrimination practices and (in a unionized environment) negotiating collective bargaining agreements and addressing grievances—these are all core competencies of a great Human Resources manager. These skills also overlap significantly with legal skills and knowledge. Lawyers with people skills may find themselves very much at home fulfilling the human resources function in a nonprofit.

Finance   Lawyers with an appropriate finance, business, or accounting background can be very effective in a chief financial officer role. Deal-making on behalf of a nonprofit organization uses many of the same business analysis and negotiation skills as deal-making on the for-profit side, but with the additional layer of nonprofit and tax considerations described in Chapter 6. The planning and budgeting required of a nonprofit financial officer is not unlike managing these elements of a law practice.

Project Management From time to time, lawyers step into roles as project managers, web designers or other kinds of managers, depending on their skills and interests. Sometimes these jobs take on a legal advisory element as the person's law background becomes evident. Once the job starts morphing into a counsel job, however, it is important to formalize the counsel function, so that there is no ambiguity about whether the person is acting as the organization's lawyer. This clarity is important from many standpoints including professional ethics, malpractice insurance, role definition, attorney-client privilege, and more.

Translate Your Resume

For lawyers seeking a job in a nonprofit organization, the task is to do the translating for the hiring person. Don't just submit the same resume as for another job like the one you have or have just left, as if looking to be hired to do the same work elsewhere. An attorney who has spent the last several years as a litigator, conducting depositions of hostile witnesses and answering demands for bills of particulars, should find a different way to express how they can be of service to the nonprofit. Unless you are applying for a post doing impact litigation for a nonprofit, these specific skills will likely not be in much demand. Attorneys seeking to make the transition must connect the management/leadership/executive dots and customize their resumes to demonstrate value to a prospective hiring organization.

> **Example:** A prominent historical museum hired an assistant United States attorney (federal prosecutor). Her role is as both general counsel and chief administrative officer.
> **Example:** A dance company that has recently moved into an iconic new physical complex hired an attorney to become its director of operations. She has since taken on a legal role as well.

Example: A large YMCA took on a project manager to handle a digital initiative. The project manager, also a lawyer, has become in-house counsel now that the technology project is complete.

Example: A leading ballet school hired an ex-entertainment lawyer, who spent 10 years as a volunteer with a nearby ballet company while her children were young, to be its executive director. She regularly draws upon legal acumen as well as executive skills and knowledge gained during volunteer service, in running a first-class organization.

Attorneys in private practice who seek to transition into non-legal jobs should spend some time thinking about how their skills and experiences—managing, advocating, persuading, and leading—might translate. And lawyers who have been cocooned in private practice for a long time may do well to remember that lawyers are not a profession beloved by many in the outside world; they may need to do some unexpected work counteracting negative stereotypes. (See Chapter 11.)

Consider a Regulatory Role

Another great career step that lawyers can take if they ultimately wish to end up as in-house counsel at a nonprofit is to consider applying for a position within the Charities Bureau of their state's attorney general's office or the Exempt Organizations division of the IRS. These regulatory roles are a way to gain first-hand knowledge and insight about what can go wrong with governance and compliance before heading in-house. By knowing the kinds of problems a nonprofit organization will face before you get there, you'll be able to nip problems in the bud before they start and you'll be able to easily identify issues before they become problems.

Don't Believe the Myths

There are many myths and preconceived notions about landing—and doing—an in-house legal job. There is really no ideal path to becoming in-house counsel at a nonprofit. The age, level of experience, and backgrounds of in-house counsel are as varied as the organizations they serve. Here are some of the prevalent myths and why they are false.

"I can't get an in-house legal job because . . . "

- *I have no in-house experience.* A lot of people in in-house roles end up there with no prior in-house experience. They may have been selected for the job because they have served as outside counsel to businesses or organizations and gained a level of understanding in that role. Volunteer counsel or trustees certainly gain translatable skills and valuable insight into the kinds of issues in-house lawyers face. Sometimes the greatest expertise a lawyer can demonstrate in a job interview is that of a generalist; private practice in a general service firm or department may be the best preparation possible for the vast array of issues that in-house counsel face.
- *I'm too young/old.* There is no ideal age for in-house counsel. Depending on the size of the organization or the work culture of the organization, it could be looking for fresh young lawyers or seasoned attorneys with the proven ability to handle all of the pressures that come with a fast-paced or intense legal practice. A small start-up enterprise with youthful leadership may feel more comfortable with counsel in their peer age range, while a more experienced management team in a well-established organization may be looking for something entirely different.
- *I'm a litigator, not a corporate/tax-exempt organizations lawyer.* Although conventional wisdom says that only corporate lawyers get in-house jobs, many in-house lawyers at nonprofits started their careers as litigators, or courtroom lawyers. The kinds of experiences gained as a litigator can translate well, because litigation exposes lawyers to a wide range of legal issues, requires lawyers to learn about new fields with every case, encourages efficient time management, requires multitasking, hones writing and oral advocacy skills, and more. Litigation also helps attorneys see around corners, anticipating problems that may not be obvious to others who have not seen similar situations break down. Being a litigator is not a detriment to finding an in-house position; it may even be good preparation for an in-house role in unexpected ways.
- *I'm a lawyer and they hate lawyers.* In-house lawyers occupy a delicate position, balancing their roles as enforcer, confidante, and facilitator. As described in Chapter 11 and elsewhere, coworkers may view him or her as a hurdle to

overcome or as someone to be avoided in the pursuit of a new project or initiative. Attorneys interviewing for in-house jobs, particularly in nonprofits but probably more generally speaking, should demonstrate an awareness of and sensitivity to these issues.

And, to be fair, here are some myths about working in the sector that are equally ill-founded.

- *Nonprofits don't pay very well.* While this used to be true and may still be true for many nonprofits, *The Chronicle of Philanthropy* recently published its report on executive compensation at nonprofit organizations.[4] It finds that these positions sometimes pay very well indeed. Leaders at hospitals and medical centers fared the best in the report, but universities and some cultural institutions also paid well.
- *Non-profits are unsophisticated in their legal needs and business challenges.* Part of the reason that nonprofits are paying more is a change in perception about the nature of nonprofit executives. Jobs are harder due to increased visibility in the press and heightened pressure from donors and government to run nonprofits more efficiently and with greater accountability. Nonprofit jobs are no longer seen as do-gooder jobs that any well-meaning person can do. Organizations and companies now understand that to run a nonprofit successfully you need people with professional business and legal backgrounds who understand (social) return on investment. Business lawyers who think they will be greeted as a savior doing the organization a favor when they interview for a non-profit executive post will quickly learn otherwise.
- *Nonprofit work is women's work.* Nonprofit work may be unfairly considered by some to be women's work, or a variant on volunteer work, an end game or step toward semi-retirement after a satisfying paid career in the for-profit business world. In fact, women (including women of color and older women) as well as men have made more strides in achieving equal opportunity as leaders and board members in the nonprofit sector than in many other business settings, and in those roles have made enormous impacts addressing society's ills and improving lives.

- *People in nonprofits don't work hard.* This is perhaps the biggest misconception of all. Nonprofit work, especially the role of in-house counsel, is demanding, visible, and meaningful. While in-house positions are generally thought to require fewer hours than the 80-hour workweeks sometimes associated with private legal practice at a large law firm, in-house counsel positions can require long, engaging days and weeks that are often taxing due to the wide variety of skills, the broad range of issues, and the high-impact work and visibility of the organization.

Counsel committed to finding in-house work at an organization should not be daunted by stereotypes.

Parting Thoughts about Nonprofit Legal Work

Attorneys, professors, and clinical instructors in and around the nonprofit sector should devote time to mentoring students, young professionals, and those seeking to make a career change. The nonprofit world is vast. The needs are compelling. There is a great deal of good to be done and a large number of people interested in doing it. Mentoring and peer counseling is one important way of connecting needy nonprofits with willing sources of labor. Through career fairs, networking receptions, public interest affinity groups, and other means, colleges, law schools, business schools, and professional associations can demonstrate that nonprofit work is a viable and meaningful career path.

In Sum/Coming Up Next

Attorneys considering entering the nonprofit sector as in-house counsel can use the ideas in this chapter to begin or enhance their search. Although paid work as in-house counsel at a nonprofit is hard to find, there are ways of locating or creating such jobs. Myths abound, so honestly examine preconceptions before embarking on such a search.

What happens once you land a coveted position as counsel to a nonprofit? The amount and range of legal needs can seem overwhelming. Organizations that may not have previously had in-house counsel (and until recently did not realize that they needed one) may in fact have an enormous array of legal matters to tackle. The next and final chapter sets forth some ideas for marshaling others to help the cause.

CHAPTER

13

Mobilizing Other Legal Forces for the Good

Good counsel need not act alone. In fact, it's impossible for one attorney to know enough about all the different areas of law to be able to address all the organization's legal needs single-handedly. Fortunately, there is plenty of good will for good causes, and a lot of legal resources to help. This chapter will describe how counsel for a non-profit can build a network of legal advisors—paid, discounted, and (best of all) pro bono.

The first step to locating great legal assistance is to survey the organization's legal needs. The Work Plans in this book are designed to provide an initial assessment of the kinds of legal issues that arise in nonprofit organizations.

The issues that emerge from the Work Plans are likely to cluster around some or all of these various categories:

- Nonprofit corporate law and governance
- Compliance with the tax exemption
- Contract law
- Copyright law and rights clearances
- Fundraising law
- Laws relating to the finance and accounting function
- Labor and employment law
- Trademark law
- Consumer regulatory law
- Real estate law
- Municipal law/governmental violations, permits, and approvals
- Government relations (lobbying)

Organizations working in technical or highly regulated fields such as health care, the environment, or education will have specialized legal needs to add to the list, as will organizations undergoing major construction or expansion. Organizations with significant operations overseas face yet other issues.

After identifying the organization's primary legal needs, including those listed and others that may be specific to the organization's work or the location(s) in which it operates, the organization and its counsel should activate their networks to find legal help to match their needs.

Paid and Pro Bono Representations

In light of the wide variety and complexity of legal matters, organizations may decide that they need to retain one or more outside counsel. This help can be in the form of paid, discounted, or pro bono legal services.

In-house counsel is the glue between outside counsel and the organization. Often the work of outside counsel is transactional, focusing on the details of specific issues or assignments rather than on the totality of the organization's legal well-being. Their role as advisor may be much more circumscribed and they may feel (and be) out of the loop. In bringing on outside counsel, the organization's in-house counsel may have to do a fair amount of translating, interpreting, and facilitating. If there is no in-house counsel to fulfill this role, other executives or lawyer/board members may pinch-hit, but there is no substitute for an in-house counsel's global perspective of the organization's legal context.

Retaining a Private Law Firm

Organizations may reach out directly to reputable full-service law firms that have the resources to address the wide range of issues that arise. There are also boutique law firms or departments within larger firms that specialize in counseling nonprofit organizations, sometimes called the *Exempt Organizations* practice. Some of these law firms even have the capabilities to fulfill the role of outside general counsel to a nonprofit. Legal fees can be billed in accordance with the firm's established hourly rates, discounted rates (often law firms will offer discounts to nonprofit clients as a matter of course), or on a project-by-project basis.

In-house counsel is responsible for overseeing all outside counsel relationships, reviewing the billings, and coordinating their work. If the organization does not yet have in-house counsel, another responsible executive such as the CFO or CEO may do this work; in that case, a lawyer on the board of directors may be in a position to provide appropriate oversight.

Locating Pro Bono Outside Help

For those organizations that cannot afford to hire counsel, many good organizations exist for the purpose of connecting lawyers and needy nonprofits. Pro Bono Net, www.probono.net, is a nationwide resource that provides resources for pro bono and legal services attorneys and others working to assist low income or disadvantaged clients. State or local bar associations can also refer organizations to qualified attorneys. A leading organization called Lawyers Alliance for New York, www.lawyersalliance.org, provides business and transactional legal services locally for nonprofit organizations helping the poor. The Lawyers Alliance webiste also publishes a list of providers of business and transactional legal services for nonprofit organizations around the country.

Other organizations, such as Catchafire, www.catchafire.org, match volunteer professionals, including legal professionals, with nonprofits calling for help. Law school clinical programs may also have resources to help organizations meet their legal needs.

Some of the nation's largest law firms have institutionalized the practice of providing pro bono legal services to worthy nonprofits. The legal departments of some major corporations have formally launched programs for their attorneys to provide volunteer legal advice to nonprofit organizations as part of their community outreach efforts. Lawyers on the board of an organization may help craft a pitch and facilitate introductions to law firms and corporations with pro bono practices.

Once legal assistance has been referred or suggested, it's a good idea to independently research and verify the attorney's or firm's suitability for the work—even if the services are being offered for free.

How to Ask for Pro Bono Help

It's amazing how many lawyers want to help—some experts believe there are more prospective legal volunteers than organizations that know how to ask for help! Pro bono legal services are quite literally yours for the asking.

How does an organization most effectively cultivate, activate, and manage in-kind contributors? In the same way that it cultivates, activates, and manages other kinds of contributors—with care, foresight, planning, and follow-through. Here are some steps an organization can take to shape an effective pro bono legal program:

- Peers respond best to peers, so if the organization is approaching a law firm for the first time, it helps to cite examples of other similar law firms that are already providing pro bono legal assistance to the organization.
- Have a clear and well-defined "ask" in mind. Crystallize the project by developing an interesting and well-defined assignment, accurately estimate the duration of the project and the amount of attorney time needed to complete it.
- Minimize administrative drain on the volunteer by gathering all the information and documents needed to launch the project at the outset.
- Wherever possible, arrange for an initial, face-to-face meeting to introduce the people and the problem.
- Clearly state the deliverables needed and the deadline by which they are required.
- Follow-up is key—even if it's only a brief e-mail at some point between the initial meeting and the deadline with the subject line, "Just checking in."
- A face-to-face meeting is best to receive the volunteer attorney's presentation of his or her work product, ask follow up questions, and express sincere gratitude.
- Implement the work—release the memo, file the brief, augment or revise the policy—and be sure to let the volunteer know what a difference his or her work made.

Speak to Legal Volunteers' Interests   Part of the pitch to a prospective legal volunteer is appealing to their self-interest. Describe how doing the work for the organization will benefit the lawyer and their firm. Pro bono work builds expertise, provides training opportunities for up-and-coming professionals, and assists in the recruitment, retention, and morale-building efforts of law firms.

Students from elite law schools working on pro bono projects for nonprofit organizations as part of their summer jobs at law firms report that the experiences reflected positively on the host law firm, strengthening the tie between the student and his future employer.

In addition to their sense of contributing meaningfully to the mission, lawyers working on pro bono legal projects report gaining valuable additional insights into what it means to be part of the profession, and an opportunity to evaluate and reflect positively on their association with the firm.

Pro bono work also provides for meaningful client exposure, presentational opportunities, and project management responsibilities that may be far greater than a junior or even mid-level attorney has experienced for paying clients. These experiences contribute to the attorney's professional development as well as building the firm's knowledge base.

Pro bono work helps a law firm align with a charity its members care about, fostering a sense of esprit de corps, and enticing future paying clients who may share the firm's values and mission orientation. If a firm is looking to expand into a new area of practice or break into a geographic market, there may be no better way to burnish its brand than to align with a respected and beloved local organization.

Get Help from Law Students   Other opportunities for pro bono service include law students on summer break and recent law grads awaiting bar admission, which can take up to a year. These soon-to-be attorneys cannot yet practice law, but they can carry out research and writing projects under the supervision of an admitted attorney.

Law students can also be put to work on other kinds of activities that align with their training. Research skills certainly come in handy when the fundraising department is researching donor prospects. Persuasive writing skills translate easily into writing grant applications, writing ad copy, and drafting press releases. That moot court champion can repurpose his superior oral advocacy skills to craft the perfect donor pitch. The former Capitol page or legislative staffer can use her knowledge of the inner workings of government to help with the organization's lobbying, policy, and government relations projects.

The American Bar Association has recently adopted a resolution urging law schools to more adequately prepare law students for legal practice by providing opportunities to gain the knowledge, skills, values, habits and traits that make up the successful modern lawyer. To that end, a small but growing number of law schools have clinical programs specializing in nonprofit law, or business law transaction clinics that work with nonprofit clients. Neighboring organizations can benefit enormously from the participation of supervised law students in a clinical program. Organizations can also harness the energies of law students looking to fulfill mandatory community service hours by crafting appropriate projects for them to complete.

Get Help from Lawyers in Transition   Even credentialed and seasoned lawyers sometimes find themselves in transition. They may be seeking to move from private practice to an in-house job, relaunching after their department has been downsized or eliminated following a merger, or returning to the paid workforce after taking time off to be with a child or an aging parent. Volunteering as in-house counsel to a nonprofit can provide a valuable opportunity for transitioning lawyers to freshen skills and rekindle passion for the practice of law. A few forward-thinking law schools even have special internships to help mid-career lawyers regroup or reinvent their legal path. Enterprising organizations can help advance such attorneys' professional interests in the short to medium term by creating volunteer engagements for a semester or two.

These ongoing voluntary engagements can provide a hands-on opportunity to deal directly with clients on quality work, stretching skills outside of the attorney's usual practice area, and provide a welcome contrast to the increasing specialization commonly found in the private practice of law. Working as an in-house volunteer can also help an attorney sharpen up skills that are hard to come by in private practice: providing abbreviated advice instead of encyclopedic memoranda; crystallizing an opinion that provides real direction instead of hedging bets with an "on the one hand, on the other hand" approach; and recognizing how legal advice fits in with other important considerations such as mission, tax, accounting, governance, strategic, and other matters. Working within an organization reinforces that legal counsel is not a stand-alone commodity but an integral part of the business objectives of the client.

Lawyers serving in these capacities should be aware there are fewer resources available than they may be accustomed to—secretarial, duplicating, package services, information technology, and like services. There may not be a law library or access to paid online legal research databases. They should also be sure that their work is covered by the organization's malpractice insurance (sometimes subsumed as part of directors' and officers' liability insurance), or maintain malpractice insurance of their own.

The lack of creature comforts should be kept in perspective—money not spent on these expenses is used instead to serve a mission.

Thank Legal Volunteers   Wise organizations thank their volunteer lawyers early, consistently, and often. Be sure these special contributors are listed in the organization's annual report and other publications where donors are acknowledged. If a project is on the agenda for a board meeting or management presentation, consider inviting the volunteer attorney to present the work or at least attend and be thanked.

Consider making a guest appearance at the law firm's offices—perhaps at a lunch-and-learn session or an affinity group meeting—both to express thanks and also to educate lawyers who are not involved with the representation about the organization, its mission and the benefits of pro bono service.

Offer follow-on projects to keep good volunteers engaged. Show an interest in their career development and progress in their firm, and encourage them to reflect on their experiences with the organization and how these experiences have contributed to their professional successes and growth.

If the names of law students who have passed the state bar exam are published in the local law journal, keep an eye out for law students who have worked on a project for the organization. Be the first to send a congratulatory note, and invite further involvement by the newly minted lawyer now that he or she has been admitted to practice.

A Broad-Gauge Role for the Legal Profession in the Nonprofit Sector

Beyond the obvious benefits of having its legal needs met, the organization may benefit in other ways from having members of the legal profession invested in its activities and its success. Lawyers often accompany their commitment of expertise with commitments of money and other kinds of support.

Sometimes rendering legal or governance advice inspires a lawyer to join a board or, in the case of newer lawyers, may serve as a feeder for a junior board or young patrons group.

The Payoffs of Pro Bono Work for the Volunteer Attorney

Identifying and meeting legal needs on a pro bono basis is worthwhile for its own sake. The lawyer who waives his fee has enabled the organization to reinvest critical resources in mission-related expenditures. He may also take satisfaction that his legal work benefits the organization far beyond the narrow definition of meeting the legal needs: It may also fulfill certain donor requirements of good governance, help meet certain grant restrictions, shore up internal controls, and provide reassurance to governmental or private funders. Each chapter in this book shows how good legal advice can help the organization better execute its mission.

In some professions, including the law, being a small cog in a big wheel is a common and mind-numbing experience. If a volunteer engagement permits a professional to work on a project from start to finish, and then see how his work has been implemented or disseminated, the lawyer can obtain professional satisfaction far outweighing the forgone fee.

Working on a large-scale project also provides a better perspective on legal work and how it fits into the overall objectives of the organization. The lawyer can help shape the outcome of an organization's new business initiative and can take pride in lessening risks or enhancing the bottom line by reducing regulatory implications or tax consequences. These skills translate readily and profitably into the private sector, to the advantage of the attorney and his future clients.

Counseling for the good can make Good Counsel even better.

In Sum

Meeting the legal needs of nonprofits serves so many worthwhile interests. A good legal, compliance, and governance function allows the board to envision the future with confidence. It empowers the organization's program professionals and business units to go forth and execute. It reassures customers and clients that the services they receive from the organization meet all required standards. It inspires private donors and governmental funders that a gift or grant to the organization is a sound investment. It helps outsiders assure themselves of the integrity of the organization's statements. It aids regulators to know that there are knowledgeable eyes and ears within the organization, taking good care of legal business from the inside so that the regulators can direct scarce resources to help address only the most serious problems.

While the array of legal issues may at first be daunting—corporate laws, tax-exemption requirements, governance considerations, contracts, copyrights, trademarks, fundraising laws, financial rules and regulations, labor and employment considerations, rights clearance, consumer regulatory matters, operations, political activity restrictions, and other matters relating to the nonprofit's state and local laws and its activities within regulated fields—it's important to start somewhere.

The preceding chapters are a start, providing a common playbook for executives, trustees, lawyers, students, social entrepreneurs and others to begin the journey together.

Additional materials, including fuller versions of the case studies, consolidated work plans, glossaries of terms pertaining to the legal needs of nonprofits, and listings of further resources, are consolidated on the companion web site to this book at www.wiley.com/go/goodcounsel.

> *Our calling in life is to find the place where our great joy and the world's great needs meet.*
> —*Frederick Buechner,* Wishful Thinking: A Seeker's ABC

Notes

Introduction

1. The charitable sector employs more people than the finance, insurance, and real estate sectors combined. www.fas.org/sgp/crs/misc/R40919.pdf at p. 15.
2. In 2009, the charities that filed Form 990 with the Internal Revenue Service reported approximately $1.4 trillion in revenue and reported holding nearly $2.6 trillion in assets. Charitable organizations are estimated to employ more than 7 percent of the U.S. workforce, while the broader nonprofit sector is estimated to employ 10 percent of the U.S. workforce. Nonprofit institutions serving households (largely charities) constituted more than 5 percent of GDP in 2008. www.fas.org/sgp/crs/misc/R40919.pdf and http://www.councilofnonprofits.org/files/crs-overview-nonprofit-charitable-sector.pdf.
3. A Report to the Board of Regents of the Smithsonian Institution, June 18, 2007, available at www.smithcompensationconsulting.com/smithsonianreport.pdf.
4. Complex organizations may have more than one such board.

Chapter 1

1. The 501(c) organization types are set forth in the Organization Reference Chart of IRS Publication 557, *Tax-Exempt Status for Your Organization*, 2010 WL 4931140 (I.R.S. Oct. 2010).
2. The National Taxonomy of Exempt Entities (NTEE) system is used by the IRS and NCCS to classify nonprofit organizations. National Center for Charitable Statistics, available at http://nccsdataweb.urban.org/PubApps/nteeSearch.php?gQry=allMajor&codeType=NTEE.
3. *See generally* Bruce R. Hopkins, *Legal Responsibilities of Nonprofit Boards* (2d ed. 2009). In New York, the duty of care is set forth in N.Y. Not-for-Profit Corp. Law § 717 (McKinney 2010). The duty of loyalty is the product of judge-made common law, while the duty of obedience owes its existence to the holding in *Manhattan Eye, Ear and Throat Hospital* v. *Spitzer*, 715 N.Y.S.2d 575 (NY Cty. Sup. Ct. 1999).
4. *See generally* Lesley Friedman Rosenthal, "'Redeveloping' Corporate Governance Structures: Not-for-Profit Governance During Major Capital Projects," 76 *Ford. L. Rev* 929, 932–933 (2007) and sources cited therein.
5. For example, the child and dependent care credit and the Low-Income Housing Tax Credit (LIHTC) may make services provided by nonprofit organizations more profitable, therefore increasing the demand for such services. *See* Steven

Rathgeb Smith, "Government Financing of Nonprofit Activity," in *Nonprofits & Government* 219 (Elizabeth T. Boris and C. Eugene Steuerle, eds., 2d ed. 2006).

6. The Big Stuff, available at www.blueavocado.org/print/544 (estimating that the federal tax exemption is worth about $72 billion annually); *see also* Tax Exemptions of Charities Face New Challenges, available at www.nytimes .com/2008/05/26/us/26tax.html (estimating that the charitable tax exemption costs local governments between $8 and $13 billion); Nonprofits Fear Losing Tax Benefit, available at www.nytimes.com/2010/12/03/business/03charity.html?_r=1&scp=2&sq=nonprofit+sector&st=nyt (citing Congressional Joint Committee on Taxation calculations that the charitable deduction (versus exemption) will cost the federal government about $237 billion between 2009 and 2013).

7. Most nonprofits are small nonprofits: Of all those filing with the IRS, 82.3 percent have expenditures of less than $1 million. Nonprofits by the Numbers, available at www.councilofnonprofits.org/telling-our-story/nonprofits-numbers.

Chapter 2

1. For the Internal Revenue Service to recognize an organization's exemption, the organization must be organized as a trust, a corporation, or an association.

2. Organization Reference Chart, Publication 557 *Tax-Exempt Status for Your Organization*, 2010 WL 4931140 (I.R.S. Oct. 2010) (containing suggested language), available at www.irs.gov/charities/article/0,,id=96117,00.html.

3. Model Nonprofit Corp. Act § 8.03 (2008). The Model Nonprofit Corporation Act (in either its 1964 or 1987 version) had been adopted by 31 states in 2004. Harry J. Haynsworth, *The Unified Business Organizations Code: The Next Generation*, 29 Del. J. Corp. L. 83, 87 (2004).

4. *See generally* Model Nonprofit Corp. Act (3rd ed. 2008).

5. *See* Appendix and Sample By-laws, available at www.lawhelp.org/documents/487501Microsoft%20Word%20-%20Notice%20of%20Organizational%20Meeting.pdf.

6. *Cf.* other types of tax-exempt organizations, such as social clubs, which may distribute assets back to members.

7. Exemption from tax on corporations, certain trusts, etc. 26 U.S.C.A. § 501(3)(c) (2010), guidelines available at www.irs.gov/charities/charitable/article/0,,id=96099,00.html.

8. Form available at www.irs.gov/pub/irs-pdf/f1023.pdf. Three groups are not required to file Form 1023: churches, public charities that do not have gross receipts of more than $5,000 in each year, and subordinate organizations exempt under a group exemption letter. Other types of organizations described in Code section 501(a) may submit an application for recognition of exemption on Form 1024. To get the most benefit from the tax exemption, organizations should file within 27 months of incorporating.

9. Organizations with gross receipts greater than $200,000 or total assets greater than $500,000 must file Form 990. Organizations with gross receipts greater

than $50,000 and less than $200,000 and total assets less than $500,000 may file a short-form return, Form 990-EZ or a complete Form 990. Many organizations with gross annual receipts of $50,000 or less are eligible to file a simplified version, Form 990-N, (an e-Postcard). Supporting organizations of any size, however, must file the standard Form 990 or, if eligible, Form 990-EZ. Private foundations of any size must file the standard Form 990-PF. More information, including links to all forms, is available at www.irs.gov/charities/article/0,,id=184445,00.html. Late filers incur fines, and failure to comply with the reporting requirements for three consecutive years' results in the automatic loss of the organization's federal tax-exempt status. The requirement for small tax-exempt organizations, other than churches and church-related organizations, to file an annual notice with the IRS was created under the Pension Protection Act of 2006.

10. Exemption from tax on corporations, certain trusts, etc. 26 U.S.C.A. § 501(3)(c) (2010) (emphasis added).

11. Example modeled on Douglas Feiden, "'Dorm King of New York' and Wife Grab Millions through 'Nonprofit' Housing Services Company," *Daily News*, February 13, 2011, available at www.nydailynews.com/ny_local/2011/02/13/2011-02-13_financial_aid_101_dorm_king__wife_grab_millions_with_nonprofit.html. Allegations remain unproven, and the case was still under investigation as of this writing.

12. *Summers* v. *Cherokee Children & Family Services, Inc.*, 112 S.W.3d 486, 504 (Tenn. Ct. App. 2002) (citing *Johns* v. *Caldwell*, 601 S.W.2d 37, 41 (Tenn. Ct. App. 1980), holding that directors bear the burden of proof in establishing that a conflict of interest is not present, if the appearance of a conflict of interest is present).

13. Treas. Reg. §1.502(c)(3)-1(d)(1)(ii).

14. *American Campaign Academy* v. *Commissioner*, 92 T.C. 1043 (1989).

15. This period culminated in a congressional hearing entitled, "Charity Oversight and Reform: Keeping Bad Things from Happening to Good Charities," available for watching and transcript download at http://finance.senate.gov/hearings/hearing/?id=48ca4cce-afe1-db95-0fcb-8ff9255e780a. The Sarbanes-Oxley Act was also passed in 2002, expressly and indirectly affecting standards of nonprofit governance. Sarbanes-Oxley Act, Pub. L. No. 107-204, 116 Stat. 745 (2002).

16. Remarks of Steven T. Miller, Commissioner, Tax Exempt and Government Entities, Internal Revenue Service, October 22, 2007, available at www.irs.gov/pub/irs-tege/stm_isector_10_22_07.pdf; *see also* introduction to *Governance and Related Topics – 501(c)(3) Organizations*, available at www.irs.gov/pub/irs-tege/governance_practices.pdf.

17. See Government and Management Policies section in *Governance and Related Topics—501(c)(3) Organizations*, available at www.irs.gov/pub/irs-tege/governance_practices.pdf.

18. Sample Conflict of Interest Policy, available at www.irs.gov/instructions/i1023/ar03.html.

19. *Id.*

20. The organization may also have whistleblower policies for other kinds of alleged wrongdoing, such as harassment or other employment-related misconduct.
21. Samples are downloadable through Boardsource, www.boardsource.org/ Bookstore.asp?Type=epolicy&Item=1027.
22. The IRS publication *Starting a Business and Keeping Records*, Publication 583 (Jan. 2007) sets forth recommended and required retention times for various categories of documents. www.irs.gov/pub/irs-pdf/p583.pdf.
23. Samples are downloadable through Boardsource, www.boardsource.org/ Bookstore.asp?Type=epolicy&Item=1071.
24. *See generally* Reynold Levy and Glenn Lowry, "Entrepreneurialism in Nonprofits," 76 *Fordham L. Rev.* 647 (2007) (discussing modern manifestations of the entrepreneurial spirit in nonprofit ventures); *see also* Darryll K. Jones, "Third-Party Profit-Taking in Tax Exemption Jurisprudence," 2007 *B.Y.U.L. Rev.* 977, 980 (2007) (arguing that joint ventures are necessary to the survival of nonprofits in a market economy).
25. For a brief introduction to joint venture activities by nonprofits, *see* Gene Takagi, "Nonprofit Joint Ventures," Nonprofit Law Blog (October 11, 2006), available at www.nonprofitlawblog.com/home/2006/10/nonprofit_joint.html. *See also, e.g.,* Rev. Rul. 2006-27, 2006-1 C.B. 915.
26. Rev. Rul. 98-15, 1998-1 C.B. 718 (1998).
27. For example, New York State's Executive Law § 174-c, Sales Advertised to Benefit a Charitable Organization, requires that "All advertising, of every kind and nature, that a sale of goods, services, entertainment or any other thing of value will benefit a charitable organization shall set forth the antici-pated portion of the sales price, anticipated percentage of the gross proceeds, anticipated dollar amount per purchase, or other consideration or benefit the charitable organization is to receive."

Chapter 3

1. For a thoughtful discussion of different board committee structures and options, *see* "Board Committee Structure," Eileen Morgan Johnson (ASAE Center for Association Leadership, Jan. 2006), available at www.asaecenter .org/Resources/whitepaperdetail.cfm?ItemNumber=24191.
2. Anthony Mancuso, "Nonprofit Meetings, Minutes & Records: How to Run Your Nonprofit Corporation So You Don't Run Into Trouble" (2008) contains information and sample forms for calling meetings, taking minutes, making resolutions, and other corporate secretary functions.
3. Several states have adopted rules requiring charities of a certain size to form an audit committee. *The Sarbanes-Oxley Act and Implications for Nonprofit Organizations* 3-4 (BoardSource, and Independent Sector 2003, rev. 2006), available at www.boardsource.org/clientfiles/sarbanes-oxley.pdf.
4. IRS Form 990 Part VII, Section A, Question 1a asks about the compensation of the highest paid employees or officers from the organization or any related organizations.

5. Indep. Rev. Committee, A Rep. to the Board of Regents of the Smithsonian Institution at 46-51 (2007).
6. 2010 Instructions for Form 990 Return of Organization Exempt From Income Tax 76 (I.R.S. 2010), available at www.irs.gov/pub/irs-pdf/i990.pdf.
7. A great deal of information on the complex subject of executive compensation appears in Bruce R. Hopkins, *The Law of Tax-Exempt Organizations* 571 (9th ed. 2007).
8. Excerpted from Letter of Reynold Levy to Lesley Friedman Rosenthal, December 20, 2010 (on file with author).
9. 20 U.S.C. § 42.

Chapter 4

1. "What Is Intellectual Property?" World Intellectual Property Organization web site, available at www.wipo.int/about-ip/en/.
2. Article I, Section 8, Clause 8 of the United States Constitution, known as the Copyright Clause, empowers the United States Congress: "To promote the Progress of Science and useful Arts, by securing for limited Times to Authors and Inventors the exclusive Right to their respective Writings and Discoveries."
3. 17 U.S.C. § 106.
4. Electronic Copyright Office, available at www.copyright.gov/eco/.
5. Note that post-1978 copyright protection begins with creation, whereas pre-1978 copyright begins with publication.
6. Copyright Term and the Public Domain in the United States, chart first published in Peter B. Hirtle, "Recent Changes to the Copyright Law: Copyright Term Extension," in *Archival Outlook* (1999). The January 1, 2011 version is available at http://copyright.cornell.edu/resources/publicdomain.cfm.
7. Berne Convention Art. 7(1) (Paris text 1971), www.wipo.int/treaties/en/ip/berne/trtdocs_wo001.html.
8. 17 U.S.C. § 101.
9. 17 U.S.C. § 106(2).
10. *See, e.g., Martha Graham School and Dance Foundation, Inc v. Martha Graham Center of Contemporary Dance, Inc.,* 380 F.3d 624 (2d Cir. 2004), available at http://openjurist.org/380/f3d/624/martha-graham-school-and-dance-foundation-inc-v-martha-graham-center-of-contemporary-dance-inc-l.
11. 17 U.S.C. § 507(b): "Civil Actions.—No civil action shall be maintained under the provisions of this title unless it is commenced within three years after the claim accrued."
12. *Advance Magazine Publishers, Inc. v. Leach,* 466 F. Supp. 2d 628, 636 (D. Md. 2006).

Chapter 5

1. Charitable Contributions – Quid Pro Quo Contributions, available at www.irs.gov/charities/charitable/article/0,,id=123201,00.html.

2. IRS Publication 526: *Charitable Contributions*, 2009 WL 5083490 (I.R.S. 2009), also available at www.irs.gov/publications/p526/ar02.html#en_US_2010_ publink1000229650.

3. Charity Auction, www.irs.gov/charities/charitable/article/0,,id=123204,00.html.

4. IRS Publication 526: *Contributions You Cannot Deduct: Contributions From Which You Benefit*, www.irs.gov/publications/p526/ar02.html#en_US_2010_ publink1000229696.

5. The National Association of State Charities Officials, or NASCO, is an association of state offices charged with overseeing charitable organizations and charitable solicitation in the United States. NASCO's web site contains state-specific information, helpful contacts, training sessions and more, available at www.nasconet.org/category/info-charities/.

6. E.g., Georgetown University Law Center, in conjunction with BoardSource, offers an annual program on representing and managing tax-exempt organizations. The IRS also offers periodic workshops for small and mid-size charitable exempt organizations. IRS Exempt Organizations Upcoming Events, available at www.irs.gov/charities/article/0,,id=96083,00.html.

7. Bureau of Consumer Protection Business Center, Q&A For Telemarketers & Sellers About DNC Provisions in TSR, available at http://business.ftc.gov/ documents/alt129-qa-telemarketers-sellers-about-dnc-provisions-tsr.

8. Information and forms available at www.multistatefiling.org/.

9. Charities retained only 39.5 percent of the funds raised by telemarketers in a 2009 study in New York. Some 60.5 percent was paid to the fundraisers and/ or used to cover the costs of conducting the campaigns. These results were consistent with similar studies conducted in prior years. Pennies for Charity, New York State Department of Law Charities Bureau's 2009 Annual Report, Telemarketing by Professional Fund Raisers, available at www.charitiesnys. com/pdfs/2009_Pennies.pdf.

10. *See, e.g.*, N.Y. Exec. Law § 172 (McKinney 2002).

11. Kathleen Blythe and Margie Guthrie, *Corrupt El Paso charity boss exposed by The Oregonian gets 10 years in federal prison*, February 18, 2011, available at www.oregonlive .com/portland/index.ssf/2011/02/corrupt_el_paso_charity_boss_e.html.

12. Tax Exempt Organizations and Gaming, available at www.irs.gov/pub/irs-pdf/p3079.pdf.

13. I.R.C. § 513(i) (2006).

14. A summary of this area of fundraising law appears in Jeffrey Tenenbaum's "Corporate Sponsorship: The Final Regulations," available at www.asaecenter .org/Resources/whitepaperdetail.cfm?ItemNumber=12199; *see also* 26 C.F.R. § 1.513-4(a).

15. *Tax on Unrelated Business Income of Exempt Organizations*, www.irs.gov/pub/irs-pdf/p598.pdf.

16. I.R.C. § 170(f)(8); *see also* IRS Publication 1771: *Charitable Contributions-Substantiation and Disclosure Requirements* at 5, available at www.irs.gov/pub/irs-pdf/p1771.pdf.

17. A directory of fiscal sponsors is available at www.fiscalsponsordirectory.org. A sample fiscal sponsorship agreement appears at www.fracturedatlas.org/site/ fiscal/contract.pdf.

18. 2011 CFC Applications, www.opm.gov/cfc/Charities/ModelCharityApp.asp.
19. *Superior Beverage Co.* v. *Owens Illinois*, 827 F.Supp. 477 (N.D.Ill. 1993).
20. A list is available at http://ohiolawyersgiveback.org/charities/.
21. Stephanie Strom, "To Help Donors Choose, Web Site Alters How It Sizes Up Charities," *New York Times*, November 26, 2010, at B1 (quoting Sean Stannard-Stockton, consultant on philanthropy).

Chapter 6

1. *See generally* Edward J. McMillan, *Not-for-Profit Budgeting and Financial Management* (4th ed. 2010); Sharon Farris, *Nonprofit Bookkeeping & Accounting For Dummies* (2009); Murray Dropkin et al., *The Budget-Building Book for Nonprofits: A Step-by-Step Guide for Managers and Boards* (2nd ed. 2007); Carter MacNamara, *All About Financial Management in Nonprofits*, available at http://managementhelp.org/finance/np_fnce/np_fnce.htm; *Financial Management of Not-for-Profit Organizations* (2004), available at www.blackbaud.com/files/resources/downloads/WhitePaper_FinancialManagementForNPO.pdf.
2. Some interesting examples of nonprofit business model statements are available at www.blueavocado.org/content/nonprofit-business-model-statements.
3. Molly F. Sherlock and Jane G. Gravelle, Congressional Research Service, *An Overview of the Nonprofit and Charitable Sector* at 17 (citing Wing, Pollak, and Blackwood, *The Nonprofit Almanac*, 2008, p. 134 and CRS calculations), available at www.fas.org/sgp/crs/misc/R40919.pdf.
4. Jennifer Hewlett, "Ex-office Manager for Big Brothers Big Sisters is Sentenced to 4 Years," *Herald-Leader*, Oct. 14, 2011, available at http://www.kentucky.com/2011/10/14/1919825/ex-office-manager-for-big-brothers.html. Ultimately the missing funds meant that 500-600 fewer underprivileged children were served by the mentorship program.
5. O'Ryan Johnson, "DA: Ex-Payroll Clerk Lived in Luxury Duping Health Nonprofit, *Boston Herald*, May 26, 2011, http://news.bostonherald.com/news/regional/view/2011_0526da_ex-payroll_clerk_lived_in_luxury_duping_health_nonprofit/.
6. Bob Carlson, *Embezzlement Happens. It's What Charities Do Next That Matters*, http://philanthropy.com/blogs/watchdog/embezzlement-happens-its-what-charities-do-next-that-matters/24359.
7. Frank L. Kurre, *Maintaining Sufficient Reserves to Protect Your Not-for-Profit Organization* at 5 (2010), www.grantthornton.com/staticfiles/GTCom/Not-for-profit%20organizations/NotForProfit%20files/NFP_Sufficient-Reserves_WP.pdf.
8. *Id.* at 9.
9. *Id.* at 5.
10. GAAP applicable to nonprofits is derived from standards of private and public entities, including the Financial Accounting Standards Board (FASB), Government Accounting Standards Board, Committee of Sponsoring Organizations (COSO), and American Institute of Certified Public Accountants (AICP). See *Statement of Financial Accounting Standards (SFAS)* 117, Financial Accounting Standards Board, www.gasb.org/pdf/fas117.pdf.

11. For a historical perspective on investing charitable funds and a description of the modern total return approach, *see* "The Total Return Approach to Investment Management," William A. Schneider, CIMA, available at http://www.land.nd.gov/constmeasure/DimeoSchneiderstudy.pdf.

12. Uniform Law Commission, www.nccusl.org. For more information on UPMIFA, see Susan Gary, *UMIFA Becomes UPMIFA*, http://uniformlaws.org/Shared/Docs/UMIFA%20Becomes%20UPMIFA.pdf

13. Josh Nathan-Kazis, "Madoff Trustee Sues to Recoup So-Called Profits," *The Jewish Daily Forward*, Dec. 10, 2010, available at http://forward.com/articles/133613/#ixzz17JmhzPaE.

14. Employee Retirement Income Security Act, Pub. L. No. 93-406, 88 Stat. 829 (1974).

15. A helpful resource for nonprofits with insurance questions is the insurance blog http://scottsimmondsinsurance.blogspot.com/.

16. For general guidance see I.R.S. Pub. 598, www.irs.gov/pub/irs-pdf/p598.pdf.

17. I.R.C. § 512(a)(1).

18. 26 C.F.R. § 1.513-1 (2010).

19. I.R.C. § 513(a).

20. *Supra* note 17.

21. Rev. Rul. 73-104, 1973-1 C.B. 263.

22. I.R.C. § 512(b).

23. I.R.C. § 513(a).

24. N.Y. Real Prop. Tax Law § 420-a (McKinney 2010).

25. *See, e.g., Genesee Hospital* v. *Wagner*, 364 N.Y.S.2d 934 (N.Y. App. Div. 1975).

26. Daphne A. Kenyon and Adam H. Langley, *Payments in Lieu of Taxes (Policy Focus Report): Balancing Municipal and Nonprofit Interests* (2010), available for purchase and download at www.lincolninst.edu/pubs/1853_Payments-in-Lieu-of-Taxes.

27. *See* Janet Kleinfelter, *Boards Can't Just Abandon an Insolvent Nonprofit*, available at http://philanthropy.com/blogs/watchdog/boards-cant-just-abandon-an-insolvent-nonprofit/24376?sid=&utm_source=&utm_medium=en.

Chapter 7

1. The Worker Adjustment Retraining and Notification (WARN) Act is a federal law requiring employers, including nonprofit employers, with 100 or more employees to provide 60 days notice before a group layoff. *See* "The Worker Adjustment and Retraining Notification Act: A Guide to Advance Notice of Closings and Layoffs," U.S. Department of Labor Employment and Training Administration Fact Sheet, available at www.doleta.gov/programs/factsht/warn.htm. The Age Discrimination in Employment Act of 1967 (Pub. L. 90-202) prohibits employment discrimination against persons 40 years of age or older. The Older Workers Benefit Protection Act (Pub. L. 101-433) amended several sections of the ADEA. In addition, Section 115 of the Civil Rights Act of 1991 (Pub.L. 102-166) amended Section 7(e) of the ADEA (29 U.S.C. § 626(e)).

2. Understanding the Value of an Effective Employee Handbook – Avoiding the Pitfalls that May Take that Value Away, by Elizabeth L. Peters (Sept. 2010), available at http://saginawchamberleadingbusiness.wordpress.com/2010/09/27/understanding-the-value-of-an-effective-employee-handbook-%E2%80%93-avoiding-the-pitfalls-that-may-take-that-value-away/.

3. Fair Labor Standards Act, 29 U.S.C. § 201 (1938); *see Tony and Susan Alamo Foundation* v. *Secretary of Labor*, 417 U.S. 290, 296 (1985) (holding that FLSA applies to nonprofit employers).

4. United States Department of Labor Fact Sheet #17A: Exemption for Executive, Administrative, Professional, Computer & Outside Sales Employees Under the Fair Labor Standards Act (FLSA), available at www.dol.gov/whd/regs/compliance/fairpay/fs17a_overview.htm.

5. *Tony and Susan Alamo Foundation* v. *Secretary of Labor*, 417 U.S. 290, 302-303 (1985).

6. *Id.* at 295 (citing *Walling* v. *Portland Terminal Co.*, 330 U.S. 148, 152 (1947)).

7. NY Labor Law § 650 (McKinney 1962); *NY Dept of Labor Memorandum* (June 19, 1989).

8. NY Labor Law § 651 (McKinney 2010).

9. *Dept. of Labor Wage and Hour Division Opinion Letter* (Apr. 6, 2006), www.dol.gov/whd/opinion/FLSA/2006/2006_04_06_12_FLSA.htm.

10. US Department of Labor Advisory: Training and Employment Guidance Letter No. 12-09 (Jan. 29, 2010); *see also Dept. of Labor Opinion Letter* (Apr. 6, 2006).

11. Hilary Stout, "Students Chafe Under Internship Guidelines," *New York Times*, July 2, 2010 at ST1; Steven Greenhouse, "The Unpaid Intern, Legal or Not," *New York Times*, April 2, 2010 at B1; U.S. Dept. of Labor Wage and Hour Division Fact Sheet #71: Internship Programs Under the Fair Labor Standards Act, April 2010, available at www.dol.gov/whd/regs/compliance/whdfs71.pdf.

12. "Independent Contractor (Self-Employed) or Employee?" http://www.irs.gov/businesses/small/article/0,,id=99921,00.html.

13. "Exempt Organizations: Independent Contractors vs. Employees," www.irs.gov/charities/article/0,,id=128602,00.html.

14. "Exempt Organizations: Who is a Common Law Employee?" www.irs.gov/charities/article/0,,id=131137,00.html.

15. "Exempt Organizations: Who is a Contractor?" www.irs.gov/charities/article/0,,id=131136,00.html.

16. *Barfield* v. *New York City Health and Hospitals Corp.*, 537 F.3d 132, 141 (2d Cir. 2008).

17. "Present Law and Background Relating to Worker Classification for Federal Tax Purposes," IRS publication available at www.irs.gov/pub/irs-utl/x-26-07.pdf; Rev. Rul. 87-41, 1987-1 C.B. 296 (setting forth a list of 20 factors that may be examined in determining whether an employer-employee relationship exists. The IRS emphasizes that factors in addition to the 20 factors listed may be relevant, that the weight of the factors may vary based on the circumstances, that relevant factors may change over time, and that all facts must be examined). More recently, the IRS has identified three categories of evidence that may be relevant in determining whether the requisite control exists under a common-law test. *See* www.irs.gov/businesses/

small/article/0,,id=99921,00.html. *See generally* Charles J. Muhl, *What is an employee? The answer depends on the Federal law,* available at www.bls.gov/opub/mlr/2002/01/art1full.pdf.

18. *Lourim v. Swensen,* 977 P.2d 1157, 1159-60 (Or. 1999).
19. *Zirkle v. Winkler,* 585 S.E.2d 19, 22 (W. Va. 2003); *see also* Liability of charitable organization under respondeat superior doctrine for tort of unpaid volunteer, 82 A.L.R.3d 1213.
20. *Riviello v. Waldron,* 47 N.Y.2d 297, 303 (N.Y. 1979).
21. National Labor Relations Board summary of legislative purpose for NLRA, 29 U.S.C. §§ 151-169, available at www.nlrb.gov/national-labor-relations-act.
22. Guidelines available at www.sba.gov/content/providing-employee-benefits.
23. *Id.*
24. I.R.C.§ 4980H.
25. USCIS. Form I-9, available at www.uscis.gov/files/form/i-9.pdf.

Chapter 8

1. If the mark is used to identify services rather than goods, then technically speaking the mark is called a service mark rather than a trademark; but most people just refer to trademarks or marks as an all-inclusive term.
2. U.S. Patent and Trademark Office web site, available at www.uspto.gov.
3. *WWP, Inc. v. Wounded Warriors Family Support, Inc.,* 628 F.3d 1032 (8th Cir. 2011). Wounded Warrior Project logo available at www.woundedwarriorproject.org/.
4. The federal trademark registration law is at 15 U.S.C. § 1051.
5. The United States Patent and Trademark Office Official Gazette for Trademarks, available at www.uspto.gov/news/og/trademark_og/index.jsp.
6. *E.g.,* N.Y. Gen. Bus. Law § 135 (McKinney 1965) (providing that "[n]o person, society or corporation shall, with intent to acquire or obtain for personal or business purposes a benefit or advantage, assume, adopt or use the name of a benevolent, humane or charitable organization incorporated under the laws of this state, or a name so nearly resembling it as to be calculated to deceive the public with respect to any such corporation.").
7. *Freecyclesunnyvale v. The Freecycle Network,* 626 F.3d 509 (9th Cir. 2010).
8. Freecycle logo available at http://www.freecycle.org/.
9. Further information about trademark law is available at: International Trademark Association (www.inta.org); World Intellectual Property Organization (www.wipo.int); J. Thomas McCarthy, *McCarthy on Trademarks and Unfair Competition* (4th ed. 2011); Anne Gilson Lalonde and Jerome Gilson, *Gilson on Trademarks* (Rel. 76 2010); Seigrun D. Kane, *Kane on Trademark Law, a Practitioner's Guide* (5th ed. 2010); web site of the U.S. Patent & Trademark Office (www.uspto.gov), which includes the Trademark Manual of Examining Procedure (TMEP) and the Trademark Board Manual of Procedure (TBMP), along with U.S. trademark laws and regulations, a search and status database, and many other resources. Trademark search companies include: Thomson CompuMark (www.compumark.thomson.com), CT Corsearch (www.ctcorsearch.com), and Corporation Service Company (www.cscglobal.com).

10. *See* Madrid System for the International Registration of Marks, WIPO IP Services, www.wipo.int/madrid/en/; *see also* Lesley Friedman Rosenthal, Dana J. Rosen and Allison N. Engel, "International Trademarking Under the Madrid Protocol: Efficiency Gains, But Not One-Stop Shopping," *NYSBA Entertainment, Arts and Sports Law Journal* 12, no. 3, at 65 (Fall/Win 2001).

11. Collections of images that organizations may search to locate the copyright owner include: Academic Image Cooperative; Allan Kohl's Art Images for College Teaching; American Society of Media Photographers; Artists Rights Foundation; Artists Rights Society; Aurora Picture Network International; Lantern Slides of Classical Antiquity; Media Image Resource Alliance (MIRA); Saskia/Luna Imaging Project; Society of Architectural Historians' Image Exchange; and Visual Artists and Gallery Association.

12 Web site available at www.corbis.com/bettmann100/ImageDonation/Image Donation.asp.

13. The Harry Fox Agency administers mechanical rights for many music publishers, available at www.harryfox.com.

14. Licensing available at www.ascap.com/, www.bmi.com/, and www.sesac.com/.

15. Searchable database available at catalog.loc.gov/.

16. CCC's web site available at www.copyright.com/ccc/home.do.

17 Web site available at www.ingentaconnect.com/.

18. Web site available at www.whorepresents.com/.

19. Web site available at http://creativecommons.org/.

20. Web site available at http://commons.wikimedia.org.

21. 17 U.S.C. §107.

22. In the nonprofit educational context, helpful guidelines have been developed for teachers struggling to understand when they can and cannot use portions of copyrighted works without permission for educational projects. Fair Use Guidelines for Educational Multimedia, available at www.adec.edu/admin/papers/fair10-17.html. Adopted by the House of Representatives Committee on the Judiciary on September 27, 1996. These guidelines do not supplant the fair use factors, which still apply when undertaking a legal analysis of such uses.

23. *Harper & Row Publishers, Inc. v. Nation Enters.*, 471 U.S. 539 (1985).

24. *Roy Export Co. Establishment v. Columbia Broad. Sys., Inc.*, 672 F.2d 1095 (2d Cir. 1982).

25. *Video-Cinema Films, Inc. v. Lloyd E. Rigler-Lawrence E. Deutsch Foundation*, 2005 WL 2875327 (S.D.N.Y. Nov. 2, 2005).

26. *Sony Corp. v. Universal City Studios, Inc.*, 464 U.S. 417, 451 (1984).

27. *See, e.g., Princeton Univ. Press v. Michigan Document Servs., Inc.*, 99 F.3d 1381 (6th Cir. 1996); *Basic Books, Inc. v. Kinko's Graphics Corp.*, 758 F.Supp. 1522 (S.D.N.Y. 1991).

28. *E.g., Salinger v. Colting*, 607 F.3d 68 (2d Cir. 2010).

29. Section 43(a) of the federal Trademark Act prohibits false representation. Trademark Act, Pub.L. No. 79-489, 60 Stat. 427 (1946).

30. *See, for example, Marcus v. Jewish Nat'l Fund*, 158 A.D.2d 101, 557 N.Y.S.2d 886 (N.Y. App. Div. 1990) (state law); Lanham Act, 15 U.S.C. § 1125(a)(1) (pro-

hibiting use in commerce of any word, term, name, symbol, or device, or false or misleading description, which is likely to cause confusion as to the origin, sponsorship or approval of the commercial activities).

31   39 U.S.C. §§ 3001, 3005, 3012(d) and 3017; a summary appears at www .dmaresponsibility.org/Sweepstakes/.

32.   39 U.S.C. § 3001(k)(1).

33.   Sample Sweepstakes Mailing is based on an example conceived by Barry Agdern and Donald Saelinger.

34.   The Digital Millenium Copyright Act (DMCA) shields Internet service providers from liability for infringement resulting from copyrighted materials posted by third-parties at the direction of third-parties, provided the service provider does not have actual knowledge of the infringing material, does not receive a financial benefit directly attributable to the infringing material, and removes the infringing material promptly upon receipt of a DMCA-compliant notification.

35.   Controlling the Assault of Non-Solicited Pornography and Marketing Act, Pub. L. 108-187, 117 Stat. 2699 (2003); *see* Stored Communications Act, Pub. L. 99-508, 100 Stat. 1860 (1986); *see also* Council Directive 95/46/EC, 1995 O.J. (L 281) (Eur. Union).

Chapter 9

1.   The International Code Council (ICC) develops codes and standards used to construct and operate homes, workplaces and schools, to enhance building safety and prevent fires. Fifty states and the District of Columbia have adopted the comprehensive, coordinated set of building safety and fire prevention codes known as I-Codes. Web site available at www.iccsafe.org/Pages/default.aspx.

2.   Americans with Disabilities Act, Pub. L. 101-336, 104 Stat. 327 (1990). Web site available at http://www.ada.gov/.

3.   OSHA web site available at www.osha.gov/.

4.   *See, e.g.*, N.Y. Gen. Bus. Law § 89-g (McKinney 1994). More information on licensing procedures in New York is available at www.dos.ny.gov/licensing/ securityguard/sguard.html.

Chapter 10

1.   I.R.C. § 4955 (1996). Section 4955 is sometimes used as an intermediate sanction, instead of the stiffer penalty of revoking tax-exempt status. *See, e.g., Catholic Answers v. United States,* 09 NO. 202 BNA Taxcore 001 (S.D. Cal. 2009). However, the IRS may revoke the organization's exempt status altogether. *See* Letter from Steven T. Miller, Commissioner of Tax Exempt and Government Entities Division, Internal Revenue Service, to America First National Committee, Constitution Party National Committee, Democratic National Committee, Green Party of the United States, Libertarian National Committee, Inc., Natural Law Party of the United States, Republican National Committee (June 10, 2004), www.irs.gov/ pub/irs-utl/eo_letter.pdf.

2. *Branch Ministries, Inc. v. Comm'r,* 40 F.Supp.2d 15 (D.D.C. 1999), *aff'd,* 211 F.3d 137 (D.C. Cir. 2000); *Branch Ministries, Inc.,* v. *Comm'r,* Brief of Defendant-Appellee, 1999 WL 34835366 (C.A.D.C.), 11-16.
3. Rev. Rul. 78-248, 1978-1 C.B. 154; Rev. Rul. 80-282, 1980-2 C.B. 178.
4. Letter from Marsha A. Ramirez, Director of Exempt Organizations Examinations, to United Church of Christ (May 13, 2008), available at www .ucc.org/news/pdf/irsmayltr.pdf.
5. IRS's definition of lobbying on lobbying page of its web site, available at www .irs.gov/charities/article/0,,id=163392,00.html.
6. Definition of legislation, *id.*
7. For more information, see the IRS's web site, at www.irs.gov/charities/chari-table/article/0,,id=163395,00.html, and www.irs.gov/charities/article/0,,id= 163392,00.html.
8. A good place to start is the National Council of Nonprofit Associations' pub-lication, *Election Activities for 501(c)(3) Charities,* available at www.npaction.org/ resources/Election_tool_kit2.pdf.
9. 26 U.S.C. § 501(h) (2006); Treas. Reg. § 1.501(c)(3)-1(c)(3) (2008). All dollar figures in this chapter are current as of 2011.
10. *Christian Echoes Nat. Ministry, Inc. v. United States,* 470 F.2d 849 (10th Cir. 1972).
11. *Regan v. Taxation With Representation of Washington,* 461 U.S. 540, 544 (1983) (holding that a Section 501(c)(3) organization may establish a Section 501(c)(4) affiliate, and that an organization with a dual 501(c)(3)/501(c)(4) struc-ture that had been denied Section 501(c)(3) status by the IRS was still eligible for Section 501(c)(4) status).
12. I.R.C. § 504(a) (1987); 34 Am. Jur. 2d Federal Taxation ¶ 20681 (2011). There are no state parallels to this limitation.
13. *See generally* "Lobbying: What Does It Mean for Nonprofits?" available at http://www.venable.com/Lobbying-What-Does-It-Mean-for-Nonprofits-09-15-2011; "Mythbusting: The Top 10 Fallacies of 501(c)(3) Lobbying," available at http://www.venable.com/Mythbusting-the-Top-10-Fallacies-of-501c3-Lobbying-12-01-2010.

Chapter 11

1. *See generally* 15 Am. Jur. 2d Charities § 183 (2011).
2. 42 U.S.C. § 14503(a).
3. Ronald J. Levine, "Not-for-Profit Institution Litigation," in *Commercial Litigation in New York State Courts* at 1025–1026 (3rd ed. 2010).
4. Philip Kennicott, "Kennedy Center and Others Should Take Note of Lincoln Center Redesign," *Washington Post,* December 29, 2010, available at www.wash ingtonpost.com/wp-dyn/content/article/2010/12/29/AR2010122903685.html.

Chapter 12

1. Remarks of Joyce Slocum, National Association of Women Lawyers 6th Annual General Counsel Institute, Nov. 4, 2010, Opening Plenary Session; *see also*

Elizabeth Wasserman, *All Things Joyce Slocum,* available at www.superlaw yers.com/washington/article/All-Things-Joyce-Slocum/77e81476-132d-4f74-ba0e-89816c3df3e3.html.

2. Web site available at http://boardnetusa.org.
3. Remarks of Carl Hum, President and CEO, Brooklyn Chamber of Commerce, NYC Bar Association program on Careers at Nonprofits for Lawyers, November 3, 2010.
4. *See* www.nptimes.com/salarysurvey/executivepositionssalary.html (available with paid subscription).

Index